Nineteenth-Century Germany

Nineteenth-Century Germany

Politics, Culture and Society 1780–1918

EDITED BY
JOHN BREUILLY
Professor of Modern History, University of Birmingham

A member of the Hodder Headline Group
LONDON
Distributed in the United States of America by
Oxford University Press Inc., New York

First published in Great Britain in 2001 by
Arnold, a member of the Hodder Headline Group
338 Euston Road, London NW1 3BH
Except for Ch. 12, originally published as part of
Mary Fulbrook, ed., *German History since 1800*

http://www.arnoldpublishers.com

Distributed in the United States of America by
Oxford University Press Inc.,
198 Madison Avenue, New York, NY 10016

© 1997 and 2001 Edward Arnold (Publishers) Ltd

British Library Cataloguing in Publication Data
A catalogue record for this book is available from the British Library

Library of Congress Cataloging-in-Publication Data
A catalog record for this book is available from the Library of Congress

ISBN 0 340 76234 9 (hb)
ISBN 0 340 76235 7 (pb)

2 3 4 5 6 7 8 9 10

Typeset in 10/13pt Plantin by Phoenix Photosetting, Lordswood, Chatham, Kent
Printed and bound in India

What do you think about this book? Or any other Arnold title?
Please send your comments to feedback.arnold@hodder.co.uk

Contents

Part I   1780–1871

Part II   1871–1918

List of maps

List of illustrations

List of tables

Preface

In 1997 Arnold published *German History since 1800* edited by Mary Fulbrook. I acted as advisory editor, taking especial responsibility for parts 1 and 2 of the book which covered the period 1800 to 1918. The book has been well received. However, it is a large volume containing many illustrations as well as maps and figures. This makes it rather bulkier and more expensive than is suitable for many readers, especially students with specific interests in either nineteenth- or twentieth-century German history but less so for the whole of that period. With this in mind it has been decided to make the four chronologically organized sections of the book available as two smaller volumes covering the nineteenth and twentieth centuries respectively, omitting the thematic section and many illustrations.

The nineteenth-century volume of which I am editor differs in certain respects from the first two parts of the original book. A new introduction written by me replaces the general introduction by Mary Fulbrook. There is an additional chapter on Germany during the First World War written by Roger Chickering. The other contributors have made slight alterations to their essays as and where this was considered beneficial.

John Breuilly

1
Introduction

John Breuilly

Introductory remarks

At the end of the eighteenth century Germany was an idea in the minds of some intellectuals and statesmen and a phrase in the title of a loose association of states – the Holy Roman Empire of the German Nation. In 1918 Germany was a state and society which had lost a war of unprecedented scale and destruction against the other major world powers. In 1800 most Germans lived in the countryside and agriculture dominated the economy. By 1918 Germany was an urban society and industry had overtaken agriculture. In 1800 most people travelled by foot and communicated by word of mouth; by 1918 there was mass transportation by rail and road; telegraph, telephone, cinema, letter writing and a mass print media had transformed communication.

It is difficult to provide a comprehensive description and interpretation of German history over this period. To emphasize long-term transformations, as I have just done, can lead to neglect of the experiences of particular groups and individuals which do not fit into that pattern of change, a pattern which can take on an air of inevitability. To switch attention to such experiences risks fragmentation and incoherence and the loss of any sense of large-scale change over several generations. To gain some hold on the range and diversity of experiences, actions and outcomes historians have to select particular topics and approaches which in turn exclude other topics and approaches. There can be no 'total history' and no definitive intepretation.

This collection of essays makes no such claims. It recognizes that the sheer scope of the subject makes it difficult for any one historian to do justice to different periods and themes. The range of expertise provided in this collection is intended to provide the reader with a sense of the distinctive ways in which social, economic, political and cultural historians work, without privileging one period within this 'long century' over any other.

Part I addresses the period from the end of the eighteenth century to 1871. The first two essays by Whaley and Clark provide broad characterizations of the periods 1780–1815 and 1815–48 respectively. The essays by Siemann and Breuilly focus on the political changes of the 1848–9 revolutions and the events leading from revolution to unification. Friedrich and Lee provide essays in cultural and economic history for the whole of this period. Part II considers the period from 1871 to 1918. In two essays Lerman focuses on the political institutions and history of the Second Empire in the period up to 1890 and from 1890 to 1914. Chickering looks at the last four wartime years of the Second Empire. Jefferies and Berghahn provide essays in cultural and socio-economic history for the whole period.

Themes and approaches

The greatest problem confronting the historian of large-scale transformation over a number of generations is that of definition. Is there a subject which varies in space and changes over time but in some essential sense remains present throughout, producing or accepting all these changes and variations? Or is the essence in that very variety and change which means there is no unifying subject to be identified?

The unifying subject identified in the title of this book is 'German'. It is this national idea which provides at least a framework, if not a subject or agency. The nation can be seen as having a unifying effect over space and time. Yet the various essays make clear the dangers of using the national idea in this way.

At no time did all those who might be defined as 'Germans' live under common political institutions. There always were some overarching 'German' institutions – the Holy Roman Empire (to 1806), the Confederation of the Rhine (1806–13), the German Confederation (1815–66), the German Customs Union (*Zollverein*, 1834 onwards), the North German Confederation (1867–71) and the German Second Empire (1871–1918). However, none of these institutions ever extended over all the territory occupied by those who considered themselves to be German and they always included people who did not consider themselves to be German. Furthermore, these national institutions often meant very little to 'Germans'. This is obvious for the earlier part of the period when individual state, regional and even local institutions had a much greater impact on people than national institutions. However, it is also arguably true for much of the later period as well. For example, most direct taxation and educational provision remained the domain of individual states within the Second Empire. When one turns from political institutions to cultural, social and economic history the problems with the national framework become even more obvious. Differences between Catholics and Protestants, men and women, workers and employers, Prussians and Austrians, Rhinelanders and Brandenburgers often appear more important than any common interest or identity these people shared as Germans. Not only is the nation but one possible historical subject, arguably it is a less important historical subject than many others. How therefore can one justify a focus on 'German' history?

To this there are a number of answers, some of which are more acceptable than others. The nationalist answer is simply to deny the claims for other frames and subjects. There is a German nation even if at times this subject is obscured by other identities, loyalties and interests, and it represents the most important of collective identities and historical subjects. Apart from the fact that only nationalists can accept such a view, there is the additional problem that there are conflicting forms of this nationalist claim. Austrians or Catholics could be German nationalists, i.e. want to see all Germans living in a single state, but their ideas about the territorial extent and institutional structure of this state could run directly counter to what Prussians or Protestants wanted. The national idea did not only matter little to many Germans in this period; even when it did matter it did so in different, changing and conflicting ways.

A more credible answer is to see national history in terms of *becoming* rather than *being*. It is much easier to argue for the marginality of the national idea in 1800 than it is in 1918. In 1800 there was little social or geographical mobility, national institutions were weak, and the (non-national) state had little positive impact on the everyday life of most people. By 1918 people changed jobs and locations within a common national space and the nation-state made decisions about such matters as food rations and the content of newspapers. Ideas about a 'national society' or 'national economy' make more sense in the period considered by Berghahn than by Lee, and ideas of a 'national culture' appear more valid in the essay by Jefferies than in that by Friedrich. The historian can legitimately consider the way the national idea moved from the margins to the centre.[1]

The great danger with this answer is that it can impose inappropriate perspectives, especially upon the earlier period. If 1871 or 1918 (or later 1933 or 1945 or 1990) is seen as the destination to which German history is moving, everything prior to that terminal date can be seen in terms of their positive or negative contributions to the journey. Thus the 'Prussian' school of history which flourished after 1871 took the fact of Prussian leadership, transformed this into the only possible instrument of national unification, and treated the pre-1871 history of the other German states as a series of obstructions and distractions. That particular approach took a 'positive' view of national unification. Since 1918 and especially since 1945, some historians have instead taken a 'negative' view. Many of the essays which follow refer to what is known as the *Sonderweg* (special path), the view that German history in some way departed from the normal path to modernity taken by other states like Britain, France and the USA. This approach has also been criticized for its teleological view, even if the concepts used and the values applied are very different from those of the Prussian school.[2]

These are powerful criticisms but they can be taken too far. One can recognize that certain things came to pass without assuming that they had to come to pass. Prussia *did* take the lead in creating a national state and that is something that the historian must seek to describe and explain but without necessarily taking the view that this was the only way national unification could come about. Precisely such an approach makes the historian sensitive to the variety of views contemporaries held about the national question, for example within the national parliament that met in Frankfurt am Main in 1848–9. Recent research to which Whaley and Clark refers has looked positively at the national achievements and/or possibilities of the Holy Roman Empire, the Rhenish Confederation and the German Confederation and not regarded the Prusso-German state created in 1871 as the only possible nation-state. Such perspectives are as much a product of hindsight (e.g. the positive valuation of federalism in the Federal Republic and more broadly the European Union) as the Prussian or *Sonderweg* schools.[3]

There is nothing wrong in principle with hindsight; indeed it is difficult to see how the historian could or should dispense with it. The major advantage the historian has over those he or she studies is knowing what came afterwards and it is not an advantage to be lightly thrown away. Rather the arguments should be about regarding the actual outcome as the only possible outcome and the methods to be used in trying to account for that particular outcome. To interpret national unification in terms of 'national character or awakening', for example, is to take a very different approach from those who employ such ideas as that of class interests or the functional needs of a modern economy or culture or the power relationships between different states. There are a diversity of theories about why nationalism and the nation-state have become so important in the modern period and they are quite properly reflected in debates over modern German history.[4]

Yet at the same time it has to be recognized not merely that the national idea has changing and conflicting forms but that it must be related to other concepts.

First, all the essays in this book make it clear that one cannot understand German history outside a European context. This is above all clear at the political and military level. The transformation of German states between 1800 and 1815 was but one aspect of the revolutionary and Napoleonic wars. The revolutions of 1848–9 in Germany were part of a series of European revolutions which interacted in important ways. The formation of the Second Empire was achieved through three wars, two of them against non-German states. The Second Empire was ended through defeat in world war. However, the European dimension is present not only during periods of war and revolution. The Holy Roman Empire only functioned under certain European conditions and with the formal involvement of non-German powers; the Rhenish Confederation was created by Napoleon; the German Confederation was a product of the international peace settlement reached at the Congress of Vienna in 1814–15.

This European dimension can be taken further. As Friedrich and Jefferies make clear, many themes in German cultural history are but variants on broader European, even global concerns – romanticism in music, historicism in architecture, the advances of modern science. Even if some of these themes are given a national emphasis, that very national emphasis is something which frequently takes similar forms from one national framework to another. Equally, German economic development cannot be understood outside a European, even global context; for example, food exports to Britain and other industrializing regions in western Europe have as much impact on the agriculture of eastern Germany as do laws passed by the Prussian state. The possibility of emigration to the USA is as important to explaining the failure of political radicalism in and after the 1848 revolutions as is state repression.

Second, in the other direction all the essays make clear the importance of the sub-national. To begin with there are the various German states. As Whaley points out, very often the term 'national' in the Napoleonic period referred to state loyalty rather than national loyalty. In the cases of the two major states, Prussia and Austria, this could mean appealing to the loyalty of non-Germans – for example, Polish speakers in eastern Prussia or Slav speakers in the eastern half of the Habsburg Empire. At the level of political and military history it is these two states which are the principal actors within 'Germany' up to 1866. After 1871 the individual states within the

Second Empire remain important objects of loyalty and control many aspects of people's lives even if this is increasingly placed within a national framework and new national institutions are created and grow in importance. Jefferies shows how, for example, federalism promoted the cause of cultural diversity, as with the challenge Munich posed as a cultural centre to Berlin.

However, it is also important to realize that these states are not themselves fixed blocks. There are periods when states are subject to great institutional and territorial change. Prussia, for example, acquired much Polish territory in the partitions of the late eighteenth century, suffered huge territorial losses in 1806–7, expanded again in 1815 and yet again in 1867 and 1871. There is a 'core' territory of Brandenburg–Prussia but that cannot be identified with the Prussian state. This is reflected in institutional arrangements: Prussia had different systems of government in various provinces and indeed Prussia was first referred to officially as a single state in the constitution issued in December 1848. Modern Baden, Bavaria and Württemberg are Napoleonic creations which in turn were reshaped territorially in 1814–15. Consequently, even while recognizing the importance of individual states within Germany over this whole period, one should not imagine that these can be represented as fixed territories, institutions or identities which might be used to complement or replace ideas about the German nation.

Some historians have looked instead to the concept of region rather than state, especially where it is recognized that states such as Prussia or Bavaria included distinct regions like Brandenburg and Franconia. In the early part of the century such regions sometimes came into conflict with their rulers, e.g. Protestants in the Bavarian Palatinate with the central state in Munich and Catholics in the Rhineland with the central state in Berlin. By contrast, by the end of the Second Empire there was something of a cult of *Heimat* which presented the German nation as the overarching product of a series of such regional identities which knitted together to produce harmony in diversity. Yet closer analysis in turn dissolves any constancy to the concept of region, above all because different groups in these various regions took very different views of their relationship to state and national institutions. By the end of our period, for all the cult of *Heimat*, very large numbers of Germans were moving from one region to another in search of work and most of the electorate voted for national rather than regional or state parties in *Reichstag* elections.

What I think this means is that ideas about the supra-national, national, and sub-national (both individual state and region) can only be used as framing devices as well as specific and changing outcomes requiring explanation, rather than as the actual subjects or agents of history. The way these ideas will be deployed and related together will in turn change from one period and type of history to another. Yet the meaning of any one of these ideas will hang upon those interrelationships.

I can only briefly refer to a few examples. Lee in his essay considers interpretations of the origins of the *Zollverein* which suggest that this 'national' institution was initially formed to serve the fiscal interests of individual states rather than as an instrument of national economic development or unification. Indeed, some historians have gone further and suggested that the operations of the *Zollverein* in that earlier period actually impeded certain kinds of economic development, for example, by disrupting regional trade flows which crossed *Zollverein* boundaries.

A second example: in the early period of the 1848 revolution leading activists in regions which strongly resisted state control, like the Bavarian Palatinate and the Prussian Rhineland, were inclined to favour the construction of a strong national state as one means of limiting the power of the individual states. Here, arguably, a strong sense of regional identity could ally rather than conflict with a strong national commitment. However, if the project of the national state appeared to fall into the wrong hands, such a view could rapidly reverse itself. Such a reversal might be related to confessional or class identity or to one's political values, depending on how liberal or democratic it appeared a national state might be.

These examples suggest that 'national' institutions can have their origins in non-national interests although later coming to take on national functions; that national commitments might be the product of strong rather than weak regional concerns; that a pro-national commitment could quickly reverse itself under certain conditions and *vice versa*; and that what was planned to have a national function might well not work in the way intended and *vice versa*. Thus rather than thinking about the supranational, the national and the sub-national as fixed institutions, interests, functions or identities which become more or less important over time, it might be better to think of them as so many fields or frames of action which change their meaning and interrelationships over time. What matters is what gets people to operate within the national field of action rather than some other field at a particular time and in relation to a particular objective. The more people operate within that national field of action, the more firmly embedded will become feelings of national identity, even if these often conflict with one another.

Sometimes the shift into the national field of action can take place quickly, for example during the revolution of 1848–9 or around the time of the war of 1866. In these cases the fast and unpredictable changes in the balance of power between different political groups or states meant that the 'national question' suddenly acquired significance. Usually this was accompanied by a constant need to re-evaluate what the outcome was likely to mean. Frequently we find people declaring that it was only at such times that they 'discovered' their nationality; this is true, for example, of people who 'realized' that they are Germans or Czechs rather than Bohemians or Habsburg subjects in early 1848. (Sometimes there are examples of brothers coming to different realizations.)

It can be that at the end of such a period of rapid change a particular set of identities and interests are crystallized in institutional forms. These can then be reproduced in an apparently routine way over a number of years. Thus, for example, it seems possible to locate a gradual and continuous growth of a positive sense of national identity produced by the expansion of the organized labour movement in the latter period of the Second Empire and its intensifying involvement in national institutions. At no time does this lead to consensus; rather it leads to the increasing importance of orientation to national institutions and roles in relation to supra- or sub-national levels of action.

Yet one should never imagine that any particular set of identities or relationships just naturally occur and recur and are so stable and embedded that they cannot be quickly altered or revalued. Clearly the society of the German Second Empire was, by 1914, a 'national society' in ways which were unimaginable even forty years earlier, let alone in 1800. In many ways orientation to the national level of action intensified with the militarization of the economy in the following years. Yet that did not necessarily make German society more national in any consensual sense. Rather, as Chickering shows, intolerable pressures produced great changes and revaluations of the national idea from 1916 to 1918. In some cases it led to more intense (if conflicting) commitments to the national idea. In other cases, for example within the peace and socialist movements, it led to a more intense commitment to supra-national ideals and movements.

In every case it is the duty of the historian to demonstrate the continuities with what had gone before (for example, how tensions within the pre-war Socialist Party can be linked to the splits which took place after 1916) but also to demonstrate how new pressures and problems lead people to change their values and the fields of action within which they operate. In doing this the historian can use the supra-national, national and sub-nation as linked fields of action within which groups and individuals with a variety of identities and interests (gender, class, confession, etc.) operate.[5]

All the essays that follow sketch out in different ways the interactions between supra-national, national and sub-national levels of action in this way. The national dimension *does* become increasingly central to more and more people over the course of the period, although this is not a simple linear process or one necessarily productive of greater consensus. Yet arguably this process is itself part of a broader, international trend and one which also leads not to the erosion but rather to the transformation of supranational and sub-national identities and institutions. It would be inappropriate (even if it were intellectually possible!) for me to offer any overarching interpretation of German history in the 'long 19th century'.[6] These essays reflect the divergent interests of cultural, social, economic and political historians; the variations between sub-periods; whether the emphasis is upon understanding short-run or long-run sequences of events; and much else. The purpose of the book is to convey to the reader something of the complexity and plurality of interpretations which in turn I hope will open up many avenues for further reading and reflection.

Notes:

1. See, for example, *Becoming National: a Reader*, edited by Geoff Eley and Ronald Suny (1996).
2. See chapter by Stefan Berger, 'The German Tradition of Historiography, 1800–1995', in *German History since 1800*, edited by Mary Fulbrook (1997), pp. 477–92.
3. See the chapter I wrote on 'The national idea in modern German history' in *German History since 1800*, pp. 556–84.
4. For recent considerations of these various approaches and theories see Anthony D. Smith, *Nationalism and Modernism* (1998) and Umut Özkirmli, *Theories of Nationalism: a Critical Introduction* (2000). For attempts to put such approaches and theories to use in historical analysis see Benedict Anderson, *Imagined Communities* (2nd edn., 1991); John Breuilly, *Nationalism and the State* (2nd edn., 1993); Ernest Gellner, *Nations and Nationalism* (1983); Eric Hobsbawm, *Nations and Nationalism since 1789* (1991).
5. Some of these other identities and interests were considered in a more general, thematic way in Part 5 of *German History since 1800*. See for example the essays by Jürgen Kocka, 'The Difficult Rise of a Civil Society: societal history of modern Germany', and Ute Frevert, 'Gender in German History'.
6. See the title of the book by Blackbourn cited in the select bibliography.

Select bibliography

Each of the contributors provides reading suggestions relating to his or her particular field. Here I cite three good, recent general studies in English that cover the same period of German history dealt with in this book. These books contain substantial bibliographies of English-language literature.

Part I

1780–1871

Introduction to Part I: 1780–1871

The essays dealing with the period from the late eighteenth century to the formation of the German Second Empire cover a variety of topics. The concern is mainly political in the contributions by Whaley, Clark, Siemann and Breuilly. Lee considers social and economic issues while Friedrich focuses on culture. In this brief introduction I will make two basic points.

First, Germany did not exist as a national state until the very end of the period covered by this section. Even then a major part of pre-1871 Germany, the German part of the Habsburg Empire, was excluded from the new state. Not only were there many states in 'Germany' but these states were themselves subject to territorial alteration through processes of war and diplomacy as well as undergoing considerable institutional and social change. One should also draw attention to the great regional variations within the larger states. Sometimes there were different institutional and legal arrangements in different parts of the same state. Inhabitants of one Prussian province had little contact with those from other provinces. Catholic culture differed enormously from Protestant culture; social divisions were much greater than today; life in east Germany was very different from that of west Germany; town and countryside were almost different worlds, often with different tax and governmental arrangements. One could multiply such examples of variation, difference and distance. Conversely, Germans in border regions often had closer contacts with non-Germans in the same region than with Germans in other regions, for example Rhenish Prussians with Belgians. Even how we make a judgement on that depends on whether we define a German as a native speaker of German, a subject of a German state, a participant in 'high' German culture, or people who in some way or another consciously regarded themselves as German. All this makes the terms 'Germany' and 'German' problematic and this is a point one will encounter frequently in the various essays and which needs to be kept constantly in mind.

Second, it is quite impossible to cover every aspect of the history of Germany in this period. The essays by Clark and Friedrich touch upon religion, philosophy and popular literature but it was simply impossible to provide a full survey either of the history of ideas or of popular culture. Instead the focus is upon organized religion, the work of philosophers which had a contemporary social or political significance, and upon the development of a new and distinctive culture associated with the bourgeoisie. War was a major feature of the Napoleonic period and the period between 1854 and 1871 and was also important in 1848–49 but there is no especial focus in these essays on the military history of this period. (See, however, in the original edition of *German History since 1800*, chapter 26 by Charles Maier: 'German War, German Peace', pp. 539–55.)

Nevertheless, the essays cover a great deal of ground and provide many details. There is perhaps a danger that the reader will lose sight of the 'big picture'. Some historians would dispute the validity of such an idea and suggest that this simply means imposing some preconceived view of what is important on the period. However, I do think there are certain major transformations in German history in this period that underpin much of the detail. Most obviously, by 1871 Germany had been brought under the control of a single state, that of Prussia. Germans moved around their country much more by 1871 than a century earlier (and many more of them also emigrated abroad). Furthermore, that movement, insofar as it was long-distance, was largely from east to west, reversing an earlier pattern. From mid-century, urban population growth outstripped that of the countryside. The imagination of contemporaries was coming to be captivated by the rapid expansion of railways, coal, iron and steel. This new technology shaped the wars of unification in ways which sharply distinguished them from those of the revolutionary and Napoleonic period. By 1871, compared to 1780, Germans were more prosperous, more mobile and more conscious of being Germans. Not only had a national state been formed but the elements of a national economy, society and culture were more clearly visible than a century earlier.

Of course, one should not exaggerate how far this had gone or imagine that what had happened was inevitable. The essays constantly point to underlying continuities and the extent to which 'Germany' remained a land of diverse regions, cultures and possibilities during this period. Still, it is much easier to write something called 'German history' by the end of this period than it was at the beginning.

2

The German lands before 1815

Joachim Whaley

In the decades before 1815 the German lands underwent a process of revolutionary change, but there was no revolution as such, nothing to compare with events in France in 1789. Yet contemporaries experienced this period as one of profound and rapid transformation. Most obviously, the map of Germany in 1815 looked very different from what it had been in, say, 1780. The Holy Roman Empire had ceased to exist after a thousand-year history; a bewildering patchwork of several hundred quasi-independent territories had been replaced by 41 sovereign states in a loose confederation. This 'territorial revolution' was accompanied by other equally profound changes: the transformation of political and legal institutions; a new relationship between church, state and society in the Catholic regions; new social and economic structures resulting from the massive transfer of Catholic ecclesiastical property; new cultural attitudes and novel perceptions of what 'Germany' and the very identity of the Germans was or might be; a new political vocabulary and new concepts with which Germans described the world in which they lived. The sheer magnitude and pace of change struck many contemporaries as the major characteristic of their age. The Gotha bookseller and publisher Friedrich Perthes (1772–1843) expressed the sense of many when he reflected in 1818 that while previous periods in history had been characterized by gradual change over centuries, 'In the three generations alive today our own age has, in fact, combined what cannot be combined. No sense of continuity informs the tremendous contrasts inherent in the years 1750, 1789 and 1815; to people alive now . . . they simply do not appear as a sequence of events.'[1]

Much of this complexity was lost in the classic accounts of this period by German historians of the later nineteenth and early twentieth centuries. They constructed a narrative which showed the inevitability of the emergence of a Prussian-dominated nation state in 1871. For Treitschke and others, German history was Prussian history. The Holy Roman Empire was portrayed as decayed and moribund, the German territories as backward and corrupt. When challenged by the ideas and the armies of the French Revolution, German political institutions, both imperial and territorial, collapsed. Yet out of Napoleon's humiliation of the Germans, according to the traditional view, a new sense of German destiny arose. Prussia, which had emerged as a great power under Frederick the Great, became the focus of a new national movement, while the Prussian reforms after 1806 supposedly embodied the German answer to 1789. Most leading historians, like Friedrich Meinecke (1862–1954), held that Stein and Hardenberg transformed Prussia into a bastion of the German national movement, the driving force in the Wars of Liberation which defeated Napoleon and finally expelled the French from Germany.

Elements of the traditional view survive even in some recent surveys. Thomas Nipperdey's account of Germany in the nineteenth century (published in 1983) opens with the words: 'In the beginning was Napoleon'.[2] Nipperdey cannot be accused of being an exponent of the '*kleindeutsch*' tradition of Prusso-centric history. Yet his portrayal of Napoleon as the 'creator' echoes the teleological ideology of the nationalist historians. German nationalism is presented as a response to French domination characterized by a reaction against French ideas (the 'ideas of 1789'), the problematic inception of modernity in Germany.

Tradition dies hard, but in the last few decades virtually every aspect of the period before 1815 has been the subject of revision. Some scholars have explored the 'modernization' of Germany in this period. Others, working primarily from an early modern perspective, have found continuity as well as change. Above all much recent research has sought to investigate alternatives to the Prusso-centric view of German history. The insistence that the emergence of the Prussian-German nation state in 1871 was not inevitable has focused attention on other options, such as a Holy Roman Empire or the Confederation of the Rhine. This has in turn shed new light on the history of nationalism and on the significance of reform movements outside Prussia, particularly in south and west Germany. At the same time a growing emphasis on lines of continuity, from enlightened absolutist reform before 1789 to the bureaucratic reforms after 1800, has challenged the view that the modernization of the German states, including Prussia, was purely defensive. Furthermore, in the European context, it appears increasingly that revolutionary France rather than reforming Germany was the exception. Some aspects of this tendency to 'normalize' German history before 1815 may be as much reflections of the *Zeitgeist* of the Federal

Republic of the 1980s and 1990s as the Prusso-centric view was of the political ideology of Germany between 1871 and 1945. Yet recent research has done much to undermine the view that German history between 1780 and 1815 represents a stage in a straightforward progression towards the nation state, still less a *Sonderfall* with disturbing implications for the history of the later nineteenth and twentieth centuries.

I The Holy Roman Empire in the eighteenth century

The Prussian-German tradition viewed the Holy Roman Empire as inadequate because it failed to become a nation state. Modern scholars, by contrast, argue that the system worked effectively. Under the Emperor as *Schutz- und Schirmherr* (protector and guardian), the Reich fulfilled a vital role after 1648 in the areas of law, defence and peace in central Europe. As a *Friedensordnung* (a peace-preserving order), it both guaranteed the peace and stability of Europe as a whole and ensured the survival of the myriad small German territories, none of which, except Prussia, were capable of survival as independent units in the competitive world of European powers. As a *Verteidigungsordnung* (a system of defence), the Reich ensured protection from external threat. As a *Rechtsordnung* (a legal system), it provided mechanisms to secure the rights both of rulers and, more extraordinarily, of subjects against their rulers. Its institutions, such as the imperial courts in Wetzlar and Vienna, provided legal safeguards for many of the inhabitants of the German territories.

Conditions varied enormously amongst the territories which made up the Reich. Some were characterized by corruption, mismanagement and stagnation. Many of the smaller south German Imperial Cities, the miniature territories of imperial knights or independent abbeys and the like, were incapable of significant innovation even if the will to change was there. In many territories, however, the decades after 1750 saw significant changes. Inspired by enlightened rationalism and driven by the need for revenue, particularly acute in the economic crisis which followed the end of the Seven Years War in 1763, many German princes embarked on ambitious reform programmes. Even in the ecclesiastical territories, commonly regarded as anachronisms by the end of the eighteenth century, wide-ranging reforms were introduced in education, poor relief and administration generally. Other states saw the beginnings of codification of law and a rationalization of fiscal administration. As the term 'enlightened absolutism' indicates, the process was initiated by the princes, but it was driven and implemented by a growing army of educated officials. For many of them the reforms represented the first stage of the emancipation of

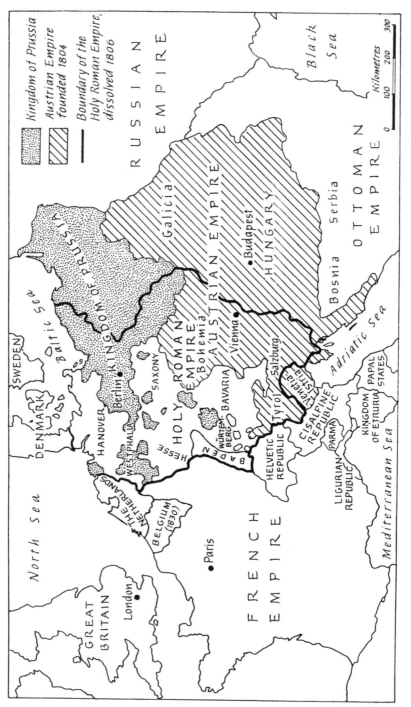

Map 2.1 Germany and the Austrian Empire, 1800–6

society that formed a central ideal of the German Enlightenment (*Aufklärung*). In the upheavals after 1800 the inherent contradiction between absolutism and emancipation became glaringly apparent. Yet in this first phase there was periodic tension but little conflict. The German educated classes were not composed of disaffected intellectuals, but of active and often enthusiastic participants in the reform process.

There were, of course, limits to what could be achieved by even the most ambitious enlightened prince. The most significant constraint was the imperial system itself. The German princes were not sovereign rulers: their power was qualified by a feudal subordination to the Reich which guaranteed the status quo, especially the rights of estates and corporations which in many territories impeded the imposition of rationalized central control. This limitation was only seriously challenged in the Habsburg lands and in Prussia, with fundamental implications for the future of the Reich and for the subsequent history of German lands.

From the early eighteenth century, Habsburg policy was characterized by a growing tension between dynastic interests and imperial duties. The succession crisis of 1740 underlined the need to consolidate the Habsburg inheritance, a collection of territories which straddled the southeastern frontier of the Reich. The creation of a Habsburg unitary state meant removing the western Habsburg lands from the Reich. In Austria, therefore, enlightened reform aimed to construct a closed unitary state. Under Joseph II from the late 1770s that involved policies hostile to the Reich, in particular a plan to exchange Bavaria for the Netherlands (with or without the consent of the Bavarian estates). Joseph only succeeded in uniting the Reich against him, but the idea of 'rounding off' a consolidated Habsburg state in southeastern Europe, including Bavaria if possible, remained an *idée fixe* in the corridors of the Hofburg even after his death.

A similar tension between Reich and territorial state characterized Brandenburg-Prussia. The construction of a formidable administrative and military machinery began before 1700 and reached a peak in the reign of Frederick William I (1713–40). The reform process was energetically promoted by Frederick II (1740–86) and shaped by his enlightened precepts. It culminated after his death in the publication of a general legal code in 1794 (*Allgemeines Landrecht*), significant for the way in which, technically illegally, it transcended imperial law to provide a unitary legal framework for the Prussian territories. At the same time Prussia's geopolitical position, straddling the Reich's northeast frontier, was similar to that of Austria. Her rulers were not, however, constrained by imperial obligations, and Frederick II in particular used this freedom to exploit every weakness in the Habsburg position. As significant as his military annexation of Silesia in 1740 was the virtuosity with which he manipulated the imperial constitution thereafter, becoming a kind of 'anti-Emperor' in the Reich.

It has often been argued that the power struggle between Austria and Prussia after 1740 doomed the Reich. It is, however, anachronistic to speak of Austria's 'departure' from Germany in the eighteenth century or of Prussia's extension of hegemony over it. Despite being torn in other directions, both states remained deeply wedded to the Reich. Their mutual antagonism was carried out through the mechanisms of the Imperial constitution: not by outright confrontation but through a constant jockeying for position in the Reich's representative institutions.

Furthermore, the other territories were not merely pawns in the larger game. The response of what became known as the 'third Germany' (the smaller territories and ecclesiastical principalities of the south and west) was a series of initiatives to reform the Reich after the 1760s. This new *Reichspatriotismus* (imperial patriotism) failed to generate a renewal of the Reich. The League of Princes (Fürstenbund) of 1785, its one concrete result, did not prove durable or effective in promoting the interests of the smaller territories, formed in opposition to Joseph II's aggressive policies. It foundered in 1788 because it fell into the undertow of Prussian policy. Despite this, the reform initiatives demonstrate three important points: first, the continuing interest in the Reich of many of its members, for whom it fulfilled a vital function; second, the inability of either Austria or Prussia to subvert the Reich against the determined resistance of the other territories; but third also the inability of the Reich to reform itself. In the last resort its durability derived from the fact that it was securely bedded into the old European state system. It was only when that international system itself was plunged into crisis in the 1790s that the Reich was acutely threatened. Once the buttresses were removed the ancient imperial edifice rapidly began to show the effects of the disintegrative tendencies that had so far been held in check.

II   The impact of the French Revolution on Germany

The French Revolution of 1789 transformed the German political landscape. The revolutionary slogan of 'liberty, equality, fraternity' created a new context for German politics, while the revolutionary wars after 1792 unleashed forces which led directly to the dissolution of the Reich in 1806 and to the emergence of a new constellation of reformed German states. There was no German revolution, but the way in which the German territories responded to the revolutionary challenge and adapted to the ideas of 1789 shaped the development of German politics and society into the twentieth century.

The first response of most German commentators to the events of 1789 was overwhelmingly positive. Figures as diverse as Kant, Herder, Hegel and Fichte hailed the news from France as the dawn of a new age of freedom for mankind, a watershed of world historical significance. In many German towns in 1790 clubs were formed and liberty trees planted, while journals and newspapers carried enthusiastic reports of the progress of events in France. At the same time, however, there was a strong feeling that the revolution had specifically French causes and a conviction that Germany did not need a revolution because conditions were better there. Some argued that the Reformation had effected a kind of 'pre-revolution' in Germany, which the *Aufklärung* had built upon to bring about a society capable of peaceful change. Others argued that the French monarchy was simply more despotic and hopelessly corrupt than anything to be found in the Reich. The consensus was clear: Germany did not need to emulate the French Revolution because many of its ideals and objectives could be, indeed were being, achieved by evolutionary means. As the revolution became more radical, so the distinction made between France and Germany became more emphatic. After the execution of the king in January 1793 and the emergence of Robespierre's reign of terror the enthusiasm of the early years largely dissolved. Some held on to the ideals of 1789, explaining that the revolutionary regime had betrayed them. Others turned against both the *Aufklärung* and its reforming ideals and rediscovered the virtues of 'German liberty' in the world of the traditional estates, and by 1800 at the latest the debate had been 'internalized' and revolved not around the French example but around variations on the 'German way'.

The reaction of intellectuals alone cannot explain the lack of a German revolution. More significant was the fact that the preconditions of the explosion in France were quite simply absent in Germany. The nobility, the educated classes and the lower clergy, all of whom played a key role in the French crisis, were in one way or another integrated into the machinery of the state in Germany. The middling classes in the Imperial Cities were deeply conservative. Rural conditions were either not so bad (west of the Elbe over 90 per cent of peasants owned some land, compared with 35 per cent in France) or rigidly under noble control (east of the Elbe). Lacking a powerful capital city, the decentralized Reich, with its legal conflict resolution mechanisms, was able to absorb more minor shocks than the unwieldy centralized French monarchy.

These structural factors inhibited a serious revolutionary crisis.

Widespread unrest in the Rhineland in 1789 and 1790, uprisings of artisans in Hamburg and elsewhere in north Germany remained localized. Substantial peasant uprisings in Saxony in 1790 and in Silesia in 1792–3 were brutally put down by military force. The most colourful revolutionary episode, the attempt to establish a republic in Mainz after Custine's occupation of the city in 1792, was a short-lived farce conducted by a small number of 'Jacobins' without popular support. If the Mainz radicals were leaders without a following, the problem elsewhere was the lack of real revolutionaries. Individuals such as the Liepstadt rope-maker Benjamin Geißler, who proclaimed a genuinely revolutionary programme inspired by French ideas in Saxony, remained an exception.

Few of the German Jacobins were in fact committed to revolutionary change. The agitation of the 1790s had, however, two important results. First, among many rulers and thinkers the unrest, compounded by increasingly alarming news from France, provoked a fierce reaction. In Prussia (after 1793) and Austria (particularly after the discovery of a 'Jacobin conspiracy' in Vienna in 1794) this stifled the last impulses of the enlightened reform process. In many other areas the unrest generated demands for participation often coupled with a growing criticism of princely absolutism. In many areas of south and west Germany this was manifest in the renewed vigour and stridency of the representatives of the estates in the territories. In other areas enlightened officials and non-revolutionary 'Jacobins' pressed more urgently than ever for reform before it was too late, echoing the maverick (and sometime alleged Jacobin) Freiherr von Knigge's exhortation to the princes: 'While there is yet time, O princes, lend your own helping hands for the improvement that is needed!'[3]

III   The French Revolutionary Wars and the end of the Holy Roman Empire

Knigge was wrong: the German princes did not have time. After 1792 the Reich became embroiled in the revolutionary wars which led to its dissolution, to the dispossession of many princes and independent rulers, and to the reorganization of the territories that remained. The crisis revealed that the Reich lacked the capacity to defend itself against armed force. Neither Austria nor Prussia showed any desire to coordinate and lead a sustained defence of the Reich. Indeed both pursued policies which explicitly undermined the very principles on which the Reich was founded and both contributed as much as France to its dissolution in 1806.

A divergence between the interests of the Reich on the one hand and the concerns of Austria and Prussia on the other became apparent as early as 1789–90. The abolition by the French revolutionaries of feudal rights and the confiscation of church property represented an attack on both German secular princes who held lands in Alsace and Lorraine and on those prince bishops whose dioceses extended into French territory. These actions struck at the very foundations of the Reich: the inviolability of feudal principles and the continued existence of the ecclesiastical states which formed its core. The radical implications of the French actions were immediately clear to the German rulers of the Rhineland and the southwest.

Yet nothing was done. The smaller territories were incapable of acting alone. Neither Austria nor Prussia moved to support their cause, for each was motivated by other concerns and preoccupied with larger strategies. Both Vienna and Berlin viewed the Revolution as a purely domestic problem. It was also felt that the French troubles might bring about a welcome absence of France from the European stage. The mutual distrust between Austria and Prussia persisted, but in 1790 pragmatic considerations dictated a reconciliation sealed by the Convention of Reichenbach.

For the Reich the new Austro-Prussian *détente* was ominous. First, in entering into an alliance with Prussia the Emperor had apparently abandoned his own imperial role as impartial mediator. Second, the reconciliation revived Austrian plans to exchange the Netherlands for Bavaria, this time potentially with Prussian consent. Third, as the tension with France escalated in 1791 it became clear that neither Austria nor Prussia would fight without territorial compensation. Hardly surprisingly the smaller states viewed the situation with alarm. As the Bishop of Würzburg told the Austrian envoy in December 1791: 'If Austria and Prussia agree then the Reich will be finished.'[4] In fact the only immediate result of the new Austro-Prussian understanding was to bring them both into conflict with France. Their declaration of solidarity with Louis XVI inflamed the radicals in the National Convention and led directly to the French declaration of war in April 1792.

Initially the Reich remained neutral. The German princes only agreed to enter the war with an independent imperial army in March 1793 after the French had advanced to the Rhine and occupied Mainz. The decision was made with reluctance: it was rightly pointed out that Austria and Prussia alone were to blame for the war, and that it was not being fought to defend the interests of the Reich. The anxieties expressed in the Reichstag proved amply justified. In military terms the princes gained nothing. The hopes raised by a successful campaign against the French in 1793 were dashed the following year when the revolutionary armies reoccupied the Rhineland, this time permanently. Nor did their entry into the war win them the gratitude of the two major protagonists, who remained wedded to their own objectives. In Vienna grandiose and unrealistic schemes for a reorganization of the Reich proliferated. By contrast, Prussia rapidly lost even formal interest in developments in the west. The opportunity to acquire territory in Poland in 1793 diverted troops and money to the east, and the conflict with France became an unjustifiable expenditure with no prospect of reward.

The failure of the 1794 campaign, undermined in part by the half-hearted participation of the Prussian military, generated a widespread desire for peace. Even that was, however, frustrated by renewed antagonism between Austria and Prussia, by Austria's determination not to give in to the French, and by a deepening mistrust on the part of many German princes of the motives of the imperial court. Prussia alone withdrew in 1795 after signing the Peace of Basel with France which deferred all territorial issues until a future settlement between France and the Reich. In the meantime Prussia agreed to cease hostilities and to recognize the legitimacy of the revolutionary government. In additional secret clauses, however, Prussia accepted French occupation of the left bank of the Rhine, in return for which she was to be compensated by territory on the right bank. Prussia also agreed to seek to secure the withdrawal from the war of all the north German territories, while the French undertook to respect the neutrality of the Prussian sphere of influence.

The treaty effectively divided the Reich by removing most of Germany north of the Main from the war for the next 10 years. Prussia's 'treachery', rapidly emulated by her neighbours, forced the territories south of the Main to turn to Vienna. They needed the Emperor's protection more than ever, against the French armies and against the spectre of domestic revolution. Yet Austrian protection had its price. The Austrians were not slow to present their bills to their protégés. Furthermore, the very proximity of Austrian troops both threatened the independence of the smaller territories and generated anxiety in Bavaria, whose estates remained acutely aware of Austria's annexationist ambitions. The position was the more threatening now that Austria's northern rival, so often the protector of the smaller territories in recent decades, basked in the safety of French-guaranteed neutrality. Attempts by Baden, Württemberg and Bavaria to hedge their bets only made matters worse. In 1796, fearing the renewed failure of the Austrian army, each concluded a secret agreement with France recognizing the loss of the left bank of the Rhine to France in return for compensation with secularized ecclesiastical property. When the Archduke Charles then defeated the French at Amberg and Würzburg, the south Germans were treated like a defeated enemy.

Austria's behaviour towards those she was supposedly protecting ensured that the Emperor gained no moral advantage from shouldering the full burden of the war against France. Furthermore her own position was soon undermined by defeat at the hands of Napoleon in Italy. Forced to conclude peace at Campo Formio in 1797, Austria followed Prussia and the three larger south German territories by agreeing (in secret clauses) to French annexation of the left bank of the Rhine in return for compensation on the right bank. As a reward Austria was promised the archbishopric of Salzburg and parts of eastern Bavaria.

If the willingness of Baden, Württemberg and Bavaria to abandon the Reich had been exposed by Austria, the intention of Prussia and Austria to do likewise was only revealed at the Rastatt conference convened in December 1797 to draw up terms for a general peace with France, though negotiations broke down in April 1799 once the secret clauses of Basel and Campo Formio became known. Perhaps the most significant outcome of Rastatt was a new French policy towards the German territories, for the conference exposed the potential isolation of Austria and Prussia. In November 1799 the Directory clearly recognized that the German princes were more promising allies than German republicans: ideological aggression waned as the Directory adopted the traditional Bourbon policy of dividing and ruling in southwest Germany.

Austria's attempts to resume the war merely resulted in less favourable terms being dictated to her by Napoleon at Lunéville in 1801: she was obliged to accept all of the concessions of the Campo Formio settlement without any of the rewards. Now, however, the majority of the princes, who had latterly scarcely been able to conceal their lack of enthusiasm for the Austrian cause, agreed with alacrity to conclude peace. Indeed several went further and concluded individual peace treaties with France which guaranteed them territorial enlargement. Acutely aware of Austria's isolation in Germany, the Emperor refused to preside over a conference to reorganize the Reich: indeed by now he and his advisers were simply concerned to secure sufficient compensation from France in return for relinquishing the imperial crown. As a result, the Reichstag itself appointed a commission which in March 1803 produced the *Reichsdeputationshauptschluß* (final constitutional law). This re-drew the map of Germany along lines dictated by France (with the agreement of Russia, the third guarantor power of the Reich). The changes were massive: the left bank of the Rhine was formally ceded to France; on the right bank three electorates, 19 bishoprics and 44 abbeys disappeared; in all about 10,000 square kilometres of land and some three million people were incorporated into new territories. The major winners were Prussia (in the Rhineland), Baden, Württemberg and

Bavaria. The disappearance of the ecclesiastical states gave the Protestant princes a majority for the first time, a further threat to the Habsburg position in the Reich.

Further changes soon followed. In 1804 Francis II assumed the title of Emperor of Austria, anticipating his abdication as Holy Roman Emperor in 1806 after another disastrous defeat and humiliating peace at Pressburg in December 1805, which also recognized the full sovereignty of Bavaria and Württemberg as kingdoms and of Baden and Hesse-Darmstadt as grand duchies. Even before the final dissolution of the Reich on 6 August 1806, 16 south and west German princes abandoned it by joining the Confederation of the Rhine. Another wave of changes began in 1806. Prussia's fatal decision to resume hostilities with France after 10 years of neutrality resulted in her crushing defeat at Jena and Auerstedt in October. Most of her recent territorial acquisitions were incorporated into new Napoleonic satellites: the kingdom of Westphalia and the grand duchies of Berg and Warsaw. In south Germany some 70 further minor territories were either secularized or 'mediatized', i.e. Imperial Cities and the lands of imperial knights were incorporated into the new sovereign states. By the end of 1807 the territory of the former Reich was divided into three fairly distinct areas: the left bank of the Rhine under France; the states of the Confederation of the Rhine (Rheinbund) under French influence and control; Austria and Prussia, both diminished in size and 'excluded' from Germany.

The main driving force in the dissolution process was clearly the success of the French armies. The eventual outcome was, however, shaped by the reactions of many of the German rulers. Since the early 1790s both Austria and Prussia had aimed at aggrandizement, which could only succeed at the expense of the smaller territories. Military inferiority, but also vacillation, deceitfulness, blindness and woeful miscalculations ensured by 1807 that neither achieved anything. The same ambition pursued after 1795–6 by the three largest south German territories led to success because they worked with Napoleon rather than against him. Of course they had little choice in that; even so, spectacular rewards fell into their tied hands.

Nationalist historians reserved harsh judgements for those who swam vigorously with the French tide. Recent scholars have adopted a more balanced view. Ambition and greed were clearly strong motives. The newly promoted rulers of Baden, Württemberg and Bavaria were determined to survive as independent sovereigns. On the other hand, idealism and a desire to rescue something from the Reich also played a part in the 'third Germany'. Some hoped that Napoleon might be persuaded to become head of a new reformed Reich. The driving force behind many of these

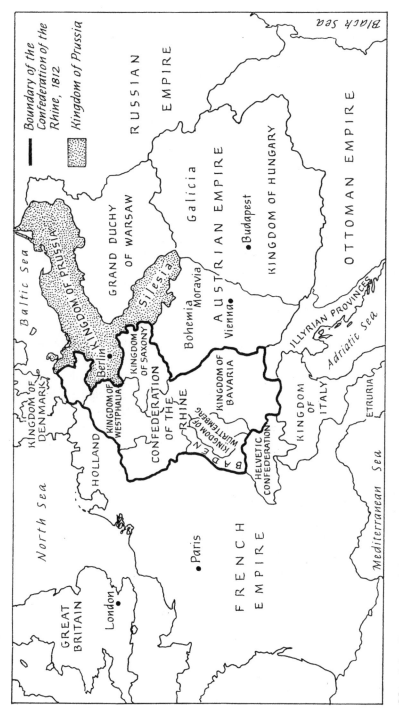

Map 2.2 Germany and the Austrian Empire, 1812

ideas was Karl Theodor von Dalberg, Elector of Mainz and Imperial Archchancellor. His self-interest is clear. While other ecclesiastical princes were dispossessed, Dalberg managed to have himself translated to Regensburg in 1803, made apostolic administrator of the whole Rhineland in 1805 with the title of Prince-Primate, made nominal head of the Rheinbund in 1806 and created Grand Duke of Frankfurt in 1810. Yet he too was captivated by the idea that a new Reich might be forged out of the old, with Napoleon as the new Charlemagne at its head.

Dalberg was not an isolated visionary. His ideas were echoed in the lively periodical literature devoted to the Rheinbund and found support among leading constitutional theorists such as Joseph Görres. Indeed in 1808 concrete proposals were made to transform the Rheinbund into a kind of national state of the Germans. It failed to become anything of the kind because of the opposition of Bavaria and Württemberg and above all because Napoleon himself had no interest in anything other than a loose federation which might serve his own military ends. His position as 'protector' of the Rheinbund was stronger than it might have been as ruler of a coherent German state capable of turning against him.

Though it ceased to exist in 1813, the Rheinbund was of exceptional importance. Its federal constitution looked both forward and backward. The central institutions envisaged in its constitution (though never in fact implemented) translated many of the representative mechanisms of the Reich into a modern idiom. At the same time the sovereign status of its members marked a clear break with the past. It was, in fact, neither a reformed Reich nor a nation-state. On the contrary it provided the framework for the creation of a new type of reformed sovereign territorial state in Germany.

IV   Reform and renewal in the German states

The nature and extent of the changes which took place in the so-called 'German reform era' have been the subject of intensive research in recent decades. Nationalist historians concentrated on the 'German' or 'organic' reforms in Prussia, as opposed to the allegedly superficial 'rationalist' reforms elsewhere, either imposed by Napoleon or at least derivative of French models. More recently, however, it has been recognized that the Rheinbund states made significant progress towards modernization in this period. At the same time it is still debated whether the reforms represented a 'defensive modernization', a 'revolution from above' forced on the German states by Napoleon, or whether they represented the continuation of an indigenous reform process begun in the 1770s and 1780s.

Despite regional differences, the reforms had many common features. The question of why the absolutist state collapsed in the face of the French armies was as acute in Baden and Bavaria as it was in Prussia. The answer too was broadly similar. Enlightened absolutist reform had created a gulf between state and society, the significance of which was driven home by the triumph of the new French nation of *citoyens*. This dictated that participation and representation, emancipation in the broadest sense, became a major theme of the reforms, though the remedies proposed ranged from traditional forms of representation based on estates to modern constitutional models. At the same time the reform process was shaped by more practical necessities. The new sovereign states, enlarged by secularization and mediatization, had to integrate new territories and mould them into a coherent governable whole: the new duchy of Nassau, for example, was made up of no fewer than 23 previously independent entities. Secularization meant that the state had to take up the functions previously exercized by the churches, which ensured that educational reform, with particular emphasis on the universities, was as central in south Germany as it was in Prussia. Confessionally uniform territories gave way to confessionally mixed states with complex legislation that guaranteed religious freedom and that tended to separate church and state.

At the same time long years of war and occupation financially exhausted many of the German territories, and the problems were exacerbated as the new states assumed the debts of the territories they took over. The result was a 'financial revolution' of the German states: the creation of state budgets, centralized financial administration, the distinction between public and dynastic finances. The sheer scale of the task ensured that the post-1806 reforms were not carried out by enlightened princely dilettantes but by experts and bureaucrats. Württemberg was exceptional in that the reforms there were implemented, against all opposition, in a fit of late absolutism by King Frederick I (1754–1816). In general, however, one of the most significant results of reform was the creation of the bureaucratic state, even in Württemberg. The problem of participation and representation was nowhere satisfactorily resolved before 1814–15, but everywhere the 'enlightened reform state' gave way to 'bureaucratic state absolutism'. The leading reformers embodied continuity between the two forms. Montgelas (Bavaria), Reitzenstein (Baden), Marshall von Bieberstein (Hessen) Barckhausen and Du Thil (Nassau), Hardenberg (Prussia) and the like, for all their differences, were the intellectual heirs of the enlightened princes of the 1780s. In the 1790s they had perceived the limitations of enlightened reform. The events of 1806 provided the opportunity to implement the remedies they had formulated in the light of the lessons taught by France since 1789.

The scope and intensity of reform was varied. In many smaller middle and north German states the impact was minimal. In some, the nobility frustrated all attempts at change. In others, the territorial reorganization had less impact and there was consequently less incentive and less perceived need to change.   Austria was another, more important, exception. Here the catastrophic political failure of Joseph II's state absolutism, combined with the crises of the 1790s, revived the alliance between crown and nobles, a reassertion of the traditional status quo. This reinvigorated *ancien régime* undermined efforts to reform the Austrian monarchy after the collapse of 1806. Neither Sinzendorff's French-inspired modernization plans nor the Stadion brothers' conservative programme (inspired by Herder) for the revival of the traditional estates made any significant impact. Johann Philipp Stadion succeeded in introducing universal conscription and in forming a Landwehr (territorial militia) in 1808. But his programme collapsed with Austria's renewed defeat by Napoleon in 1809. His successor, Metternich, saved the Austrian monarchy by accommodating himself with Napoleon and by restoring sound financial management. Survival for Austria in 1809 meant making the old status quo work.

The significance of Austria's failed reform, and the gulf that opened up between her and the other German states, becomes apparent when set beside the reforms elsewhere. Four areas and types of reform may be distinguished: the left bank of the Rhine; the Napoleonic satellites of Westphalia, Berg and Frankfurt; the south German states; and finally Prussia.

In the first two areas, French influence was clearly paramount. The left bank of the Rhine was integrated into the French *département* system in 1802. After ten years of often brutal occupation, exploitation and military activity, the introduction of the Code Napoleon and the French administrative system brought a measure of relief. Furthermore, the sale of former church lands, often to prosperous town dwellers, seems to have loosened the social structure more effectively than it did elsewhere, while local industry profited from the continental blockade. As a whole the changes in these areas – legal, institutional and social – were profound, and were recognized as such by the new governments after 1815, which ensured the Code Napoleon remained in force until 1900. Ironically, that was not the fate of the reforms undertaken in the satellite states of Westphalia (under Napoleon's brother Jerôme) and Berg (under Murat until 1808, then under Napoleon as regent for his nephew Napoleon Louis). Their 'model' status was undermined because they were ruthlessly exploited: their finances were milked and state demesne used to provide rewards for the new Napoleonic nobility. Thus the Westphalian constitution of November 1807 (the first German constitution ever) was never fully implemented and like most of the changes effected during the French period was swept away when the kingdom of Westphalia was dissolved in 1815. The same fate befell the French reforms in the duchy of Frankfurt and grand duchy of Warsaw, and the occupied areas of northern Germany (e.g. Hamburg).

The reforms in the new sovereign states of Baden, Württemberg and Bavaria together with Hesse-Darmstadt and Nassau were more durable. In Bavaria, for example, Montgelas implemented a programme which he had outlined in his 'Ansbach memorandum' of 1796. Some measures were introduced as early as 1799, but the major reform drive began in 1806. Montgelas set about reforming the central administration, creating a new state bureaucracy, consolidating all state debts and setting state finances on a secure footing, marking out a distinction between state and dynasty. At the same time the secularization process required the state to take over the universities and schools, as well as other former ecclesiastical institutions. Montgelas's vision of a state based on the equality of all before the law led to an assault on noble privileges and to the promulgation of a constitutional edict which envisaged a representative system.

It is significant that Montgelas resisted French pressure to introduce the Code Napoleon. Where he borrowed from the French model, for example in devising regional divisions based on the *départements*, it was for pragmatic reasons, in this case the erosion of traditional loyalties and of local noble power bases. Equally important, however, were the limitations. Most obvious was the enormous accumulated debt and Napoleon's continuing financial demands: Bavaria was at war almost continuously throughout the reform period and was obliged by her French alliance to maintain an over-large army. Second, noble resistance to the reforms was strong and thwarted the full implementation either of peasant emancipation (until 1848) or of a representative constitution (until 1818).

Reform had its limits. On the other hand the fact that a constitutional movement did prevail in south Germany (including Württemberg) after 1815 has prompted a re-evaluation of the Rheinbund reforms in recent years. They are now viewed as an extension of *Aufklärung* reforms of the 1780s, the more revolutionary for the fact that they were based on the idea of *bürgerliche Freiheit* (bourgeois freedom), with all that implied for the limitation of royal power and the participation and representation of the individual.

If constitutionalism, or at least the introduction of a constitution soon after 1815, is taken as the ultimate criterion of successful modernization, then Prussia must be regarded as a failure. Some have argued that this reflected the complete triumph of the bureaucracy, which resisted constitutionalism because it regarded itself as a kind of representative body. Others emphasize the entrenched nature of the noble opposition to the reform process as a whole, and argue that Hardenberg held back on the constitutional question for tactical reasons. The debate underlines the continuing importance of Prussia in German historiography: the question about Prussia's 'delayed' constitutional history inevitably raises larger questions about later German history as a whole.

Prussia experienced a different pattern of reform within a different institutional and social context and with some different motivations. For one thing Prussia already had a kind of constitutional law in the form of the *Allgemeines Landrecht* of 1794 (a framework of rights as well as a code of law). Second, many historians emphasize the theoretical and philosophical sophistication of the Prussian reform movement which contrasts strikingly with the pragmatic late-Enlightenment rationalism of south German reformers. In economic terms the reforms were characterized by a systematic and rigorous application of the principles of Adam Smith. The reformers aimed to liberate the economic potential of man. This involved both relaxing trade and craft restrictions and dismantling the constrictive feudal agrarian order. The emancipation of 1807 gave little to the peasant, though he now had the freedom to realize his potential if he could. The estate owners, by contrast, profited immediately since it now became possible to intensify the agricultural production process. Other areas of activity (education, military reform) were also characterized by a distinctive philosophical inspiration. Nipperdey has argued that Prussian reforms transcended the *Aufklärung*; they embodied the new post-Kantian philosophical idealism which aspired to enable man to achieve ultimate freedom. Certainly the influence of Kant on the Prussian bureaucracy was profound, and the Prussian reform is characterized by the involvement in many different areas of individuals who were highly gifted theoreticians as well as practitioners. Humboldt in education, Scharnhorst, Gneisenau and Boyen in the army, are merely the best known of a whole phalanx of philosophically minded protagonists of change.

Prussian reform was also the product of humiliating military defeat and, in many minds, motivated by the desire for revenge. Nationalist historians believed this gave the movement a profound moral dimension and a higher 'national' purpose. They regarded Stein as the central figure: a conservative romantic nationalist who aimed to make Prussia into the foundation of a Germany capable of withstanding Napoleon.

This myth obscures two important points. First, as elsewhere, the origins of reform ideas in Prussia lie in the 1780s and 1790s: defeat in 1806 provided the reformers with their opportunity but not with their agenda. Second, recent research has tended to emphasize the significance of Hardenberg. Stein's period of office was short (he was dismissed in November 1808 after only 14 months in office); Hardenberg was *Staatskanzler* from 1810 until 1822. Their ideas also differed fundamentally. Stein *was* a nationalist who dreamt of an uprising of the Germans against French tyranny. He was also a conservative. In his view the only conceivable form of representation was that based on property, i.e. the traditional estates. The mobilization of society, Stein believed, meant the reinvigoration of historically grown forms of participation and representation. If Stein wished to 'reorganize' the Prussian state, Hardenberg aspired to 'revolutionize' it. Stein's 'Nassau memorandum' (1806) concentrated exclusively on administration; Hardenberg's 'Riga memorandum' (1807) spoke of 'unleashing' all abilities, of bringing about a 'revolution' which would lead to the 'great end of the ennoblement of mankind, through wise government and not through violent force either from within or from outside'. The most appropriate form for the 'current *Zeitgeist*', he declared, was 'democratic principles in a monarchical system'.[5] Hardenberg's emphasis on the *Zeitgeist* indicates that he saw no going back: 1789 marked the start of a new era in human history; the task of all wise politicians was to adapt to it successfully. Military reform played a central role in the programme. 'All inhabitants of the state are born defenders of the same', Scharnhorst wrote; 'the government must enter into an alliance with the nation' in order to bolster its independent spirit.[6] Gneisenau declared that the state must be established on the 'threefold foundation of arms, education and constitution'.[7]

If there are many elements of similarity between Prussia and, say, Bavaria, the obstacles to success were much greater in Prussia. Financial ruin in 1806 dictated that much of the reform process was driven by fiscal needs rather than by constitutional ideals. The resistance of the nobility to change was formidable. Military reformers were denounced as 'Jacobins' because they wanted to arm the peasantry. Any hint of constitutional plans aroused intense opposition, even amongst many bureaucrats. Like Montgelas, Hardenberg was a virtuoso tactician and combined his philosophical convictions with wily pragmatism. The reformers succeeded in their fiscal, economic, administrative and educational measures. The military reform represented a compromise; the constitutional issue remained in suspension. The outcome was a bureaucratic absolutism serviced by a sophisticated educational system which presided over an economic system shaped by the spirit of Adam Smith and a traditional society still dominated by the nobility. The tensions inherent in that formula were only later revealed, in particular when the system was overtaken by the effects of the dramatic demographic explosion of the decades since 1740.

It is tempting to see the diminution in the number of German territories from over 1000 to around 40 as part of a long-term progress of integration, another stage in the delayed progress of the Germans towards a nation state under Prussian leadership. The point is apparently reinforced by the similarities generated by the reform process between many of the new states and by Austria's failure to reform. This ignores, however, one of the central characteristics of the thinking and language of most leading reformers. They were concerned with the nation, but primarily with the Bavarian or the Prussian nation, rather than the German nation. When Montgelas wrote that elementary schools must help shape the *Nationalgeist*, he meant the Bavarian national spirit.[8] When Hardenberg wrote of 'stamping a single "Nationalcharakter" upon the whole', he meant a sense of national identity for the whole Prussian state.[9] The similarities between the reforms cannot obscure the fact that they were explicitly intended to create differences between the new sovereign states. This immediately raises important questions about the origins of German nationalism in this period. If *Nationalgeist* pertained to the new sovereign states, what did *die deutsche Nation* mean at this time?

V   The Wars of Liberation and German nationalism

In traditional historiography the most important feature of the Napoleonic period was the birth of German nationalism. Napoleon's defeat and humiliation of Prussia, it was argued, generated a sense of German national resentment against French tyranny: ideas developed in Prussia by men such as Fichte, Arndt and Jahn provided the inspiration for a national uprising of the Germans led by Prussia. In this view the Wars of Liberation (1813–15) were interpreted as the first collective action of the German nation, its first violent rite of passage in an ordeal by fire. In fact this 'birth myth' of the German nation was an artificial construct of nationalist ideology. Later Prussian nationalism wrote its own history and then declared it to be the history of Germany as a whole.[10] From an eighteenth-century perspective, however, the development of German nationalism appears much more diffuse. It leads neither to a single coherent ideology nor to a firm political or state orientation by 1815.

Since the 1760s there had been a growing preoccupation among many German intellectuals with questions of patriotism and German identity. There was no single movement, rather a variety of lines of development. One strand led to the *Reichspatriotismus* of the 1780s and then on to the debate over reform of the Reich around 1800. Another strand can be identified in the tradition of lyric poetry from Klopstock to Hölderlin, in which the quasi-religious identification with a German fatherland forms a persistent theme. Related to that was the so-called 'German movement' of the 1770s and 1780s: young *Sturm und Drang* writers and their successors whose interest in 'Germany' formed part of their rebellion against society in the name of freedom. The main emphasis was on the 'cultural nation', 'Germany' defined by language and a common literary and philosophical culture. Yet this 'cultural nationalism' was not unpolitical: its tendency was anti-absolutist and democratic.

In the 1790s Herder's notion of the individuality of all peoples took on a new meaning in the context of the German response to the French Revolution. The argument that Germany did not need a revolution formed part of a world historical perspective in which the Germans, from medieval freedom through revolutionary Reformation to *Aufklärung*, emerged as the nation of true freedom as opposed to anarchic French liberty. The idea of the unique mission of the Germans was central to this view: as Schiller put it in 1797, their day had yet to come; it would be the last day, the final and highest stage in the development of human freedom. Parallel to this some writers of the 1790s, often associated with early Romanticism, renewed older poses against French cultural imperialism in literature, once more emphasizing the gulf between 'Germany' and France. A revived literary patriotism responded to the French threat. In areas such as the Rhineland this also connected with the bitter experience of invasion and occupation, and a deep popular resentment against the exploitative and militantly secular French revolutionary authorities.

In so far as any of these diverse preoccupations with 'Germany' were anchored on a political system they were focused on the Reich (even though constitutionally the 'nation' of the Reich only included the higher nobility). The Reich manifestly failed from the mid-1790s. Yet the sense of the functions that it had served was still strong, and there was a wide sense of the need to find something that would replace it. The Reich's dissolution in 1806 created a new situation since it left 'the German nation', however defined, without any institutional framework. Nationalist historians argued that the 'nation state' led by Prussia stepped into the breach. The reality is more complex. In south and west Germany much 'national' thinking focused on the Rheinbund, sometimes with Napoleon envisaged as the new Emperor of the Germans. That vision soon lost credibility, but arguments for some form of equivalent to the Reich played an important part in discussions right up to 1815.

The reaction against Napoleon elsewhere had no coherent political programme, no clear ideology, no clear preference for the leadership of the German nation. The anonymous pamphlet *Deutschland in seiner tiefen Erniedrigung* (Germany in her deep humiliation) (May 1806), generally regarded as the first blast of the anti-Napoleonic movement in Germany, was deeply critical of both Austria and Prussia, particularly for having abandoned the German people. Indeed much of the patriotic literature after 1806 contains many echoes of the anti-absolutist rhetoric of the 1780s and 1790s.

Inevitably, however, the 'German' patriots gravitated towards Vienna, Dresden and Berlin outside the sphere of direct French control. Vienna attracted conservative patriots, Romantic political theorists of the reaction, Catholics or converts to Catholicism, and others who wanted to revive the old Reich (now idealized as an Arcadia of traditional politics and religion). After 1805 intellectuals such as Friedrich Schlegel, Adam Müller, Friedrich Gentz (the 'German Burke') and Heinrich von Kleist (significantly, a Brandenburg nobleman disillusioned by Prussian neutrality before 1806) provided the ideological foundations for Stadion's conservative reform programme for the Austrian monarchy. In Berlin the movement was more diffuse. Military reformers drew up plans for a *levée en masse*. Stein propagated the idea of a conservative estates-based nation state version of the old Reich. The literary patriotism of Arndt, Jahn and Theodor Körner drew on pietist traditions in propagating a religious identification with a German fatherland, calling for an uprising of the German *Volk* and a fight to the death against France. Fichte appealed for a new *Nationalerziehung* (national education), necessary because the princes had betrayed the *Volk*. Romantic conservatism combined with 'national democratic' tendencies in a broad church united only by a common desire to end the French tyranny.

One should be wary of overestimating the contemporary significance of this flood of patriotic literature. The 'national' interests of Prussia and Austria were not submerged in the German cause, though both governments exploited the ambiguity of the 'national' idea. In Berlin, Stein, inflamed with hatred for 'French filth' and infuriated by the admiration for Napoleon of young Romantics such as Tieck, actively coordinated the activities of the patriotic writers, promoting journals and offering financial inducements. In Austria too Stadion coordinated a literary campaign which provided the ideological dimension to the Austrian rebellion against Napoleon in 1809. Inspired by the Spanish insurrection, the Stadion faction persuaded the Emperor to appeal to all Germans to rise up against the French. The appeal failed and after an initial triumph at Aspern in May 1809, the Austrian army was decisively crushed at Wagram in July. Indeed the whole affair revealed a deeply ambivalent attitude to the whole concept of popular insurrection: when the Tyrolean peasants rebelled and triumphed over the French under the charismatic Andreas Hofer the Austrians failed to support them.

Austria under Metternich had no more truck with patriotic uprisings. The case of Prussia is more complex. Fundamentally, of course, Napoleon was brought down by the progressive collapse of his empire after 1810. The disastrous Russian campaign of 1812 was the final straw. Furthermore, when Prussia joined forces with Russia in December 1812, it was the result of the deeply conservative Yorck von Wartenburg's rebellious defiance of the king's orders: not a national patriotic uprising but an insurrection of the reactionary East Prussian nobility. None the less Yorck forced the king's hand and allowed the reformers in Berlin to implement their plans for a people's army. The king's call to arms 'An Mein Volk' (significantly directed at 'Brandenburger, Preußen, Schlesier, Pommern, Litthauer!' not Germans) unleashed a ferocious patriotic wave.[11]

Many did give 'gold for iron'; the military reforms allowed the formation of an army of 280,000 with impressive speed; some 28,000 volunteers joined up. How decisive all this was is another matter. Soon after the battle of Leipzig (16–19 October 1813) it became clear that the future of Germany would not be decided by German patriots but by the particularist interests of the sovereign states. Bavaria had left the Rheinbund just before Leipzig. Württemberg, Baden, Hesse-Darmstadt and Hesse-Kassel left just after. The plans of Stein and his secretary Arndt for a strong German national imperial state served only as a useful foil in the complex negotiations over the future of the German lands which were dominated by Hardenberg and Metternich, both at root sceptics on the 'national' issue.

VI Conclusion

Heinrich Heine later wrote that the Germans had become patriots and defied Napoleon because their princes ordered them to. That fails to do justice to the strength of anti-Napoleonic sentiment in many parts of Germany by 1813–14. But there was no 'national uprising' or 'national crusade'. There remained a world of difference between the nationalism of some intellectuals and the 'nation' they aspired to lead. Heine's comment also underestimates the ambivalence of contemporary governments towards the very idea of arming the peasantry for an uprising of the *Volk*, as envisaged by the likes of Arndt or Jahn. In the excitement of victory the issues became confused, and later the veterans of 1813 constructed a myth of the Wars of Liberation that bore little relation to reality. That mythology, formed around the canon of patriotic writing of the period 1806–15, is an important legacy of the period. It provided the foundation for later nationalist ideology which increasingly drew on everything but the democratic tenor of the first phase: the image of the French *Erbfeind* (hereditary enemy); the glorification of the *Volk*; Germany as the nation which had defeated the ideas of 1789 and which had developed its own superior 'idea'; the myth of a strong Reich.

Little of that could, however, have even been imagined in 1815. Far from celebrating the birth of the German nation, men such as Arndt and Jahn were bitterly disappointed. The Vienna settlement reflected not their ideas but the process of evolution and adaptation that had occurred since the late eighteenth century. Secularization, mediatization and the dissolution of the Reich had removed the obstacles to the emergence of fully sovereign states to replace the feudal patchwork of the past. What emerged at Vienna in 1815 was a confederation which placed the seal on the emergence of the German sovereign territorial states. Prussia was strengthened by the acquisition of the Rhineland; Austria was to an extent diverted by her position of strength in Italy; but both remained leading players in Germany. The settlement created a balance of power designed to maintain peace and stability, and led to the competition between Austria and Prussia ending in stalemate.

More important than anything else in 1815 was the fact that many of the new sovereign states were in one way or another 'reformed'. The path from the Reich to the German Confederation was characterized by a complex adaptation to the challenges posed by the French Revolution and the Napoleonic regime. Reformers reacted to what they perceived were the limitations of the enlightened state by reforming its structure and by aiming to overcome the gulf between the state and its subjects. Financial necessity drove a reform process which created the bureaucratic state. On the other hand, ambivalence and noble opposition undermined first attempts to mobilize the population or to secure their representation. The result in many German states was a dissonant mixture: a strong, 'modernized' state grafted on to a traditional society. Nowhere did the reformers achieve complete success. Even so, their collective efforts brought about fundamental and irrevocable changes. They ensured that for the next generation at least most politically active Germans would be preoccupied not with the national issue but with the implications of the German 'revolution from above'.

Notes:

1. Quoted by Hans-Ulrich Wehler, *Deutsche Gesellschaftsgeschichte*, Band 1: *1700–1815* (1987), p. 546.
2. Nipperdey, Thomas, *Deutsche Geschichte 1800–1866. Bürgerwelt und starker Staat* (1983), p. 11.
3. Quoted by Horst Möller, *Fürstenstaat oder Bürgernation. Deutschland 1763–1815* (1989), p. 531.
4. Quoted by Karl Otmar von Aretin, *Vom Deutschen Reich zum Deutschen Bund*, 2nd edn. (1993), p. 61.
5. The memorandum is printed in Georg Winter, ed., *Die Reorganisation des Preußischen Staates unter Stein und Hardenberg* Teil 1. Band 1 (1931), pp. 302–63; quotation from pp. 305–6.
6. Quoted by Nipperdey, *Geschichte*, pp. 51, 53.
7. *Ibid.*, p. 51.
8. Quoted in Max Spindler, ed., *Handbuch der bayerischen Geschichte*, 4 vols. (1967–1975), vol. I, pt. I, p. 7.
9. Winter, *Reorganisation*, pp. 319–20, 325.
10. See Stefan Berger, 'The German Tradition of Historiography, 1800–1995' in Fulbrook, ed., *German History since 1800* (1997).
11. Printed in Hans-Bernd Spies, ed., *Die Erhebung gegen Napoleon 1806–1814/15* (1981), pp. 254–5.

Select bibliography

Aris, R., *History of Political Thought in Germany from 1789 to 1815* (London: Frank Cass, 1936).

Beiser, Frederick C., *Enlightenment, Revolution, and Romanticism. The Genesis of Modern German Political Thought, 1790–1800* (1992).

Blanning, T. C. W., *The French Revolution in Germany: Occupation and Resistance in the Rhineland, 1792–1802* (1983).

Breuilly, John, *The Formation of the First German Nation-State, 1800–1871* (1996).

Gagliardo, John G., *Reich and Nation. The Holy Roman Empire as Idea and Reality, 1763–1806* (1980).

Gooch, G. P., *Germany and the French Revolution* (1920).

Hughes, Michael, *Early Modern Germany* (1992).

Schroeder, Paul W., *The Transformation of European Politics, 1763–1848* (1994).

Sheehan, J. J., *German History, 1770–1866* (1989).

Vann, J. A. and Rowan, S., eds, *The Old Reich: Essays on German Political Institutions 1495–1806* (1974).

Walker, Mack, *German Home Towns: Community, State, General Estate, 1648–1871* (1971).

3
Germany 1815–1848: Restoration or pre-March?

Christopher Clark

The period discussed in this chapter fell between two great European upheavals: the revolution of 1789 with its Napoleonic aftermath and the revolutions of 1848. Inevitably, this has influenced the way we think about the era. The term 'Restoration', often used for the years until 1830 or 1840 and sometimes for the period as a whole, evokes the struggle to reverse the effects of the French Revolution and underlines the reactionary, backward-looking character of the age. The term 'pre-March', generally used for the years from 1830 or 1840, is forward-looking; it suggests a prelude to upheaval, specifically to the Revolutionary unrest of the 'March days' of 1848. Both terms are problematic, since they encourage us to think of this era either as a reconstruction of the past or as a rehearsal for the future.

'Should the half-dead forms of the old regime, which still contain so much of the beautiful life of the past, be maintained?' Leopold von Gerlach asked himself in 1813. 'Or should they be boldly destroyed to make way for the new?'[1] As Gerlach himself was aware, the answers history gives to such questions are always composite and provisional, never absolute. There was no thorough-going 'restoration' of the old regime after 1815, nor, on the other hand, were traditional structures and allegiances entirely destroyed 'to make way for the new'. But the period covered by this chapter was one of heightened political and social conflict that often turned on the question Gerlach had asked. Guilds, corporate privilege, feudal tenure, dynastic particularism – all these not-so-dead forms inherited from the old regime had their defenders and detractors. It was conflict over these and related issues that made the years between 1815 and 1848 an 'epoch of polarization' across a broad range of fronts.

The conflict between modernity and tradition in its various manifestations forms the central theme of this chapter. The chapter does not provide a chronological narrative but examines five areas in turn. The first subsection deals with that unloved institution, the German Confederation, which provided the outer framework for German political life throughout and beyond the period covered by this chapter. We then turn to the bureaucratic state, which has often been seen as the most important 'modernizing' force in early nineteenth-century German society. There follows a discussion of the various forms of political mobilization that were so characteristic of the period. A section on the mass poverty and economic dislocation of the 1830s and 1840s attempts to identify what was modern and what was not about the 'social question' that so preoccupied contemporaries. This is followed by a discussion of the religious revival of the 1820s and 1830s that did much to galvanize political debate, but was also a formidable social force in its own right. Each of these topics has been the subject of extensive recent debate in the historiography of the period, and each will help to bring us nearer to what was distinctive about the decades between 1815 and 1848.

I The German Confederation

In the eighteenth century, German Europe had been divided into some 300 territories. After the secularizations and territorial resettlements of the Napoleonic period and the readjustments made at the Congress of Vienna, only 38 sovereign states (39 after 1817) remained. These were joined in a loose association of independent sovereign entities known as the 'German Confederation'. The largest and most significant were the Austrian Empire and the Kingdom of Prussia, with 9.3 and 8.1 million Confederal subjects respectively (Prussia's easternmost provinces and Austria's non-German lands were excluded from the Confederation, as they had been from the old Reich). The remaining member states ranged in size and significance from the most powerful middle states, Bavaria, Baden, Württemberg and Hanover, all of which had made substantial territorial gains since the dissolution of the Reich, to the little Duchy of Liechtenstein, with a population of only 5,000. As in the old Reich, the small states outnumbered the large. In 1818, there were only seven German states with populations in excess of one million; 21 had fewer than 100,000 inhabitants.

The Confederation managed to get by on a minimum of institutions and personnel. It had only one statutory body, the Federal Diet (*Bundesversammlung*), which met in Frankfurt. The Diet was effectively a

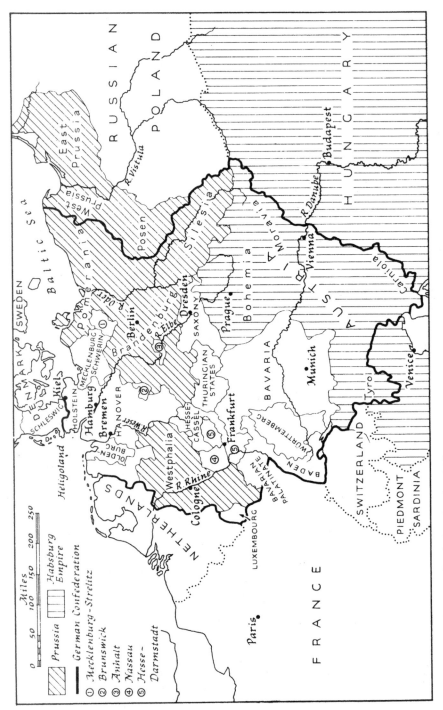

Map 3.1 The German Confederation in 1815

permanent congress of diplomatic representatives who were appointed and instructed by their respective governments. The supreme executive organ of the Confederation was the Inner Council (*Engerer Rat*); all the states were represented on this body, but only Austria, the kingdoms of Prussia, Bavaria, Württemberg, Saxony and Hanover, Electoral Hesse, the grand duchies of Baden and Hesse-Darmstadt, Denmark (on account of Holstein) and the Netherlands (on account of the Grand Duchy of Luxemburg) had the right to a full individual vote; the remaining states were organized by size in groups of between two and nine members, each of which had one vote. The Inner Council dealt with the regular administration of the Confederation; if matters arose that touched on the Confederal constitution or on the function and status of its institutions, these had to be dealt with by the Plenary Diet (*Plenum*), in which each state spoke and voted for itself. But even here, the primacy of the greater states was guaranteed by allocation of votes; with four votes each, Austria and the five kingdoms could combine to veto any unwelcome initiative from a smaller state.

The Confederation does not enjoy a good reputation. It was a bitter disappointment to those federalists and nationalists who had hoped for a more cohesive organization of the German territories and it has been much criticized since. One historian has recently described it as 'a prediluvian monster' that had no place in the age of the emergent nation state, another as an 'incarnation of illiberality and oppression'. These reproaches reflect two distinct, though related, lines of argument that have often been advanced against the Confederation.

It is certainly true that the Confederation failed to create genuinely 'national' institutions. The Act of 1815 had left open a number of important issues, including joint defence policy, the creation of a unified economic area within the Confederation, the legal status of the Jews and constitutional reform. These were to be subject to subsequent debate and deliberation by the Confederal Diet. It was thus plausible, in 1815, to believe that the following years would see the gradual extension of the central powers and responsibilities of the Confederation, and perhaps even the emergence of a genuinely 'federal' German authority.

In the event, these hopes were not fulfilled. Power remained firmly in the hands of the individual sovereigns. The promised Confederal regulation of the status of Jewish residents was not forthcoming. Instead, Jews remained subject to a bewildering variety of regional legal codes – 33, for example, in the Kingdom of Prussia alone. The question of constitutional reform was likewise left to the discretion of the individual states. Attempts to reach an agreement on customs in the German states foundered on Austrian opposition. The failure of the Diet to take the lead in organizing a German customs union was to prove highly significant, since it enabled Prussia, which had already effected a union in its own territories, to seize and retain the initiative in this area. The German customs union which emerged in 1834 was not motivated by Prussian desire to found a small German nation state, nor did it represent an irreversible step towards the emergence of such a state. But to the Austrian government, which remained excluded from the *Zollverein*, its strategic significance as a means by which Prussia might exert influence on the lesser states was clear.

National defence was one area in which the Confederation did have some limited success in establishing federal institutions. Under Article 2 of the 'Final Act' (*Wiener Schlussakte*) of 1820, a revised version of the earlier Federal Act of 1815, the Confederation was to exist as 'a community of independent states' in its domestic affairs, but as a 'politically unified, federated power in its external relations'. The 'military constitution' accepted in its final form after long debate in July 1822 provided for a single wartime army under unified command. In fact, however, the 'federal army' never became a cohesive body. Its various contingents rarely served together, there was very little common planning or policy-making, and the great royal armies, such as the Austrian and the Prussian, clung to their particularist traditions. The fact was that after 1815, the states of the Confederation had very diverse defence priorities. The small states were concerned above all to avoid any move that might subordinate their interests to those of a more powerful partner. In the event of conflict with France, the south German states were first in the line of fire; in times of crisis they drew together and looked to Prussia for support. Austria, by contrast, saw the southwest German states as a buffer zone (and possible battlefield) between France and the Austrian heartland; it was more concerned to protect its vulnerable Italian possessions. The absence of a coordinated Confederal defence policy became painfully evident during the French war scares of 1830 and 1840–1.

In marked contrast with its half-hearted efforts at reform was the vigour with which the Diet set about suppressing political dissent within the Confederation. In 1819, after the assassination of the reactionary publicist Kotzebue by the nationalist student Karl Sand, the Confederation began to acquire new powers of censorship and surveillance. The 'Karlsbad Decrees', initiated by Chancellor Metternich and passed by the Diet in September 1819, called for closer supervision of the universities throughout the Confederation, the dismissal of subversive teaching staff, as well as the establishment of a press commission for the enforcement of censorship throughout the German states and of the 'Mainz Central Investigative

Commission' for dealing with persons involved in 'revolutionary agitation'. These new federal responsibilities were enshrined in the 'Final Act' of 1820, Article 26 of which stipulated that the Confederation had the right to intervene in the internal affairs of a member state in order to suppress unrest and restore order, even if the government of that state were 'rendered unable to request help'.

In July 1832, shortly after the Hambach Festival (see p. 54 below), the Diet introduced new and stronger censorship regulations, forbade public assemblies and festivals, as well as the foundation of political clubs, organized new forms of surveillance over travellers and 'conspicuous' persons, and established procedures for the extradition of political suspects. In the aftermath of an attack by ex-student activists on the garrison buildings in Frankfurt in 1833, the Diet even founded a new political intelligence-gathering institute, the Frankfurt Investigation Authority. The new body was intended to collate information on political malefactors through informants, surveillance and interrogation, but like its predecessor in Mainz, it tended increasingly to act preventatively against those merely suspected of subversive activity. The most important Confederal powers involved the use of armed force on the territory of a member state. In October 1830, following the revolutionary unrest of that year, new laws were introduced by the Diet permitting armed intervention within member states with or without the prior request or permission of the relevant governments. This was more than a paper threat; a Confederal force intervened in revolutionary Luxembourg in 1830 and against the Free City of Frankfurt in 1833 (after the above-mentioned attack on the garrison buildings). There were also cases in which the mere threat of armed intervention was sufficient to coerce governments into following the line set out by the Diet. When Baden, for example, introduced liberal press laws and abolished internal censorship towards the end of 1831, the Diet successfully used the threat of 'federal action' (*Bundesexekution*) to reassert the validity for all territories of the Press Laws of 1819.

That the Confederation was illiberal and oppressive is impossible to deny. That it was an anachronism, a 'prediluvian monster', is a more complex claim that may require some qualification. There is no doubt that the Diet was out of tune with nationalist aspirations. The war scare of 1840–41, when loose talk by the Thiers government in Paris prompted fears that France would push her borders forwards to her 'natural frontier' on the Rhine, generated a wave of nationalist 'Rhine songs' by poets and poetasters across the German states. But it is important not to overestimate the power or homogeneity of German nationalism as a political force during this period. German nationalism as a mass phenomenon tended to be reactive, erupting in response to perceived threats (especially from France) and then subsiding again. It is true that nationalist organizations such as the Gymnasts' Movement (*Turnbewegung*) grew at an impressive rate in the mid-1840s – there were 90,000 gymnasts in 300 clubs by 1847 – but attachments to individual states and dynasties remained strong. And as the experiences of 1848 were to show, confessional allegiances divided Catholic enthusiasts for a German nation under Habsburg captaincy from Protestant 'small-Germans' who envisaged a narrower federation under Hohenzollern leadership.

Recent studies have tended to reject the teleology implicit in the nationalist critique, and to focus on the Confederation's 'forward-looking' characteristics. It was an association of sovereign entities with a commitment to the maintenance of peace and the provision of justice through interstate arbitration; in these respects, it 'anticipated' modern supranational entities such as the United Nations and the European Union. Moreover, the Confederation succeeded in reconciling a robust and peaceful solution of the 'German question' with the need to meet the security needs of the European great powers in the then-foreseeable future. Viewed from the perspective of our own day, this was a formidable achievement.

II   The modernizing state

The major German states all emerged from the years of war and internal reform with larger, better organized, and more powerful bureaucracies. Supreme executive power remained with the sovereign, but his authority was increasingly mediated through state officials. This can be seen in the changing balance of fiscal power. While revenues raised personally by the sovereign through loans or from royal domains – once staple sources of public finance – dwindled in significance, those collected by officials in taxes, tolls and tariffs accounted for an increasing portion of state income. For G. W. F. Hegel, Professor of Philosophy at the University of Berlin from 1818 whose writings profoundly influenced the thinking of generations of Germans, these were developments of the most fundamental importance. Hegel saw the rationalized, bureaucratized state as the highest form of government. As a 'universal caste' distinct from civil society, the bureaucracy was uniquely capable of providing informed and disinterested administration for the good of all.

Following in this tradition, a number of historians have seen in the emergent *Beamtenstaat* (civil service state) of the post-war decades the single most important motor of social and economic modernization. There is something to be said for this view. In Prussia, for example, one could cite the bureaucratic achievements of the era of reform discussed in the previous chapter. Bureaucrats played a crucial role in the establishment of a Prussian customs union in 1818, forerunner of the German customs union (*Zollverein*) negotiated in 1834. In Württemberg, Bavaria and Baden, bureaucrats helped to draw up 'national' constitutions (see below). One could find further evidence for the modernizing role of the state in the area of educational provision. Prussia was the first major German state to introduce compulsory primary schooling. By 1848 the state provided systematic teacher-training in 49 purpose-designed institutions. Rates of school attendance and general literacy far outstripped those in France and Britain.

Important as these achievements are, the thesis of the modernizing state requires some qualification. A distinction has to be drawn between the political and the economic spheres. The state was not, generally speaking, a *politically* progressive institution. Even Hardenberg, one of the great modernizers of the Prussian bureaucracy, took an extremely illiberal line on political dissent. Indeed, one historian has described the Prussian bureaucracy in this period as an 'agency of domination' which acted to control and contain public and even domestic life through the routine administration of violence. This contrast between political reaction and economic modernity led Thomas Nipperdey to speak of the 'Janus-head' of the Prussian state after 1815.[2]

But even in the economic sphere, the state's achievements were ambivalent. The most recent studies have tended to relativize the longer-term impact of the reform undertaken during the Napoleonic era. In Prussia, it has been argued that a resurgence of conservative forces resulted in the modification or disabling of key legislative initiatives and a 'victory for traditional society'.[3] And throughout the post-war decades, state bureaucracies did little to help and much to hinder economic development. The Prussian financial bureaucracy opposed the foundation of joint-stock companies, and thus hindered the concentration of funds necessary to facilitate investment. Moreover, government credit policies tended to favour agriculture, with the result that money was drawn away from industrial and commercial investment. In this and many other areas, government policy reflected the still formidable political power of the landed nobility. The government did attempt to promote industry by sponsoring various technical experiments and innovations, but its approach was haphazard and its successes modest.

Detailed studies of individual sectors of the economy have revealed a similarly negative picture. Mining entrepreneurs in the Ruhr valley region, for example, found their freedom of action constrained by the government's insistence on managing the industry through its own bureaucratic 'experts'. Mine-owners frequently complained of overregulation and red tape. In 1842, a water-pump had to be removed from the 'Crown Prince' mine in the Ruhr because the owner had not obtained a permit from the *Bergamt* before installation; while the machine was out of commission the mine flooded and had to be abandoned. The state's most significant contribution to the later industrialization of Prussia probably lay in the area of infrastructure (especially roads and waterways) and technical education.

State bureaucracies remained small by modern standards. It is true that after 1815 a growing percentage of government spending went into administrative costs and bureaucratically administered social services, but the lion's share still went to the military, as in the eighteenth century. Many German states were heavily indebted by the end of the wars and large payments in debt-service put pressure on bureaucratic budgets. As a consequence, the overall number of government officials remained low or gradually declined. In 1846, there were only 7.1 government employees in Prussia for every thousand subjects and only a very small proportion of these were administrative bureaucrats proper. Policemen were particularly thin on the ground, a fact which substantially qualified the state's capacity to impose day-to-day control. Indeed, one historian has spoken of a 'trickling away' of the state's power in rural areas, where the shortage of officials was most keenly felt.[4]

The situation was different in the south of Germany, where bureaucracies tended to be larger. In Württemberg, for example, the number of persons employed in 'public service' in 1821 stood at 53,849: about one in three adult males not working on the land was working for the government. In the south German states, the bureaucracy became the dominant political force, not only through its administrative functions, but also through the involvement of officials in parliamentary politics. Bureaucrats had a vital role to play in homogenizing the diverse administrative districts of the recently expanded south German states. Their special status was recognized in the state constitutions, where the public standing and function of the civil servant were formally set down and guaranteed.

However, greater size did not necessarily entail heightened effectiveness. There were practical limitations to the bureaucracy's ability to impose reforms; in Bavaria, measures taken in support of industry and manufacture proved sporadic and ineffective. The laws introduced by the Bavarian government to raise agricultural productivity foundered on the inertia and conservatism of the agrarian sector. A comprehensive reform of Bavarian agriculture was not introduced until the 1850s. In Württemberg, despite the draconian penalties meted out to those who dared to impugn the civil service, there were frequent complaints of the wasteful 'surfeit of scribbling' (*Vielschreiberei*) that so burdened public finances, and recent economic surveys have tended to confirm that the diversion of public money into the large southern bureaucracies harmed, rather than helped, economic growth and development.

Many contemporary observers were less concerned with the economic than with the social impact of bureaucratic reforms. In the south German states and to a lesser extent in Prussia, the nobility emerged from the era of wartime reforms with its privileges and political standing diminished. In this context, it is easy to understand why conservative noblemen railed in the immediate post-war years against the new 'administrative despotism, which eats up everything like vermin'.[5] But it is also important not to underestimate the continuing power and social dominance of the nobility, despite the upheavals of the reform era. In some areas, such as Bavaria and East-Elbian Prussia, nobles retained their traditional policing and judicial rights after well-organized campaigns against the modernizing bureaucrats. In Prussian Silesia, they even managed to cling on to their feudal rights until 1848. In the kingdom of Saxony, likewise, the old feudal agrarian system remained intact, though this changed after 1830, when feudal tenure was abolished in the wake of widespread social unrest. Nobles continued to dominate the agrarian sector in their capacity as large landowners – in Prussia, many estate owners bought up the smallholdings of their emancipated peasants and became successful agrarian entrepreneurs. Moreover, throughout and beyond the period covered by this chapter, nobilities dominated the political, administrative and military institutions of most of the German states: the parliaments, provincial Diets, bureaucracies and armies.

III   Political mobilization

There had been talk at the Congress of Vienna of harmonizing the various political systems within the new German Confederation: in fact, however, the individual states took matters into their own hands and the result was a diverse array of constitutional arrangements that makes any generalization problematic. Broadly speaking, one can distinguish between those states – the Free City of Lübeck, Hanover, Electoral Hesse, Mecklenburg, Saxony, Prussia and other small north German states – in which the old corporate representative bodies retained all or much of their power and those – Nassau, Württemberg, Bavaria, Baden and several of the small Thuringian states – which issued formal constitutions providing for the convocation of bicameral representative assemblies.

The constitutions of the southern states created a completely new institutional context for political participation in Germany. For the first time, parliaments became partners in the legislative process. No law, no budget, could be passed without their approval. It is important, however, not to exaggerate the 'modernity' of these new political arrangements. Almost all of the constitutions were 'issued' by sovereigns; there was no prior negotiation with constituent assemblies. The monarch remained the supreme executive with decisive powers of veto and emergency decree. Moreover, governments did what they could to prevent parliaments from becoming a focus of partisan political activity. Deputies were forbidden, for example, to choose their seats in the chamber; instead, places were pre-assigned or drawn by lot in order to prevent the coalescence of like-minded factions. The German constitutions enshrined various 'human rights', such as equality before the law, freedom of confession and of conscience and the security of property, but political rights, such as freedom of association and assembly or freedom of the press, were either not granted at all or were hedged in by conditions permitting their curtailment by law or decree. Moreover, the upper chambers of the south German parliaments, whose agreement was also required for the passing of any law, were dominated by princes of the ruling family, members of the high nobility and appointed notables.

Until 1848, elections for the lower chambers were subject to numerous restrictions. Suffrage was limited to males who met certain legal and economic qualifications and voting was indirect – enfranchised citizens voted for a college of electors drawn from the social elite, who then selected the deputies; these were themselves required to satisfy stringent economic criteria. In Baden, for example, often regarded as the most liberal of the south German polities, 17 per cent of the population were entitled both to vote and to stand for the college of electors, but only 0.5 per cent were entitled to become deputies if elected. In Bavaria and Württemberg, traces of the old corporate representation remained, even in the lower chambers, where people voted under separate franchise regimes according to occupation and social group.

Despite these and other measures designed to limit the impact of the political process on the public, the parliaments of the south German states did manage to function as the focus for a political opposition of sorts. In 1823, for example, a narrow majority of deputies in the lower chamber of the Baden parliament succeeded in blocking the government's new budget. In the early 1830s, a dispute raged between Duke William of Nassau and his parliament over the sovereign's right to dispose of the ducal domains. When the government refused in 1832 to comply with the demands of the liberal parliamentary majority, the entire lower chamber, excluding five loyalist deputies, resigned *en masse* in a public gesture of disgust. The unequal distribution of constitutional and coercive power meant that governments generally had little difficulty overcoming such opposition. They could stock the upper chambers with loyalist appointees, shift the focus of decision-making away from the legislature into government committees, dissolve uncooperative parliaments, or employ intimidation in order to prevent the re-election of opposition deputies. One example is the Heidelberg bookseller Christian Friedrich Winter, who had led the anti-budget 'faction' in the Baden parliament in 1823. The college of electors in his Heidelberg constituency were informed by the government that if they re-elected Winter their beloved university would be moved to another town.

The unevenness of the contest between sovereigns and elected deputies sometimes had the effect of moving the focus of political opposition out of the parliaments altogether. But in spite of these frustrations and setbacks, it is striking how significant the representative assemblies remained as forums of political dispute and argumentation. In Hesse-Darmstadt, a protracted struggle between the opposition and the reactionary Grand Duke Ludwig II during the early and mid-1830s resulted in the emergence of a liberal faction under the able leadership of Ludwig von Gagern; he and his movement were to win an impressive victory in the parliamentary elections of September 1847. In 1843, liberal deputies in the Baden parliament began to sit together, thereby declaring their willingness to work together under a single programme. The vote of no confidence passed by the lower chamber in the same year represented a further important milestone in the development of parliamentary politics in Germany. Even the very modest provincial assemblies of neo-absolutist Prussia, which were intended to function solely as advisory bodies, gradually became centres of liberal opposition to government policy.

What did 'liberal' mean in the context of early nineteenth-century Germany? This question is less easy to answer than one might expect. Although the term was in widespread use by the early 1830s, its meaning remained imprecise. There was no single liberal 'party' or organization with a monopoly of liberal doctrine. Generally speaking, liberals were opponents of despotism and defenders of liberty. They demanded that the power of the state be bounded by laws and constitutions and they opposed privilege by birth. Their attitude to the state was ambivalent. Many opposed the incursions of state bureaucracies; the castigation of 'paper government' was one of the stock themes of south German liberalism. But many looked upon the strong constitutional state with favour as the chief guarantor of law and order, especially in periods of heightened social unrest. Many liberals favoured free trade, but some did not: 'economic liberals' called for the removal of constraints on the free operation of markets; 'cameral liberals' (the categories are those of the German historian Dieter Langewiesche[6]) sought the implementation of liberal policies through agencies of the state.

Early nineteenth-century German liberals were far from being democrats in the modern sense. They saw themselves as representatives of 'the people', by which they generally meant the educated, property-owning elite. Liberals tended to distinguish between those whose education and economic standing justified their participation in the political process, and the 'mob' (Pöbel), though there were widely diverging views on where exactly the line should be drawn. Their political preferences and cultural outlook were those of the emergent Bürgertum: professionals, academics, men involved in commerce and manufacture. But it would be a mistake to see liberalism as confined to the 5 per cent of the population who belonged to the commercial and educated bourgeoisie. Many distinguished liberals were noblemen, such as Heinrich von Gagern in Hesse-Darmstadt and Theodor von Schön in Prussia, and it is clear that liberalism also enjoyed considerable support among the self-employed in trade, manufacture and services.

Thanks to economic restrictions on the franchise in the constitutional German states, the upper reaches of the Bürgertum tended to be overrepresented in the liberal parliamentary factions. But liberal political activity was not confined to representative institutions. There were liberal 'factions' in many of the German bureaucracies. This was certainly the case in Prussia, where it has been argued that senior officialdom functioned as a kind of 'surrogate parliament'. Although historians no longer argue that the Prussian bureaucracy as a whole was liberal it is clear that there were significant groups of liberal officials, though their influence on policy appears gradually to have waned after 1820. In Baden, liberal officials played an important role in mobilizing public opinion against the government after the reactionary ministry of Freiherr von Blittersdorf tried to prevent them from taking up seats in parliament by restricting civil service leave allowances in 1839; there were similar campaigns by civil servants in the other southern states.

Political opposition in Restoration Germany was not, of course, limited to these forms of 'institutional' dissent. A variety of extra-parliamentary groups emerged in the immediate post-war years, of which the most important was a small but active student movement organized around university fraternities known as *Burschenschaften*. The *Burschenschaftler* were romantic nationalists who hoped by the creation of a pan-German student movement to overcome the narrow confines of the dynastic polities. The political implications of the students' nationalism remained unclear. Some saw their task in terms of education and culture, others were willing to contemplate a more activist political agenda. In October 1817, members of the movement congregated to hold a political festival on the Wartburg. Here, at the castle where Luther had produced his translation of the Bible, students gathered to hear speeches exhorting them to take up the cause of the nation. It is important not to exaggerate the impact of the student movement; there were fewer than 500 students on the Wartburg in 1817, and probably no more than 1,000 *Burschenschaftler* in all. The festival's importance lies more in the emotional and theatrical character of its politics. In addition to hearing and giving speeches, the students burnt reactionary books and objects held to symbolize despotism, among them an officer's cane and a French corset. They wore jackets and hats intended to evoke the traditional 'German costume'; their colours (black, red and gold) were those of the patriotic volunteers who had fought in the Wars of Liberation. 'Festivals' of this kind, in which specific political appeals were blended with the emotive use of symbol and spectacle were henceforth to play an important role in the development of nationalist and radical movements in Germany.

The *Burschenschaft* movement suffered a serious setback in 1819 when a student from its most radical wing stabbed to death a reactionary publicist employed by the Russian legation in Mannheim. The assassination prompted a dramatic change in the political mood. The governments of the German states, egged on by the Austrian chancellor, Metternich, introduced a package of laws known as the 'Karlsbad Decrees' (see above, p. 44) to tighten controls on political activity throughout the Confederation. The student movement was banned, as was the 'old German costume', and fraternity members were hounded by the police. A censorship regime was introduced and the right to form voluntary associations was narrowly circumscribed.

Despite these constraints, the decades of the Restoration era saw the emergence of a widespread and increasingly differentiated network of voluntary organizations whose tone was predominantly liberal. In the 1820s, for example, a wave of support for the Greek uprising against the Ottoman Empire led to the formation of a dense network of 'Greek clubs' concentrated especially in the southwest of Germany. The *Griechenvereine* attracted volunteers from an unprecedentedly broad social spectrum ranging from the *Bürgertum* to urban and rural labourers. The clubs were not overtly 'political' in their aims, but they developed innovative techniques of public mobilization such as the mass distribution of posters and pamphlets and used political festivals and monuments to encourage public 'participation' in the campaign.

In 1830, the July Revolution in Paris combined with widespread shortages and price rises caused by poor harvests to produce a political crisis in several German states. The main centres of civil unrest in the autumn of 1830 were Saxony, Braunschweig, Hesse-Darmstadt and Electoral Hesse. In Braunschweig, there was open rebellion; the ducal residence was set on fire on 7 September and the duke himself forced to flee. Although the motivations for these episodes of unrest had little to do with high politics – more important was the failure of respective administrations to meet social needs – they had lasting political consequences. Constitutions were subsequently granted in all four states. Throughout the German Confederation and especially in the southwest, the events of 1830 raised the political temperature. Factional politics in the parliaments became more confrontational. There was an unprecedented flood of political pamphlets and a proliferation of new dissenting organizations. Among the best known of these was the Patriotic Club in Support of the Free Press ('Press Club'), founded in 1832 to protest against the reactionary policies of the Bavarian government and specifically its restrictive press laws. Members were distributed across 116 auxiliary associations in Bavaria and neighbouring states. Whereas the printed propaganda of the Press Club tended to focus on constitutional issues and to reflect the world-view of the commercial and academic *Bürgertum*, the speeches of individual agitators often focused on social issues and adopted a more radical tone. In this way, Press Club publicity reflected increasingly divergent standpoints within German liberalism.

Press Club agitation culminated in a political festival at the ruined castle of Hambach near Neustadt. The *Hambacher Fest* attracted at least 20,000 participants and has rightly been described as 'the first political demonstration in modern German history'.[7] Once again the internal tensions within the opposition were manifest; the extremism of some of the speeches far exceeded the intentions of the organisers. This did not escape the attention of the watchful Austrian chancellor, Prince Metternich: 'Liberalism has given way to radicalism', he commented in a letter to the Austrian ambassador in Berlin.[8] In June and July 1832, new laws were issued under the authority of the German Confederation forbidding 'festivals' and large assemblies and tightening censorship controls.

Those 'radicals' who stood to the left of liberalism placed more emphasis on social and economic reform as a precondition for the exercise of political liberties; they were likely to be republican, whereas most liberals were constitutional monarchists. They favoured a greatly enlarged or even universal male franchise – voting for women was not on the agenda. The dividing line between radicals and liberals was only gradually clarified, but the widespread unrest of the early 1830s was a crucial milestone in the emergence of a distinctive radical milieu. Radicals distinguished themselves less by their political programmes than by their greater willingness to carry out or condone attacks upon authority. They directed their appeals above all to artisans, peasants and labourers. Radical agitation among these strata was not entirely without success. A network of activist cells and small associations emerged, most of them dominated by urban artisans, and radical factions began to crystallize in some of the parliaments, but in general there was little public sympathy for radical politics. In April 1833, for example, when a small gang of ex-student and artisan activists stormed the police station in Frankfurt am Main, the stolid burghers of the city looked on with interest but offered nothing in the way of support. Radical activism was marked by amateurishness and dilettantism – 'professional revolutionaries' of the legendary type were few and far between. Meanwhile, on the socialist and communist far left, there were attempts to establish a sound theoretical basis for a revolutionary agenda. By the late 1840s, Karl Marx was emerging as an influential figure. The brilliance – and savagery – of the polemical essays in which Marx defended his views and demolished the arguments of his various rivals were to ensure him a central place in the nascent labour movement. For the moment, however, Marx and the communist left played at best a marginal role in the political experience of most German labourers and artisans.

By comparison with liberalism and radicalism, conservative politics have until recently attracted relatively little attention. Though it is clear that the states of the German Confederation often adopted reactionary policies, it is important not to conflate conservatism with the centres of government power. As often as not, conservatives found themselves in opposition to the state. In Prussia, for example, conservative political circles formed among sections of the nobility in opposition to the reforming measures of government bureaucrats. And within the bureaucracy itself, a conservative faction fought with considerable success to wrest control over policy-making from liberal senior officials. In Baden, conservative nobles rejected the constitution offered by the Grand Duke and boycotted the parliament, preferring instead to lobby the Confederal authorities in Frankfurt. The *Evangelische Kirchenzeitung*, founded in 1827 by the theologian Ernst Wilhelm Hengstenberg in Berlin, was the chief organ of north German conservative opinion in the late 1820s and 1830s, but it, too, opposed the Prussian government on various issues, especially in the area of church policy. The *Berliner Politische Wochenblatt* founded by ultraconservatives in 1831, conceived of itself as a loyalist organ directed against the subversive forces unleashed by the July Revolution, but even this newspaper was subject to constant obstruction from government censorship authorities. The public resonance of such journals was modest, but they bore witness to a growing willingness among conservatives to 'organize' for the purpose of influencing opinion. Generally speaking, conservative political theory used organic metaphors and religious argumentation to legitimate an idealized 'traditional order'. Historically given, 'natural' social relations based on paternalistic and localized structures of authority were opposed to the levelling, homogenizing thrust of bureaucratic modernization. It was not until the late 1840s, with the rise to prominence of the legal theorist Friedrich Julius Stahl, that a middle road was found between modern constitutionalism and the provincial, nostalgic politics of the old conservatives.

IV   The social question

Public discussion and debate in Germany during the last decade before the revolutions of 1848 were characterized by a growing awareness of social issues. Books such as Lorenz Stein's *History of Social Movements in France from 1789 to Our Own Day* (1842) and Friedrich Engels' *Condition of the Working Classes in England* (1845) raised public awareness of the 'social question' by focusing on the plight of factory workers and artisans. In 1841, when Bettina von Arnim published her two-volume work *This Book is for the King* in Berlin, readers were less interested in the book's political arguments than in its long appendix documenting the appalling living conditions that prevailed among industrial and manufacturing workers in Berlin. The 'social question' embraced a complex of different issues: working conditions within factories, the problem of housing in densely populated areas, the dissolution of corporate entities (e.g. guilds, estates), the vicissitudes of a capitalist economy based on competition, the decline of religion and morals among the emergent 'proletariat', the fear of revolutionary upheaval. In other words, the social question was also a political question, which turned on divergent evaluations of economic liberalism and its consequences. But the central and dominant issue was 'pauperization', the progressive impoverishment of the lower social strata. The 'pauperism' of the pre-March era differed from traditional forms of poverty in a number of important ways. It was a mass phenomenon, collective and structural, rather than dependent upon individual contingencies, such as sickness, injury or crop failures. It was permanent rather than seasonal. And it showed signs of engulfing social groups whose position had previously been relatively secure, such as artisans (especially apprentices and journeymen) and smallholding peasants. 'Pauperism', the *Brockhaus Encyclopaedia* noted in 1846, 'occurs when a large class can subsist only as a result of the most intensive labour'. The key problem was a decline in the value of labour and its products. This affected not only unskilled labourers and those who worked in the craft trades, but also the large and growing section of the rural population who lived from various forms of cottage industry.

Inevitably, the causes of mass poverty were extremely complex; generalizations are difficult, since conditions varied according to occupation and locality. The older historical literature on this subject tended to focus on state-sponsored processes of modernization, particularly industrialization, arguing that more efficient modes of production had a drastic effect on older forms of manufacture. But, as we have seen, this view is founded on on a misapprehension of the power and ambitions of the state. Industrialization had made only very modest advances in the German states by the time revolution broke out. German society remained overwhelmingly rural; in the 1840s, over 70 per cent of the population still worked on the land. There were a few sectors (such as cotton-printing, typesetting and nail-making) in which mechanized production posed a serious threat to manual labour by the late 1840s, but in the great majority of manufacturing trades, various kinds of skilled and unskilled manual labour still predominated. In 1846, for example, when there were at least 55,000 male workers in Berlin, the city could boast only 75 steam engines. In Prussia as a whole, industrial workers proper accounted for no more than 3.9 per cent of the population.

The most fundamental cause of mass impoverishment was probably demographic growth. In 1816, the population of the German Confederation, including the three provinces of Prussia outside its borders, was about 32.7 million. By 1865 this figure had risen by 60 per cent to 52.2 million. The reasons for this rapid growth are still debated and they cannot be dealt with here (see further Chapter 4 below, pp. 72–4). However, it is important to remember that the impact of demographic growth was socially very uneven. It was above all a rural phenomenon. In Prussia, for example, the population increased by 56 per cent from 10.3 million in 1816 to 15.9 million in 1846, while the percentage of the population living in cities rose only from 26 per cent to 28 per cent. A few cities, particularly Berlin, did experience dramatic growth, but the overall picture was one of stasis. Both in the cities and on the land, moreover, the effects of population growth were most apparent among the least economically secure social groups. On the land the abolition (by liberal bureaucrats) of marriage restrictions and the extension of land under cultivation raised nuptiality and fertility among the 'sub-peasant strata' (*unterbäuerlichen Schichten*), especially families on subsistence holdings and landless rural labourers. In Minden-Ravensberg, for example, the ratio of families living from the wages of hired labour to full-time peasants (*Vollbauern*) was 149/100 in 1800; by 1846, the ratio had risen to 310/100. Such families earned an increasingly marginal living from a combination of agrarian labour and various forms of domestic piece-work for merchants who dealt with supra-regional markets. Rural labourers of this kind spent most of their income on food; they were vulnerable not only to rises in the cost of agrarian produce, but also to fluctuations in the business cycle which could depress demand for the goods – especially textiles – they helped to manufacture.

There was a similarly disproportionate growth in the number of artisans. This becomes clear if we consult figures for Prussia during the period 1816–46, when, as we have seen, the population as a whole rose by 56 per cent. The number of master artisans rose by 70 per cent during the same period. Much more dramatic was the rise (156 per cent) in the number of assistants and apprentices. A similarly dramatic growth in this sector can be observed for the same period in the German Confederation as a whole.

In a buoyant, elastic economy, such changes may have been sustainable; in the stagnant conditions of the 1830s and 1840s, however, the growth in the labour supply was not matched by a corresponding demand for manufactured products. The result – leaving aside the dramatic differences between regions and sectors – was a continual net decline in the living standard of those involved in craft trades and rural proto-industrial manufacture. From the 1830s, the Poor Office in Cologne dedicated a special category of charity to master craftsmen who had fallen on hard times. A contemporary statistical survey suggested that between 50 and 60 per cent of the Prussian population were living on a subsistence minimum. The striking combination of rising population and mass poverty may lead us to suspect that the social crisis of this era was the result of a 'Malthusian trap', where the needs of the population exceeded the available supply of agricultural produce. However, it is important to remember that during the period covered by this chapter technical improvements (artificial fertilizers, modernized animal husbandry and the three-field rotation system) and an increase in land under cultivation had doubled the productivity of German agriculture. In other words, the food supply increased at about twice the rate of population growth in the German Confederation. The problem was not, therefore, chronic underproduction. But large agricultural surpluses could also have a harmful effect on manufacturing, since they depressed the prices of agricultural produce. The result was a collapse in agrarian incomes and a corresponding decline in the demand for goods from the overcrowded manfacturing sector.

More importantly, food supplies remained vulnerable despite the impressive growth in total agricultural production, because natural catastrophes – poor harvests, cattle epidemics, crop diseases – could still turn the surplus into a drastic shortfall. This is what happened in the winter of 1846, when harvest failures sent food prices up to double and even triple the normal average. The crisis was compounded by a downturn in the business cycle and a crop disease that wiped out the potato harvests upon which many regions had become dependent. The rise in prices was accompanied by a heightened frequency of civic unrest. In Prussia alone, 158 food riots – marketplace riots, attacks on stores and shops, transportation blockades – took place during April/May 1847, when prices were at their highest. Interestingly enough, the geography of food riots did not coincide with that of the most acute shortage. Extremely hard-hit areas like upper Silesia, where some 50,000 people are thought to have died from diseases related to malnutrition, remained riot-free. Riots were more likely to occur in areas which produced food for export, or in transit areas with high levels of food transportation. Such protests should certainly not be seen as 'rehearsals' for revolution; they were generally pragmatic attempts to control the food supply, or to 'remind' the authorities of their traditional obligations to provide for afflicted subjects. Rioters did not act as members of a 'class', but as representatives of a local community whose right to justice had been denied. The human targets of their wrath were likely to be 'outsiders': merchants who dealt with distant markets, customs officials, foreigners or Jews.

We have seen that despite considerable improvements in the cultivation of land and livestock German societies remained vulnerable to sudden disruptions in the agrarian sector. This primacy of agriculture led Eric Hobsbawm to describe the European crisis of the late 1840s as 'the last, and perhaps the worst, economic breakdown of the *ancien régime*'. But this view requires some elaboration: harvest cycles and climate fluctuation remained crucial as they had been in traditional societies; in this sense, certainly, the German crisis of the 1840s was a crisis 'of the old type'. But the dramatic growth and internal restructuring of the labour force in the manufacturing sector was new. It generated new social groups, who were exposed to poverty in different ways and through more complex mechanisms than the smallholding peasants and traditional artisans of the *ancien régime*. This helps to explain not only the heightened sensitivity of these groups to fluctuations in supply and demand, but also the chronic character of mass poverty in pre-March society.

V Religion

Throughout the period covered by this chapter, politics and religion were closely intertwined. We must be wary of applying anachronistic assumptions based on the relatively marginal and specialized role of religion in modern public life. Political views were often articulated in religious language and religious disputes and allegiances could easily take on political character. This was apparent, for example, in the case of those Prussian noble families – Gerlachs, Thaddens, Senfft von Pilsachs, Kleist-Retzows, Belows, Oertzens and others – whose conservatism drew upon religiously motivated opposition to government church policy. In Bavaria, likewise, conservative Catholics in Würzburg formed a 'Literary Society' whose aim was to oppose the secularizing reforms of the ministry under Montgelas. Some historians have seen this organization as a forerunner of the Centre Party. Political and religious milieux tended to overlayer each other: in Prussia, for example, conservative political mobilization remained a largely Protestant domain. In the predominantly Catholic Rhineland, conservative newspapers were rarely read outside the Protestant 'ghetto'. Even the political rhetoric of pre-March radicalism, with its evocations of brotherly love, justice, spiritual renewal and utopian prospects, was saturated with the language of the gospels.

Religious allegiances also influenced contemporary responses to social problems. The efforts by Protestants to alleviate social need among the impoverished often focused on the need to reconcile the conditions of modern manufacture with the maintenance of a strict ethical code founded on providential religion and the sacralization of labour. Typical of this tendency were the 'spinning houses' established by Baron Kottwitz in Silesia and Berlin in the 1810s, or the orphanage complex built up by Count von der Recke near Düsseldorf in the 1820s, where prayer and elementary instruction were combined with work in a variety of manufacturies. By contrast, socially minded Catholics tended to be more fundamental in their criticism of economic liberalism and the modern industrial system. In their place, Catholic theorists offered corporatist solutions: the philosopher Franz von Baader – the first writer in Germany to use the term 'proletarian' (1835) – called for obligatory corporations of workers led by priests with the right to political representation in the parliaments. Others called for state controls on the ownership of property, protective tolls, laws against long working hours and child labour, and marriage restrictions to prevent further overpopulation. The intention was to reverse the 'decorporation' and atomization characteristic of modern capitalist society. These responses doubtless reflected the fact that Catholics and Catholic regions were less involved in the modernization of manufactures and industry than their Protestant counterparts – Protestants were greatly overrepresented, for example, in the early industrial enterprises of the Catholic Rhineland.

It is important, however, not to see religion merely as a fund of language and argumentation for various forms of political discourse, or as a passive 'milieu' that coloured the public life of German communities. The dynamism of religion as an autonomous social force was arguably greater during this era than at any time since the late seventeenth century. In the Protestant north of Germany, the early decades of the nineteenth century brought a widespread and socially differentiated Christian revival movement. 'Awakened' Christians emphasized the emotional, penitential character of faith in a language reminiscent of eighteenth-century pietism; their religious commitment often found expression outside the institutional confines of the church. Characteristic for this period was the proliferation of voluntary Christian societies with a variety of purposes: the distribution of charity, the housing and 'betterment' of 'fallen women', the moral improvement of prisoners, the care of orphans, the printing and distribution of bibles, the provision of subsistence labour for paupers and vagrants, the conversion of Jews and heathens. Most of these societies were supported by networks of auxiliaries throughout northern Germany. In Prussia, they generally enjoyed the patronage of 'awakened' nobles, and in many cases, of the sovereign and his family; the auxiliary groups in smaller communities were often dominated by pious master artisans.

German Catholicism also entered a phase of revival during the period covered by this chapter. It is important to remember that the church had been the foremost victim of the secularizations carried out during the Napoleonic era. The ecclesiastical principalities of the old Reich had been dissolved and absorbed into new or enlarged secular states, some with a Protestant majority. The revival of religion among the mass of the Catholic faithful and the tightening of clerical control over popular religious life characteristic of the Restoration era have to be seen against this background. Catholic revival reflected a larger trend away from rationalism towards a greater emphasis on emotion, mystery and revelation – in this sense at least, Catholic and Protestant revival were cut from the same cloth. But it also offered a means of compensating for the church's traumatic loss of resources and political autonomy. Whereas the Protestant awakening was dominated by lay initiatives, Catholic revivalism tended to be clerically led. In Bavaria from the 1820s, the clergy used liturgical innovations, pilgrimages and processions to encourage and deepen public participation and to replace the rationalist ethics of the Catholic Enlightenment with a respect for mystery and miracle. In the Rhineland, the 1840s saw the emergence of a new style of pilgrimage characterized by mass participation – 400,000 went to view the Holy Robe at Trier in 1844 – and a high level of clerical discipline. The untidy, festive mobs of the traditional pilgrimage were replaced by ordered groups under strict clerical supervision.

Closely associated with the phenomenon of Catholic revival was the rise of ultramontanism. Ultramontanes were those who argued that the strict subordination of the church to papal authority was the best way of protecting it from state interference. They perceived the church as a strictly centralized but international body. Until around 1830, Catholic conservatives were concerned above all with 'inner' religious renewal; thereafter the focus of their activity shifted to strengthening the ties with Rome. Inevitably, the rise of ultramontanism led to increasing tension between church and state. In Bavaria, a dispute broke out in 1831 over the education of children in Catholic–Protestant mixed marriages. The ultramontanes moved on to the offensive and liberal publicists depicted the debate as a struggle between the forces of darkness and light. Six years later, a much more serious fight broke out over the same issue in Prussia, in the course of which the authorities arrested and imprisoned the ultramontane archbishop of Cologne. Such conflicts helped to accelerate the emergence of an increasingly confident and aggressive 'political Catholicism'. The *Historisch-Politischen Blätter für das katholische Deutschland*, founded by Joseph Görres in Munich in 1837, became the chief organ of this tendency. It favoured the political consolidation of the traditional corporate social bodies and the return to a Habsburg-led German Reich.

In Protestant Germany, there was a similar shift away from the 'awakening' of the early decades, with its romantic and ecumenical overtones, towards a more narrowly confessional revivalism. In 1830 the three-hundredth anniversary of the Confession of Augsburg, one of the founding texts of Lutheran Protestantism, was greeted with celebrations by Lutherans throughout northern Germany. In Saxony, it was the refusal of the Catholic sovereign to permit Lutheran celebrations that unleashed the first protest demonstrations of that troubled year. In Prussia, revived Lutheranism found itself in direct conflict with the government. Since 1817, King Frederick William III had been effecting a gradual union of the Calvinist and Lutheran Confessions in Prussia. But from 1830 an 'Old Lutheran' movement emerged in Silesia that openly rejected the Church of the 'Prussian Union'. The government responded with fines, surveillance, arrests and imprisonment, in the hope that the beleaguered Lutherans would relinquish their separatism and return to the Union. Instead, the Old Lutheran movement steadily grew; by 1840, when Frederick William died, there were some 10,000 known active separatists in Prussia. A further 2,000 had emigrated to Australia and North America to escape persecution. The conflict was only defused when Frederick William IV offered a general amnesty and granted the Lutherans the right to establish themselves within Prussia as an autonomous 'church society'.

Both Protestant and Catholic revivalism were, as we have seen, closely affiliated with conservatism. But these movements did not remain unchallenged within the two confessional communities. The 'German Catholic' movement, founded in Leipzig in 1845, called for a severing of ties with Rome and a movement of enlightened spiritual renewal which would abandon the straitjacket of traditional dogma and create the foundation for a German, Catholic–Protestant, 'national church'. Two years later, the movement had acquired 250 congregations with a total membership of some 60,000, of whom about 20,000 were converts from Protestantism. There were close ties with Germany's leading political radicals. Among the foremost supporters was Robert Blum, who used his *Vaterlandsblätter* to combine anti-Roman polemic with attacks on bureaucracy, police and censorship. Another was the radical Gustav von Struve, who was to lead the ill-fated Badenese uprising of 1849. The connection between religious critique and political radicalism was equally clear in the case of the Protestant movement known as the 'Friends of Light' (*Lichtfreunde*). Like the German Catholics, the Friends of Light combined rationalist theology with a presbyterial-democratic organizational culture in which authority was devolved on to the individual congregation and its elected elders. The movement was particularly successful in attracting poor urban and rural artisans, especially in Saxony, the most industrialized state in the German Confederation. Both the Friends of Light and the German Catholics were concentrated among social strata and in areas which later became centres of radical democratic activity: Silesia, Saxony, Electoral Hesse, Baden, Vienna. Located halfway between sect and party, these movements offer dramatic evidence of the intimate relationship between religion and politics in the pre-March era.

VI Conclusion

The fascination of the period 1815–48 for students of German history lies partly in its transitional character. The bureaucratic state was larger and stronger than it had been before 1806, but not as strong as it would later become. Parliamentary factions, political 'festivals' and mass demonstrations coexisted with corporate noble-dominated estates – a reminder that modernity was born in Germany long before the old regime had died. The result of the overlap, as we have seen, was a heightened tension between restorative inertia and the progressive movement that was briefly to win the day in 1848.

But 'transition' is in some ways an inadequate metaphor for the developments we have discussed. The mass poverty and social dislocation of the 1840s were not the consequences of a transition from a traditional agrarian to a modern industrial society. Not all movements were progressive and forward-looking, nor, as we have seen, were the forces of Restoration purely backward-looking. Revivalist religion generated a new and dynamic social force that was neither entirely reactionary, nor entirely modern. The political Catholicism that emerged in the 1830s was to play a decisive role in the public life of the Wilhelmine Empire, the Weimar Republic and, later, of the German Federal Republic. Rather than combing through the 'pre-March' for the first signs of 1848, we should remember that this era, like all eras, contained the seeds of many futures.

Notes:

1. Diary of Leopold von Gerlach, Breslau, February 1813, Bundesarchiv Abteilungen (BA) Potsdam, NL von Gerlach 90 Ge 1 (transcript), B1.45.
2. Nipperdey, T., *Deutsche Geschichte 1800–1866. Bürgerwelt und starker Staat* (1983), p. 333.
3. Nolte, Paul, *Staatsbildung als Gesellschaftsreform. Politische Reformen in Preußen und den süddeutschen Staaten 1800–1820* (1990), p. 105.
4. Kocka, J., 'Preußischer Staat und Modernisierung im Vormärz', in B. Vogel, ed., *Preußische Reformen 1807–1820* (1980), pp. 49–65; here p. 58.
5. Gerlach, Leopold von, 1 May 1816, BA Potsdam, NL von Gerlach, 90 Ge 2, Bl. 9.
6. D. Langewiesche, *Liberalism in Germany* (1998).
7. Heuss, Theodor, cited in H. Schulze, *Der Weg zum Nationalstaat. Die deutsche Nationalbewegung vom 18. Jahrhundert bis zur Reichsbründung* (1985), p. 78.
8. Metternich quoted in J. J. Sheehan, *German History 1770–1866* (1989), p. 613.

Select bibliography

Anderson, M. L., 'Piety and Politics: Recent Work on German Catholicism', *Journal of Modern History*, 63 (1991).

Beck, H., 'The Social Policies of Prussian Officials: The Bureaucracy in a New Light', *Journal of Modern History*, 64 (1992).

Billinger, R. D., *Metternich and the German Question. State Rights and Federal Duties 1820–1834* (1991).

Botzenhart, M., *Reform, Restauration, Krise. Deutschland 1789–1847* (1985).

Diefendorf, J., *Businessmen and Politics in the Rhineland, 1789–1834* (1980).

Lee, L. E., *The Politics of Harmony. Civil Service, Liberalism and Social Reform in Baden 1800–1850* (1980).

Lee, W. R., 'Economic Development and the State in Nineteenth-Century Germany, 1815–1870', *Economic History Review*, 2nd series, 41 (1988).

Lüdtke, A., *Police and State in Prussia 1815–1850* (1989).

Lutz, H., *Zwischen Habsburg und Preussen: Deutschland 1815–1866* (1985).

Nipperdey, T., *Germany from Napoleon to Bismarck 1800–1866*, Eng. trs. (1996).

Schulze, H., *The Course of German Nationalism: From Frederick the Great to Bismarck*, trans. S. Hanbury-Tenison (1990).

Sheehan, J. J., *German History 1770–1866* (1989).

Simms, B., *The Struggle for Mastery in Germany, 1779–1850* (1998).

Sperber, J., *Popular Catholicism in Nineteenth-Century Germany* (1984).

Sperber, J., 'State and Civil Society in Prussia: Some Thoughts on a New Edition of Reinhart Koselleck's *Preußen zwischen Reform und Revolution*'. *Journal of Modern History*, 57 (1985).

4

'Relative backwardness' and long-run development

Economic, demographic and social changes

Robert Lee

Any discussion of Germany's economic development during the decades of the nineteenth century prior to political unification in 1871 is still influenced by a series of hypotheses stemming from the Gerschenkronian paradigm of 'relative backwardness'.[1] On the basis of this analysis, Germany's apparent economic backwardness and the persistence of market imperfections enhanced the role of special institutional factors, such as banks and the state, and generated a more rapid rate of industrialization with a greater emphasis on producer goods, large plant size and up-to-date technology. The creation of a unified internal market with the establishment of the customs union (*Zollverein*) in 1834 and the elimination of internal tariffs and customs barriers was a 'significant step forward', and the role of the state was equally evident in the official encouragement of railway construction and extensive improvements in educational training. Recent research, however, has begun to question some, if not all, of these traditional explanations. This chapter will therefore attempt to explore the extent to which our understanding of the pattern of economic and social change in nineteenth-century Germany prior to political unification in 1871 has now been altered or modified.

I The 'relative backwardness' of Germany in the late eighteenth century

A key question, in this context, is whether Germany (or the different states that constituted Germany) was actually 'backward' in the late eighteenth or early nineteenth centuries, and to what extent? Recent views on the level and nature of economic activity at the start of this period vary considerably in terms of their interpretation of the available data. On the one hand, although there were certain well-established manufacturing centres, output levels were low and development was hindered by restricted markets and an inadequate transport infrastructure. Urban guilds constituted a major obstacle to economic growth, political divisions within the German Confederation hindered the development of both trade and industry, and specific sectors, such as the iron and steel industry, were slow to introduce more modern methods of production. In Prussia in the early 1800s over 70 per cent of the population either lived or worked in the countryside, agriculture continued to attract the lion's share of net investment and the production of capital goods was very limited. In addition, capital accumulation remained a major problem as a result of the relative backwardness of the economy and German agriculture, even by the 1840s, was apparently amongst the most backward in Europe.

Recent research, on the other hand, has helped to create a more differentiated picture of Germany's economic position at the end of the eighteenth century. The expansion of proto-industrial production, particularly in such regions as Silesia, Saxony and the Rhineland, fostered important changes in the regional division of labour and contributed to an increasing diversification in urban function. Minimal regulation in rural areas kept labour costs low and encouraged the long-term territorialization of handicraft production, so that even in Bavaria over 50 per cent of all holdings were probably dependent on some form of non-agricultural income by 1752–60. Similarly in the Kurmark Brandenburg more than half of all agricultural holdings in 1755 were held by day labourers or domestic craftsmen. In some regions, such as Lower Saxony, the expansion of rural handicrafts did not immediately threaten existing urban production, but many city guilds continued to oppose this trend. However, substantial population growth from the mid-eighteenth century onwards, together with price inflation and increased accessibility to markets, provided important incentives for a general expansion of industrial production.

The eighteenth century also witnessed the development of larger units of centralized production (*Manufakturen*) whether in Bavaria, the electorate of Mainz or Schleswig-Holstein, often as a result of direct state initiatives reflecting a concern to reduce unemployment and to promote the sale of luxury goods. In line with cameralist principles, for example, 150 new *Manufakturen* were first registered in Saxony between 1793 and 1800. It is not surprising, therefore, that many individual towns and cities had developed a respectable manufacturing and trading profile: if approximately one-third of all households in Krefeld were engaged in the linen and silk trades in 1750, the proportion had risen to over 46 per cent by the end of the eighteenth century. Despite a long tradition of city states and a substantial number of cities, Germany only had a low level of urbanization in the early eighteenth century. By 1800, however, there had been significant changes: new industrial and commercial centres had developed in the Rhine and Ruhr regions, with expanded regional capitals (such as Cologne and Frankfurt am Main); Saxony was increasingly dominated by Dresden and Leipzig, and Silesia by Breslau and Lemberg. The growth of administrative cities (*Residenzstädte*) was spectacular, with demographic growth reflecting policies which openly encouraged immigration, in contrast to the more restrictive controls retained on urban in-migration by the older German home towns.

At the same time there are indications of significant primary sector growth, including an expansion of plough land and a reduction in the extent of fallow. Further confirmation of this trend can be found in the dissemination of improved cultivation patterns (for example, the Holstein *Koppelwirtschaft*); the introduction of new crops (including clover, esparto grass, potatoes and lucerne); and buoyant grain exports, particularly from the eastern territories. Certainly by the late eighteenth century specialist areas of production had already emerged, with different field systems and cultivation patterns; for example, by 1800 almost 30 per cent of the cultivable area of Lower Saxony was devoted to flax. Moreover, the expansion of rural craft production, together with the proliferation of smallholdings had already stimulated regional specialization in the primary sector. In various regions of Germany there were clear signs of increased agricultural prosperity: higher dowry values in rural communities, a fall in the frequency of enforced sales of agricultural holdings, and a more commercial approach to market opportunities by certain types of peasant, such as the dairy farmers of Neuholland.

II   Rates of growth in the nineteenth century

It is generally accepted that the industrialization of Germany took place in three distinct phases. From the 1780s onwards there were clear signs of economic growth, but only in certain regions such as the Rhineland, Saxony and Silesia. The years after 1815 witnessed the reintroduction of restrictive guild regulations in such states as Hesse-Kassel, Hanover and Oldenburg, and a collapse of agricultural prices in the 1820s which led to indebtedness and depression in many rural communities and a fall in aggregate demand. Many rural industries in Prussia, for example, suffered from a lack of suitable markets during these years. The period between the

1840s and the early 1870s, on the other hand, was characterized by a significant acceleration in the pace of industrialization, associated with the expansion of heavy industry and extensive railway construction. In Prussia the 1840s can be seen as a watershed which marked the final acceptance by élite groups of the inevitability of industrial development and a recognition after 1848 that the private sector, rather than the state, should control the forces of production. The central decades of the nineteenth century therefore marked the beginning of Germany's industrial revolution, in line with the Gerschenkronian model that specifies a big spurt discontinuity in the growth rates of relatively backward national economies. This was then followed by a second phase of industrialization in the late nineteenth century associated with the successful development of the chemical and electricity industries (see below, Chapter 9).

However, such an interpretation of Germany's economic performance is not based on firm quantitative evidence and seriously underplays the extent and dynamic nature of economic growth in the earlier decades of the nineteenth century. In the first instance, existing estimates of the trend in agricultural output, despite certain limitations, confirm the relatively positive performance of the German primary sector during this period (Table 4.1). Within Prussia the highest growth in agricultural output in the period 1816 to 1855 was registered in Posen, Saxony, Silesia and West Prussia. In terms of total population employed in the primary sector, the rate of change in the period 1816 to 1849 was as fast as during the later

Table 4.1   The development of agricultural production per unit of labour input (LI) in Germany, 1800–50 on the basis of grain values

Period	Production in 1,000 tons					
	Arable	Livestock	Total	Labour force (1,000)	Tons per LI	Index
1800–10	14,500	7,555	22,055	9,525	2.32	100
1811–20	15,660	7,332	22,992	9,530	2.41	104
1821–25	19,140	8,100	27,240	10,100	2.70	116
1826–30	20,010	8,787	28,797	10,300	2.80	120
1831–35	22,910	11,205	34,115	10,600	3.22	139
1836–40	24,795	12,262	37,057	11,057	3.35	144
1841–45	26,825	13,719	40,544	11,662	3.48	150
1846–50	29,000	14,874	43,874	11,425	3.84	165

Note: Index shows the relative growth in output (tons per LI) from the base line of 1800–10.
Source: G. Franz, 'Landwirtschaft, 1800–1850', in H. Aubin and W. Zorn, eds, *Handbuch der deutschen Wirtschafts- und Sozialgeschichte*, vol. 2 (Stuttgart, 1976), p. 313.

period from the mid-nineteenth century to 1883. In Württemberg the rise in output more than kept pace with the increase in population, and in good years the primary sector generated a noticeable surplus. Grain output in Bavaria, for example, increased by an estimated annual rate of 4.2 per cent between 1810 and 1864, whereas total population only rose by 0.6 per cent per annum. Indeed, for Germany as a whole, the estimated rate of growth in agricultural output was higher in the first half of the nineteenth century up until 1861–5, than in the following three decades. In general, there was an improvement in yields, a significant expansion in the cultivation of potatoes and root crops, as well as a selective shift to dairy produce. The rise in arable output, however, was largely achieved through an expansion in the cultivable area and, particularly in the eastern provinces of Prussia, through continuous increments in labour supply. Undoubtedly the liberal agrarian reforms of the early nineteenth century, such as the Prussian legislation of 1807, 1811 and 1821, modified land distribution, farm organization and agricultural production, particularly within a regional context, even if their contribution to economic development has frequently been exaggerated. But the estimated increase in annual agricultural output in the 1820s and 1830s of 1.32 per cent and 2.58 per cent respectively (in comparison with an equivalent figure of 0.12 per cent between 1840 and 1850) also reflected a positive response to rising levels of aggregate demand and the buoyancy of export markets after an initial decline in the Danzig grain trade. With the revival in agricultural prices in the 1830s peasant production increased significantly: the growth in rape seed and sugar beet cultivation was symptomatic of a stronger commercial approach to agriculture by the peasantry and a willingness to respond positively to market demands.

Second, new estimates of trends in industrial investment, specifically in the case of Baden, and total net capital formation in Prussia have revealed evidence of substantial growth in the post-Napoleonic period. Industrial enterprises in a number of states showed early signs of development, and the Prussian tariff of 1818, by treating pig-iron imports as a raw material, provided an important impulse for the long-term development of the iron and steel industry. Trade in Saxony increased noticeably throughout the 1820s and various industries in and around Berlin registered substantial growth during the 1830s and early 1840s. During the first half of the nineteenth century the highest annual growth rate in textile production, in particular of cotton and woollen goods, was registered in the period 1831–40. It is not surprising, in this context, that the changes in occupational structure in the western provinces of Prussia were just as extensive during the period 1816 to 1849 as in the later nineteenth century.

Moreover, the traditional periodization of German economic development has been further undermined by a re-estimation of the available data on net domestic product. On this basis the overall performance of the economy during the 1840s, which has often been viewed as the starting point for Germany's industrial revolution, was weaker than predicted, with a significant increase in growth rates only occurring from the 1850s onwards. Industrialization, therefore, was not characterized by extensive discontinuities and economic development in Germany was essentially a cumulative long-term process with significant changes taking place in the pre-1840 period.

In terms of the overall structure of employment, agriculture retained its predominant role throughout this period. Although its relative position declined as a result of the disproportionate growth of employment opportunities in the secondary and tertiary sectors, it still accounted for 49.3 per cent of total employment in 1871. Indeed, because of the continued dependency on labour-intensive methods of production, approximately two million more individuals were now employed in the primary sector than had been the case in 1800. Although the 1850s and 1860s witnessed a substantial expansion in the output of capital goods industries (such as iron and steel production, coal-mining, and machine construction), textiles (including the leather and clothing industries) still remained the largest component in the secondary sector. Even in 1875 just over 37 per cent of the 'industrial' workforce in Germany was employed in textiles, in comparison with approximately 14 per cent in the second largest sector – metal production and manufacture. Moreover, until the mid-nineteenth century textile production, in particular cotton-spinning, led the way in terms of factory organization and management. Indeed, despite the significant changes that took place during this period in specific sectors of German industry, the general nature of industrial organization did not alter substantially. Certainly in the case of Prussia, employment levels in craft production increased two-fold between 1816 and 1861: the number of master craftsmen grew at a rate well above that of total population, but the number of registered journeymen rose on average by 3 per cent per annum. As a result the average enterprise size increased from 1.6 to 2.0 people. The introduction of freedom of trade in certain states may well have led to an initial fall in the overall number of craftsmen, but the expansion of many trades in the 1820s and 1830s gave rise to a growing concern over excess labour supply, the proliferation of unskilled and untrained workers, and the decline in income levels of master craftsmen. By the early 1840s only 407 of the 2,812 registered shoemakers in Berlin earned enough income to be liable to the *Gewerbesteuer* (trade tax), and the situation in Elberfeld and Barmen was considerably worse. But the continuing growth in the number of bakers, tailors, shoemakers, joiners and masons also reflected a long-term expansion of consumer demand which required skills that remained relatively unaffected by new techniques of production. Moreover, the construction industry in Prussia (providing employment for masons, painters, roofers, carpenters and stonemasons) underwent an even more remarkable process of expansion between 1816 and 1858, particularly in the period 1831 to 1846: there was an almost five-fold increase in the number of journeymen and a three-fold expansion in average enterprise size which reflected a significant degree of concentration within this sector as it responded to favourable economic conditions.

Unfortunately, there is little reliable information on German foreign trade prior to the creation of the customs union in 1834, but the available data reveal further evidence of a long-term growth process. Although the depression of the early 1820s cannot be denied, as the decline in the merchant fleet both in Hamburg and Bremen reveals, the value of Saxony's imports and exports nevertheless grew by 8 per cent throughout that decade. Grain exports from Prussia, via the Baltic ports of Elbing, Lübeck, Rostock, Königsberg, Stettin and Stralsund, also expanded by approximately 21 per cent between 1825 and 1831. For those states within the *Zollverein* the value of imports and exports between 1837 and 1855 rose by 4.6 per cent and 4.5 per cent annually. The estimated export surplus increased from 37.6 million taler in 1834 to 65 million in 1845 and over 101 million by 1860. Shipping capacity increased four-fold between the end of the 1820s and 1850, at a time when German merchants were establishing themselves extensively in both North and South America, as well as in other parts of the world. Although Germany's foreign trade performance in the second half of the nineteenth century was even more impressive, the process of development before 1850 was nevertheless considerable.

This interpretation is reinforced by demographic evidence. Population growth in the second half of the eighteenth century was already substantial, but this continued to be the case during the early decades of the nineteenth century (Table 4.2). Between 1816 and 1864 high rates of population growth were registered in the eastern agricultural provinces of Prussia, including East and West Prussia, Pomerania and Brandenburg, slightly lower but significant growth rates in the developing industrial centres of Saxony, the Rhineland and Westphalia, and markedly lower rates in the southern states of Baden, Bavaria and Württemberg. Indeed many German territories recorded peak population growth rates during this period, which were not exceeded until the end of the nineteenth century. Debate continues over the causal factors behind this trend, and the relative contribution of changes in nuptiality, fertility or age-specific mortality to long-run population growth. In most German states crude birth rates remained relatively high and easily exceeded contemporary mortality levels, except during the 1816–17 famine and the major cholera epidemics of 1831–2, 1848–50 and 1852–5, and the further fall in the death rate from the mid-nineteenth century has been attributed to

Table 4.2   General rates of population growth (per annum): 1816–64, 1864–1910

Province/state	1816–64			1864–1910		
	Absolute increase (000s)	%	% p.a.	Absolute increase (000s)	%	% p.a.
East Prussia	875	98.75	2.05	303	17.20	0.37
West Prussia	682	119.43	2.48	451	35.99	0.78
Berlin	435	219.69	4.57	1,438	227.17	4.93
Brandenburg	898	82.68	1.72	2,109	106.30	2.31
Pomerania	755	110.54	2.30	279	19.40	0.42
Posen	704	85.85	1.78	576	37.79	0.82
Silesia	1,609	84.59	1.76	1,715	48.84	1.06
Saxony	848	70.84	1.47	1,044	51.05	1.10
Schleswig-Holstein	302	43.32	0.90	622	62.26	1.35
Hanover	316	19.62	0.40	1,016	52.75	1.14
Westphalia	601	56.37	1.17	2,458	147.45	3.20
Hesse-Nassau	430	44.88	0.93	833	60.01	1.30
Rhineland	1,462	76.54	1.59	3,749	111.09	2.41
Hohenzollern	10	18.18	0.37	6	9.23	0.20
Total (Prussia)	9,873	72.01	1.50	16,583	70.32	1.52
Bavaria	1,168	32.38	0.67	2,112	44.23	0.96
Saxony	1,143	95.72	1.99	2,470	105.69	2.29
Württemberg	337	23.88	0.49	689	39.41	0.85
Baden	436	43.33	0.90	711	49.65	1.07
Mecklenburg-Schwerin	245	79.54	1.65	87	16.32	0.35
Gross-Sachsen	87	45.07	0.93	137	48.92	1.06
Mecklenburg-Strelitz	27	37.50	0.78	7	7.07	0.15
Oldenburg	80	34.18	0.71	169	53.82	1.17
Braunschweig	67	29.64	0.61	201	68.60	1.49
Saxe-Meiningen	57	47.10	0.98	101	56.74	1.23
Saxe-Altenberg	46	47.91	0.99	74	52.11	1.13
Saxe-Coburg-Gotha	53	47.32	0.98	92	55.75	1.21
Anhalt	73	60.83	1.26	138	71.50	1.55
Schwarzburg-Sonderhausen	21	46.66	0.97	24	36.36	0.79
Schwarzburg-Rudolstadt	20	37.03	0.77	27	36.48	0.79
Waldeck	7	13.46	0.28	3	5.08	0.11
Lippe	30	37.03	0.77	40	36.03	0.78
Elsass-Lothringen	366	30.04	0.62	290	18.30	0.39
Hesse	255	45.37	0.94	465	56.91	1.23
Total (excl. the three Hansa towns)	14,559	58.62	1.22	25,534	64.82	1.40

Source: Compiled from official sources.

a decline in the variability of mortality. However, health conditions in many cities were far less favourable than in rural areas and until the 1880s mortality was positively correlated with city size. In the five largest cities of Prussia (Berlin, Breslau, Cologne, Magdeburg and Königsberg) crude mortality rates rose from the early nineteenth century onwards. Urban population growth therefore depended to a large degree on the in-migration of craftsmen and domestic servants, who frequently came from surrounding rural areas or adjacent towns. Infant mortality remained a major component of total mortality, particularly in the south German states of Bavaria and Württemberg, and it continued to rise in most parts of Germany until the 1870s. To some extent, this may have been the result of a failure to breast-feed infants at a time when poverty and environmental factors heightened the risks associated with artificial feeding. But child mortality, at least in Prussia, had certainly fallen by the 1860s, perhaps as a result of the earlier introduction of smallpox inoculation or the reduced virulence of specific childhood diseases. The gains in life expectancy for older age groups, on the other hand, were much more limited.

It is important to note, however, that overall population density rose from 45.9 inhabitants per square kilometre in 1816 to 75.9 by 1871. Indeed such was the extent of population growth in the early nineteenth century that a number of states, including Baden, Bavaria and Württemberg, imposed legal restrictions on marriage, while Doctor Weinhold from Halle advocated infibulation as a means of restricting procreation. The legislation in Bavaria was not repealed until 1862–8, although its precise impact in terms of contemporary trends in illegitimate fertility is difficult to substantiate. A more immediate reaction to the problems created by high rates of population growth was the increase in emigration (Table 4.3). In the first wave of mass migration between 1845 and 1858, approximately 1.3 million individuals left Germany to seek a better life overseas and between 1864 and 1873 a further million followed a similar path. Particularly during the 1830s and 1840s, overseas migration was a direct result of relative overpopulation, as measured in terms of employment opportunities, as well as rising prices and harvest failure.

III   Regional variations in development

The inherent unevenness of German economic development has been highlighted by recent research. By the late eighteenth century iron and steel production was concentrated on both sides of the Rhine, in the Siegerland and Hesse, to the west in the Eiffel, in Silesia, as well as in a few other regional centres. Industrial production was particularly concentrated in

Table 4.3   German overseas emigration, 1816–1934

Period	Emigrants (000s)	Immigrants to USA (000s)	%	Annual average emigration rate[a]
1816–19	25.0			2.7
1820–24	9.8	1.9	19.4	1.0
1825–29	12.7	3.8	29.9	1.2
1830–34	51.1	39.3	76.9	2.2
1835–39	94.0	85.5	91.0	2.6
1840–44	110.6	100.5	90.9	2.4
1845–49	308.2	284.9	92.4	4.5
1850–54	728.3	654.3	89.8	9.0
1855–59	372.0	321.8	86.5	4.3
1860–64	225.9	204.1	90.4	2.5
1865–69	542.7	519.6	95.7	3.6
1870–74	484.6	450.5	93.0	2.3
1875–79	143.3	120.0	83.7	0.7
1880–84	864.3	797.9	92.3	3.8
1885–89	498.2	452.6	90.9	2.1
1890–94	462.2	428.8	92.8	1.8
1895–99	142.4	120.2	84.4	0.5
1900–04	140.8	128.6	91.3	0.5
1905–09	135.7	123.5	91.0	0.4
1910–14	104.3	84.1	80.6	0.3
1915–19	4.1	1.0	24.4	0.0
1920–24	242.3	150.4	62.1	0.8
1925–29	295.3	230.1	77.8	0.9
1930–34	88.1	62.1	70.6	0.3

Note: [a]Based on the population of the areas affected by emigration.
Source: W. Köllmann and P. Marschalck, German Emigration to the United States. Perspectives in American History, vol. 7 (1974), p. 518; F. Burgdörfer, 'Die Wanderungen über die deutschen Reichsgrenzen im letzten Jahrhundert', Allgemeines Statistisches Archiv, 20 (1930), p. 189 et seq.; W. Mönckmeier, Die deutsche überseeische Auswanderung (1912), p. 14.

Berlin, Saxony, Silesia and the Ruhr. The Grand Duchy of Berg was one of the most advanced areas on the continent and individual towns, such as Krefeld, had become important manufacturing and trading centres well before the end of the eighteenth century. On the other hand, the increasing emphasis on export-orientated grain monoculture in the eastern provinces of Prussia hindered economic diversification as the profitability of rye exports reinforced the region's relative dependency on primary sector production. At the same time there was a greater distribution of craftsmen (*Handwerker*) in the south than in the north, which, in turn, recorded a better level of provision than the east. Particularly in the case of Prussia there is clear evidence of significant regional divergence by the early nineteenth century between the eastern and western provinces, in terms of estimated per capita income, selective income proxies, and relative levels of urbanization.

The extent to which economic development in the period between 1815 and 1871 modified or aggravated the degree of pre-industrial regional economic divergence is still a subject of considerable debate and the evidence is not unambiguous. By and large, however, this period witnessed an accentuation of regional divergence. The increasingly regional concentration of industrial production in west, southwest, northwest and central Germany was accompanied by a greater emphasis on agricultural employment in other areas. This was the case in the eastern provinces of Prussia, as well as in the southern states of Baden, Bavaria and Württemberg, which became more agricultural relative to the national average. Furthermore, even within the primary sector, there is evidence of increasing regional divergence during this period – a trend that was reinforced by the selective impact of peasant emancipation legislation and reform 'from above'. The eastern provinces of Prussia (East and West Prussia, as well as Pomerania), for example, were increasingly characterized by extensive cereal production, primarily for export, and the growing emphasis on grain monoculture was accompanied by a continuing reliance on traditional cultivation methods. By contrast, there was a perceptible shift towards intensive cultivation in the western regions of Germany, with an emphasis on commercial crops and the dairy–livestock sector. In those regions of Germany where domestic textile production, particularly linen manufacture, had developed in response to growing export opportunities, flax cultivation had become widespread, whereas other agricultural areas, such as the Magdeburger Börde, had concentrated on sugar beet production as a result of official tax incentives. Regional specialization was also increasingly evident in relation to viticulture and livestock–dairy farming, although it would be false to overstate the extent of such trends during this period. Moreover, because of the ability of established landed élites to resist institutional change, agrarian reforms affected more backward regions with a noticeable time lag or not at all, thereby reinforcing existing regional differentials.

Urbanization also affected the trend towards increased regional divergence: it spread out from Saxony and Berlin at the start of the nineteenth century to the industrializing areas of the Rhineland, Westphalia and Silesia by the 1850s. Although there was only a marginal increase in the level of urbanization in Prussia between 1816 and 1871 (from 27.9 to 32.5 per cent of total population), the average size of cities in the west was already noticeably greater than in the east, and whereas urbanization levels rose slightly in the western provinces before 1840, they actually fell in the East. Moreover, there was a clear difference in the components of urban growth:

in the west urban centres developed through a combination of in-migration and natural increase; eastern towns remained almost solely dependent on in-migration. In general, both age at marriage and the proportion remaining single were higher in urban areas, but fertility was often lower than in rural areas. However, during the final period of increasing urban mortality levels during the 1860s and 1870s, it was primarily cities in eastern Germany, such as Elbing, Frankfurt (Oder), Stralsund and Görlitz, that registered a disproportionate rise in both male and female mortality. By contrast, during the 1850s some of the developing industrial cities in the Ruhr, such as Mönchen-Gladbach, had a higher migration intensity (in terms of in-, and out-migration per 1,000 inhabitants) as Berlin, and the population of Essen expanded almost exponentially from just over 4,000 in 1811 to over 180,000 by the end of the century as a result of the development of the Krupp works in the town. It is instructive to note, however, that even in 1871 almost 83 per cent of the population of the German Confederation still lived in communities with less than 10,000 inhabitants.

Further evidence of trends in regional differentials can be obtained from demographic data. Within Prussia, for example, the crude death rate throughout this period was consistently higher in the eastern provinces than in the west. Infant deaths remained a major component of total mortality throughout this period: the infant mortality rate rose perceptibly during the central decades of the nineteenth century and remained disproportionately high in the southern states of Bavaria and Württemberg, as well as in the eastern provinces of Prussia. The high variance in the infant mortality rate became even more accentuated towards the end of the nineteenth century and was still visible, although to a lesser extent, in the age group 1–15. A significant rise in the number of illegitimate births in the south, particularly in Bavaria (Table 4.4), reinforced this trend, given the higher mortality

Table 4.4   Illegitimate births in Bavaria (per 100 live births), 1835–60 to 1872

Period	Illegitimacy rate
1835–60	21.1
1860–68	22.2
1868–69	17.9
1869–70	16.4
1871	15.2
1872	14.4

Source: Die Bewegung der Bevölkerung des Königreichs Bayern im Jahre 1877, *Zeitschrift des kgl. Bayerischen Statistischen Bureaus*, Jahrgang 11 (Munich, 1879), p. 259.

rates of illegitimate offspring. Regional differences, however, were not so prominent in relation to adult death rates as life table evidence confirms. At a disease-specific level, tuberculosis mortality also displayed a pronounced east–west gradient, reflecting, in all probability, differential nutritional levels and labour intensity. Equally in terms of fertility-related indices, regional differentials remained clearly visible in the nineteenth century, both in terms of the birth rate and the practice of family limitation.

IV   The role of the state

It is generally accepted that the state was heavily involved in the industrialization process in Germany, whether in responding to the problems generated by relative backwardness and market imperfections, or in clearing away many of the obstacles hindering economic development. Indeed it is often argued that the state played a critical role in providing the preconditions for successful industrialization, specifically through the abolition of the feudal agrarian regime, the dismantling of guild controls and the introduction of more liberal trade policies, as well as through the provision of an appropriate legal framework for capitalist production. Even if political reform was strenuously avoided, the state effectively promoted economic development through financial and administrative reforms. Taxation policy, for example, showed a clear bias in favour of industrial interests and capital formation and direct government support was important in the creation of social overhead capital, particularly in the case of railway construction. The state, however, also played a more selective interventionist role by providing direct subsidies to individual sectors, such as sugar beet production, steam-engine construction or specific branches of the textile industry. In Upper Silesia, for example, the retention of the *Direktionsprinzip* until 1864 contributed to the efficiency of the mining and metallurgical industries, where expansion to a large degree was state-induced. Indeed the state was often directly involved in production. In Prussia, the *Seehandlung* (Overseas Trading Corporation), originally created as a state salt monopoly in 1772, had become a major economic force by the early 1820s, running its own enterprises (such as flour and paper mills, chemical works, and river steamers) and providing capital investment to the private sector. Finally, state support for education, it has been argued, was probably the most important contribution to industrial development, with tangible benefits in terms of technology transfer, technical training and the inculcation of appropriate attitudes within the German working class as a whole. Even during the 1860s and early 1870s, when more liberal policies tended to prevail, state intervention in the economy remained durably persistent.

Many of the leading entrepreneurs of the early nineteenth century, such as Harkort and Mevissen, had advocated government action to correct the abuses of industrialization, and the idea of state intervention, whether in the form of subsidies, monopoly grants, tariff concessions or special treatment of key industries, was always congenial.

More recently, however, the view that German industrialization was ultimately achieved with the support of state power has been challenged. It has been argued that state priorities in terms of economic policy were often inappropriate. The exercise of state power, by increased regulation, might have contributed to economic efficiency at the margin, but the lifting of traditional restrictions on trade was not a prerequisite for industrial expansion. Prussia had achieved this objective as early as 1807–11, but the absence of trade liberalization in Saxony until 1861 did not adversely affect its position as one of the most dynamic areas of economic growth during this period. The trade policy (*Gewerbepolitik*) of some of the south German states, such as Baden and Bavaria, attempted to maintain small-scale handicraft production based on a traditional concessionary system, although such policies militated against large-scale industrialization. In the case of Württemberg such a policy contributed to a general opposition to factories in the period before 1848 and in Schleswig-Holstein trade policy was concerned primarily with the maintenance of existing privileges, rather than the promotion of economic development. The efficiency of the administrative apparatus in coordinating the separate economic functions of the state has also been questioned, as well as the net contribution of government intervention in individual sectors. Even in relation to the official commitment to improved educational provision, it has been argued that the needs of industry were often neglected; the curriculum of the elementary schools (*Volksschulen*) was inadequate; trade schools remained fee-paying; and secondary education, particularly in Prussia, was characterized by a continuing conflict between classicism and modernism and limited social mobility. It is not surprising, therefore, that certain historians view the role of the state in promoting industrialization as having been circumscribed, with economic growth during this period primarily a function of growing intra-German and international competition, indigenous resource endowment, the expansion of foreign trade and the interplay of market forces.

V   Redefining the state

It is commonly agreed that the state, building on cameralist and mercantilist principles, showed a high level of interest in economic affairs between the late eighteenth century and 1871. However, the persistence of a national consensus in German economic history and the tendency to view Prussia as the paradigm of the modern German state has prevented a rigorous exploration of its role. By 1815 the complex territorial configuration of the Holy Roman Empire of the German nation had been substantially transformed, but there were still 39 federal states, ranging from Prussia with over eight million inhabitants, to minor principalities, such as Liechtenstein (7,000 inhabitants), and the free cities of Bremen, Frankfurt am Main, Hamburg and Lübeck (Table 4.5). With few exceptions, there was general support within Germany for the federal idea, which remained dominant both in the constitution of 1848–9, at the foundation of the Norddeutsche Bund in 1867, and in the Bismarckian constitution of 1871. Unfortunately there are very few modern studies of the economic history of individual German states for the period between 1815 and 1871, and even fewer historians have attempted to examine aspects of economic policy in a comparative context. In order to explore further the role of the state in German economic development during this period, three points need to be emphasized.

First, the continuing fragmentation of political power directly affected the role of the state. Many of the states that emerged from the Napoleonic period were both 'modern', in that a central authority exerted control throughout the entire kingdom, and economically important. Bavaria, for example, with a total population of 4.5 million by 1849 was the third largest state in the German Confederation after Austria and Prussia. Even in 1816 five German states, in addition to Prussia, already had a total population in excess of one million (Baden 1.3; Bavaria 3.5; Hanover 1.3; Saxony 1.7; Württemberg 1.4). Given that approximately 60 per cent of

Table 4.5   The German federal states in 1816

State	Population	Area (in km²)	Population (per km²)	%
A Empire and Kingdoms				
1 Austria[1]	9,482,227	195,228.44	48.6	31.15
2 Prussia[2]	8,042,562	185,460.25	43.4	29.59
3 Bavaria[3]	3,560,000	76,395.75	46.4	12.19
4 Hanover[4]	1,328,351	38,568.43	34.4	6.15
5 Württemberg	1,410,327	19,506.66	72.3	3.11
6 Saxony	1,192,789	14,958.15	79.7	2.39
B Grand duchies and duchies				
7 Baden	1,005,899	15,307.23	65.7	2.44
8 Mecklenburg-Schwerin	308,166	13,260.65	23.2	2.12
9 Holstein-Lauenburg[5]	360,000	9,580.44	37.6	1.53

10 Hesse-Kassel[4]	567,868	9,567.78	59.4	1.53
11 Hesse-Darmstadt	587,995	8,414.82	69.9	1.34
12 Oldenburg	221,399	6,339.06	34.9	1.01
13 Nassau[4]	301,907	4,765.44	63.4	0.76
14 Braunschweig	225,273	3,729.21	60.4	0.60
15 Saxe-Weimar[6]	193,869	3,640.57	53.3	0.58
16 Mecklenburg-Strelitz	71,764	2,724.92	26.3	0.43
17 Luxemburg[7]	154,000	2,587.82	59.5	0.41
18 Saxe-Meiningen[6]	115,000	3,549.28	45.1	0.41
19 Saxe-Gotha[6,8]		1,422.75		
20 Saxe-Coburg[9]	111,989	586.39	55.7	0.32
21 Saxe-Altenburg[6]	95,855	1,330.80	72.0	0.21
22 Anhalt-Dessau[10]	52,947	894.17	59.2	0.14
23 Anhalt-Bernburg[10]	37,046	827.55	44.8	0.13
24 Anhalt-Köthen[10]	32,454	662.92	49.0	0.11
C Principalities				
25 Waldeck-Pyrmont	52,557	1,202.51	43.7	0.19
26 Lippe-Detmold	78,900	1,129.83	69.8	0.18
27 Hohenzollern -Hechingen[11]	50,060	1,148.00	43.6	0.18
28 -Sigmaringen[11]				
29 Schwarzburg -Rudolstadt[6]	53,937	958.04	56.3	0.15
30 -Sondershausen[6]	45,125	852.33	52.9	0.14
31 Reuss Junior Line[6]	69,333	834.16	83.1	0.13
32 Schaumburg-Lippe	24,000	443.23	54.2	0.07
33 Reuss Senior Line[6]	30,293	345.78	87.6	0.06
34 Hessen-Homburg[4]	23,000	262.09	87.8	0.04
35 Liechstenstein[7]	7,000	159.67	43.8	0.03
D Free Cities				
36 Lübeck	36,000	364.50	100.4	0.06
37 Hamburg	146,109	351.83	415.3	0.06
38 Bremen	50,139	263.19	190.5	0.04
39 Frankfurt am Main	47,850	100.76	474.9	0.02
Total	30,174,590	626,725.40	48.1	100.0

[1] Only those areas belonging to the Deutsche Bund.

[2] Excluding the provinces of West and East Prussia, and Posen, which did not belong to the Deutsche Bund.

[3] Including the Pfalz which ceased to belong to Bavaria after 1920–45.

[4] Annexed by Prussia in 1866.

[5] Acquired by Prussia in 1866.

[6] Merged with Thuringia in 1920.

[7] Independent since 1866 and the dissolution of the Deutsche Bund.

[8] Acquired by Coburg in 1826 following the inheritance apportionment contract of Hildburghausen.

[9] Joined with Bavaria in 1920.

[10] After the demise of the Köthen line (1847) and the Bernburg line (1863), the dukedoms were united with Anhalt.

[11] Joined to Prussia in 1849.

Source: Kiesewetter, H., *Industrielle Revolution in Deutschland 1815–1914* (Frankfurt am Main, 1989) pp. 308–9.

Germany's population experienced a change in ruler during the Napoleonic period, it is not surprising that many of the states, such as Hesse-Darmstadt and Hanover, pursued a 'narrow particularism' in the period after 1815. Bavaria and Württemberg, for example, constantly emphasized their uniqueness and school books were explicitly redesigned to create a separate sense of 'national' identity. Although a number of banks, such as the Badische Bank in Mannheim or the Sächsische Bank in Dresden, were founded with outside capital participation, most state banks during the first half of the nineteenth century had a conservative policy in terms of capital provision and supply. They had a particular responsibility to promote local infrastructural improvements or to cater for 'national' needs, as in the case of Saxony's Landrentenbank which was the first state credit agency founded in Germany in 1832. Although capital supply frequently extended over state boundaries, the majority of firms operated within a narrowly defined local institutional framework. This was the case in Saxony and the Rhineland-Palatinate, where industrial enterprises were almost entirely supported by indigenous capital. Indeed, even in terms of money supply, policy differences continued to exist. Most states permitted the use of a wide variety of currencies (including foreign banknotes), but Württemberg, for example, only issued silver coins during this period.

Individual states generally fought for their own narrow interests and often pursued different approaches to specific issues, such as the development of the railway network, the introduction of freedom of trade, tariff policy or the maintenance of handicraft-based production. Tax policy is an instructive example, in this context, as it remained the responsibility of the federal states throughout the nineteenth century and beyond. Tax reforms were widely implemented in the post-Napoleonic period, but individual states frequently adopted a different approach which reflected local needs and divergent traditions. Baden, as a result of its substantial territorial expansion by 1815, was faced by a multiplicity of tax regimes and opted for a relatively simple tax system based on land values that could be applied without additional administrative costs. On the other hand, Württemberg consolidated its existing land tax based on net yield, and Bavaria retained an assessment system based on gross production until 1855. Indirect taxes continued to provide a significant proportion of government revenue in most states, but the actual balance between direct and indirect taxation varied considerably. Prussia failed to develop a uniform tax system: urban communities remained subject to indirect taxation, whereas direct taxes were levied in rural areas.

At the same time, there were noticeable differences in the overall distribution of the tax burden. In the case of Baden the more flexible system of tax liability assessment introduced in 1848, together with the retention of an unmodified trade or occupation tax (*Gewerbesteuer*) between 1815 and 1854, encouraged increased capital investment in the secondary sector throughout the first half of the nineteenth century. Württemberg's system of taxation also promoted economic growth by providing explicit benefits for rural manufacturing, housing construction and recipients of high incomes, as well as encouraging the replacement of labour by machinery. As a result, the specific configuration of individual tax regimes in the federal states affected a range of economic variables in a differentiated manner, including the relative balance between consumption and investment, capital accumulation, technological change, and the spatial location of manufacturing production.

In a number of policy areas, including the gradual introduction of protective employment legislation or the establishment of local craftsmen's associations, federal states often followed a common strategy. For example, there were clear similarities in the legislation adopted by Prussia in 1836 and by Bavaria in 1842 relating to the establishment of local associations of craftsmen and merchants. This reflected not only the impact of general processes of change and increasing economic integration, but also an element of competitive rivalry between the individual states and a recognition of the need to emulate policy initiatives developed in other parts of Germany. But in most other areas of policy-making, as the example of taxation policy indicates, the federal states maintained a particularist approach. In general, the overall timing, direction and extent of government intervention varied significantly and this, in turn, affected the process of economic development and industrialization in the separate federal states.

Second, the existence of numerous federal states with well-defined provincial, administrative structures facilitated both the emergence of interest groups and their articulation of economic demands. In large nation states, as Olson has demonstrated, substantial resources are frequently required to influence government policy, whereas interest groups operating within the federal state framework of nineteenth-century Germany would have had lower operational costs and greater organizational powers for collective action. On the one hand, the initiative to develop corporate industrial structures had frequently been taken by the state, whether in Prussia or Bavaria (see above), although the establishment of extended merchant corporations in the eastern ports of Danzig, Memel, Stettin and Tilsit in the 1820s followed the Danish model based on the *Kammerkollegium* (Revenue Board) which had been adopted in Altona in

1738. Corporate organizations played an increasingly active role at the federal level in registering specific demands and in exercising lobbyist functions, whether over the ruinous effect of increased taxes on small traders in Buxtehude, or the promotion of the south German cotton industry. On the other hand, the continued fragmentation of state power after 1815 allowed an effective prioritization of local issues in the federal states. In many cases a narrow policy of self-interest characterized the attitudes of both town and country members of state parliaments, but the federal structure of Germany after 1815 allowed a more effective articulation of lobbyist interests than might otherwise have been the case within the framework of a larger nation state. It also contributed, as was the case in Baden, to a provincial atmosphere that reinforced the impression of a closer proximity between the rulers and the ruled.

As a result, economic policy at the level of the federal state often reflected local needs. In Saxony, for example, the political influence of business and industry increased perceptibly after 1830 and economic development was promoted by the state through a range of administrative and financial reforms. Industrialists and businessmen were particularly active in advocating tariff protection, specifically for the textile industry, and the state helped to reshape the institutions of an industrializing society by responding effectively to their demands. The state provided considerable support for the development of the railway network and other infrastructural improvements: it subsidized the expansion of the machine-construction industry, and paid particular attention to the provision of educational and training facilities. From a modern perspective it is clear that economic policy in Saxony during this period suffered from considerable weaknesses: policy initiatives were often selective and inconsistent, and the state authorities failed to develop a long-term concept for financing industrial enterprises. Nevertheless, the localized framework of economic policy-making, within a political context that allowed entrepreneurs and industrialists considerable influence, enabled the state to adopt a more supportive approach to contemporary development issues.

On the other hand, the fragmentation of political power within a federal structure and the existence within individual states of a strong tradition of provincial representation also allowed traditional élites in relatively backward regions to maintain their position by blocking necessary reforms and by maintaining unresponsive economic institutions. This was particularly the case in relation to the agrarian reforms of the early nineteenth century. Considerable emphasis used to be given to the capacity-widening effects of these structural reforms 'from above', on the basis that they facilitated more efficient arable cultivation as well as the partition and enclosure of common lands. In contrast to eighteenth-century reforms, they made possible, in theory, the development of a free rural population, owning landed property. However, longer-term processes of structural change were evident in the German countryside well before the end of the eighteenth century and the exact nature of agrarian reform legislation differed in many respects in individual German states. In most cases peasant emancipation was only achieved as a result of extensive compromises with the local aristocracy and estate-holders, whose preferential treatment directly affected the level of compensation payments and the extent of land redistribution. Traditionally a clear distinction existed between western areas of Germany, characterized by peasant cultivation and hereditary tenure (*Grundherrschaft*) and the eastern territories dominated by extensive seigneurial estates with a dependent and largely servile peasantry (*Gutsherrschaft*). To a large extent, the specific impact of the reform legislation reflected this distinction, as well as the relative power of the provincial nobility and regional political élites. Within Prussia reform legislation reinforced the role of the Junker estate owners and large-scale peasant cultivators in the east, with their increasing dependency on an export-orientated grain monoculture, whereas land compensation in many western territories benefited a wider spectrum of peasants and further encouraged agricultural diversification. Whereas serfdom was finally abolished in Mecklenburg in 1820, the continued influence of the landed aristocracy in Baden meant that feudal rights were only terminated when revolution was imminent in 1848. Agrarian reforms, therefore, only affected more backward regions, such as eastern and southern Germany, with a noticeable time-lag, or not at all. The ability of traditional élites to resist structural change, in such cases, only served to reinforce existing regional differentials.

Third, in assessing the nature and impact of economic policy during the first half of the nineteenth century it is always important to establish how state power was constituted. Particularly at the federal level, state economic policy was often determined by the bureaucracy (for a fuller discussion, see Chapter 3, above). The expansion of the bureaucratic apparatus was a precondition for the growth of state power and most German states witnessed a significant increase in administrative personnel in the period under consideration. In Prussia, for example, the number of civil servants (including both central and local officials) rose annually by 1.4 per cent between 1846 and 1880, in contrast to an annual rise of 0.8 per cent in total population. Primarily because of the limited electoral franchise throughout Germany, bureaucrats increasingly determined state policy. In Baden, for example, a group of officials sharing a common educational and social background assumed national leadership; in Prussia civil servants felt superior to the emerging entrepreneurial class; and in Bavaria there were growing complaints against what was perceived in some quarters as civil service absolutism. Moreover, the development of an extensive state administrative apparatus preceded the creation of modern representative bodies which, in turn, tended to be dominated by civil servants. They constituted approximately 50 per cent of the federal parliament (*Landtag*) in Baden in the early nineteenth century and almost 64 per cent of the deputies in the North German parliament in 1867.

In this context, the state bureaucracy was uniquely placed to influence economic policy. In certain cases its contribution was significant. In Saxony, for example, liberal-minded bureaucrats helped to reshape the institutions of an industrializing society; civil servants in Baden during the 1830s were committed to liberal objectives, such as free trade, transport improvements and wider educational facilities; and state officials in Prussia also pursued selective policies conducive to industrial development. On the other hand, the continuing recruitment of higher civil servants in northern Germany from the landed aristocracy undoubtedly encouraged a more conservative approach to contemporary issues, just as the fusing of the old social order with the new service hierarchy in the form of the Prussian *Landrat* (or rural administrative officer) in the eastern provinces had a negative impact on government policy-making.

VI   The role of the banks

It is traditionally accepted that Germany, as a result of its relative backwardness, depended on banks far more than other Western economies (such as Britain) for both investible funds and entrepreneurial initiative. In the first half of the nineteenth century the development of an appropriate banking infrastructure was constrained by insufficient demand and an absence of commercial concentration. Although there were a number of prominent private banking houses, such as the Rothschilds and Bethmanns in Frankfurt am Main, and Bleichröder and Mendelsohn in Berlin, they were primarily concerned with government loans and state bonds. In Württemberg, for example, the main function of the Hofbank (founded in 1817) was to meet the capital requirements of the crown and private banking firms, such as the Gebrüder Benedict and Stahl und Federer, restricted their activities to mortgage lending or exchange transactions. There were very few stock exchanges: in Frankfurt am Main, as elsewhere, activities were confined to dealing in government securities and the stock exchange in Berlin was not geared to large-scale industrial transactions.

Furthermore, the activity of savings banks (except in Bremen, Hamburg and Saxony) remained restricted. Initial attempts to develop a network of savings banks (*Sparkassen*) were initiated in Bavaria (1816) and Württemberg (1822), primarily as a means of enabling domestic servants and day labourers to achieve a limited degree of economic independence. However, by the mid-1830s there were only 281 savings banks throughout Germany and it was only after Prussian legislation in 1838 that their number increased significantly. It was not until the foundation of the first credit banks, such as the Schaafhausen Bankverein (1848) and the Diskonto-Gesellschaft (1851) that an effective basis was laid for the direct promotion of industrial investment and development.

In complete contrast with this situation, historians have argued that the *Kreditbanken* (or universal banks), particularly from the 1850s onwards, helped to finance risky investments, facilitated mergers and the formation of cartels, and contributed to the stabilization of the business cycle. By the mid-1860s there is evidence of increased capital mobility: Berlin banks provided loans to Baden and 'national' bank consortia were formed in individual states to negotiate government loans. The Bank für Handel und Industrie in Darmstadt (founded in 1853), in this context, served as a proto-type: it was created as a joint-stock enterprise, provided current account facilities to several industrial firms and was involved from the outset in small-scale industrial promotion. Developments in the banking infrastructure, therefore, helped to remove traditional barriers that had restricted the flow of capital to German manufacturers. Joint-stock banks, in particular, played a major role in supporting the expansion of heavy industry and railway construction at a time when capital investment in the German textile industry also rose significantly.

However, capital supply does not appear to have been a major problem in the first half of the nineteenth century: capital costs were generally low; interest rates continued to fall, partly as a result of the liquidation of state debts; and entrepreneurs were able to employ a variety of strategies to limit short-term capital requirements. Even if capital markets remained imperfect and long-term credit was seldom available, the cost of technical innovation, particularly in agriculture, was not high during this period. Although the capital market, particularly in Prussia, had a pronounced regional character, the number of banks in Cologne with links to industrial enterprises was already considerable by 1830. This was specifically the case in relation to Rhenish textile firms, although extensive connections with enterprises operating in the Ruhr only became evident after 1850. Even before the end of the eighteenth century, Cologne merchants had financed the development of the mining industry in the Siegerland, and prior to the crisis of 1848 the Schaaffhausen Bank had acted as the mainstay of at least 170 factory enterprises with approximately 40,000 workers. Indeed, even in relation to the later nineteenth century there are continuing doubts concerning the precise role of the *Kreditbanken* in terms of their sectoral concentration on heavy industry and the specific nature of bank–industry relations. Although the Cologne banks played an important role in the formation of joint-stock companies in the Ruhr's iron and steel industry from the early 1850s onwards, their range of activity had a limited geographical radius and new banking initiatives were inevitably pro-cyclical. The marked involvement of the *Kreditbanken* in heavy industry was counterbalanced by a more limited, or even minimal, role in the development of the chemical, machine construction and electrical engineering industries. Nor is it possible to construct a uniform model of bank–industry relations: existing micro-level studies of specific enterprises confirm the continued predominance of self-financing and the important role of the credit banks in promoting industrial concentration in the late nineteenth century effectively weakened the influence of any one bank on the business activity of individual industrial enterprises. To this extent, even in the late nineteenth century, the banking system may well have played a 'permissive' rather than a 'causative' role in German industrial development and it is important not to overestimate the role of the banks in the first phase of German industrialization.

VII The *Zollverein*

As an example of enlightened state policy, the foundation of the *Zollverein* in 1834 is frequently accorded a major role in German economic development. Friedrich List even argued that the *Zollverein* and the railway system were 'Siamese twins', contributing to Germany's emergence as the focal point for intra-European trade. In the late eighteenth century there were approximately 1,800 customs frontiers in Germany and it was only between 1807 and 1812 that the three southern states of Bavaria, Württemberg and Baden finally eliminated their internal customs dues. According to Henderson, Germany's industrial development was 'undoubtedly ... stimulated' by the creation of the *Zollverein*, as the persistence of numerous customs barriers had only served to cripple trade and encourage smuggling. On this basis, the development of the customs union demolished internal trade barriers; intensified inner-German economic links; contributed to the formation of a 'national' market and a unified commercial law; provided supportive tariff protection for infant industries (particularly following the tariff of 1844); facilitated a major improvement in internal communications as a function of railway construction; and fostered increased optimism throughout the whole of Germany. The creation of the *Zollverein*, therefore, represented a significant step forward. It consolidated the achievements of the Prussian customs law of May 1818, stimulated Germany's industrial revolution, and provided substantial benefits for participating states, such as Baden, Bavaria and Saxony.

More recently, however, the role of the *Zollverein* as a key factor in German development has been subject to reappraisal. As Dumke has shown, both the immediate and longer-term welfare gains of the *Zollverein* were relatively small. Although there was an improvement in the terms of trade for the south German states through their membership of the customs union, it only accounted for a 1.5 per cent increase in national income. In the case of the three Hesse states (Kurhessen, Hesse-Darmstadt, and Nassau), *Zollverein* membership did generate some significant benefits, particularly in terms of increased competition, but it failed to promote rapid industrialization and could not prevent the serious socio-economic dislocations of the 1840s. As far as most other states are concerned, poor data quality for assessing contemporary trade flows continues to preclude a more rigorous analysis of this issue, although the economic impact of membership was almost certainly highly differentiated, depending on the overall structure of 'national' economies, as well as the extent and sectoral configuration of industrial production. Moreover, the motives behind the establishment of the *Zollverein* were primarily fiscal and not economic, as individual states sought simultaneously to maximize revenue gains from a more efficient customs system and to minimize the possibility of budgetary control by nascent parliamentary institutions. Most German states in the early nineteenth century were too small to establish an independent border tax system as an efficient source of government revenue, but this situation was radically transformed through the creation of the customs union. Bavaria's customs receipts, for example, virtually doubled in 1834 as a result of its membership of the customs union. At the same time, the creation of the *Zollverein* post-dated significant developments in the German economy (see above): the long-term growth in German trade can be traced back to the 1820s and inner-German trade links were already well established before 1834. Macroeconomic factors, therefore, including rising British demand for German primary produce and increased aggregate demand within Germany itself as a result of high rates of population growth, may have played a more critical role than the *Zollverein* in stimulating industrial development in the first half of the nineteenth century. Indeed, the economic unification of Germany had still not been achieved by 1871: it was not until 1881 and 1888 respectively that the Empire's two premier ports, the city states of Hamburg and Bremen, finally became members of the customs union.

VIII   Railway development

Traditionally, the development of a railway network has been seen as a factor that critically shaped German industrialization. In particular, from the 1840s to the late 1860s the increased demand generated by railway construction had a very positive effect (via backward linkages) on heavy industry, specifically in relation to iron and steel production and coal-mining, constituting what is often known as a leading sector complex in the German economy. Indeed, proponents of such a view have been able to mobilize a substantial amount of evidence. During this period railway construction accounted for approximately one-third of net investment and therefore directly affected the development of the business cycle; it generated an unprecedented increase in demand from heavy industry; and encouraged significant progress in terms of import substitution. For example, Germany was virtually self-sufficient as far as locomotive construction was concerned by the late 1840s. The expansion of the railway network undoubtedly contributed to a substantial reduction in transport costs; it facilitated a greater degree of market integration and industrial concentration within Germany; improved the speed and regularity of communications; extended the area of supply for perishable goods; and narrowed the gap between producers and consumers. Indeed, in line with the Gerschenkronian paradigm, railway development was also directly assisted by the state. By guaranteeing a minimum rate of return on private investment in individual railway lines, the federal states were able to boost construction and simultaneously encourage the development of the capital market. Indeed, in Bavaria the first railway line was built with state funds in 1836 and the Baden authorities right from the start of railway development in 1838 were committed to the construction of a 'national' network. Direct state investment in such cases therefore represented an enforced transfer of resources via taxation in a manner that would have promoted economic growth.

Certainly within the period 1852 to 1874 railway construction was probably the most important sector in the German economy, particularly in terms of relative growth rates (estimated at 13.6 per cent per annum), inter-sectoral linkages, and its contribution to unbalanced growth. However, even in this case recent research has contributed to a process of reappraisal.

Within the provinces of Prussia price data for rye reveal an extensive degree of market integration by the early 1820s, and little evidence of any further improvements before 1865. From a spatial perspective, the long-term process of concentration of economic activity preceded the onset of railway construction, and urban growth was not dependent on railway development. At best, it would appear to be the case that the most important pre-railway cities only obtained short-term gains from the development of the railway network, although railways played an important role in serving cities, such as Chemnitz, which were not directly located on existing waterways. Specific regions clearly benefited from railway development which encouraged, for example, the mining and use of raw materials in the Westerwald that were previously discounted as commercial propositions because of high transport costs. On the other hand, the surge in coal production in the Saarland from the early 1850s was not a result of railway development, given existing canal links with the Rhine and Main. Indeed, it should not be forgotten that during the period 1816 to 1870 a further 1,400 kilometres of canals were added to the German network. State intervention could also be counter-productive, as in the case of Baden where government officials opted for a non-standard gauge which meant that the track had to be rebuilt after a number of years. Furthermore, even by the turn of the nineteenth century the estimated social savings generated by the railway system constituted no more than 5 per cent of German GNP, although this was a slightly greater contribution than was the case in some other European states.

IX   Education and human capital

Finally, it is often stated that state support for improved educational training was a key factor in the long-term development of the German economy. The nineteenth century witnessed an increased level of state support for educational provision in all German states, which reflected not only common political objectives, but also a systematization process that was hierarchically determined. Many states showed an early commitment to the introduction of compulsory primary education, as was the case in Prussia with the decree of 1763–5, or saw improved educational provision as a means of creating a 'national' identity following the territorial changes of the Napoleonic period. In Prussia approximately 50 per cent of all children between the ages of 5 and 14 were attending elementary schools (*Volksschulen*) by the end of the eighteenth century, and by 1816 attendance rates had risen to 60 per cent. Similarly, there was general recognition of the need to widen the base of secondary education beyond the established structures of the grammar school (*Gymnasium*), in order to satisfy the more practical needs of the emergent commercial and industrial classes. This resulted in the creation of more modern secondary schools with a greater emphasis on science and languages (*Realschulen, Bürgerschulen*), as well as more specialized town schools. Vocational education was also expanded considerably during this period, which saw the development of continuation schools for various trades and businesses, the establishment of agricultural high schools (as at Hohenheim, 1818), and weaving schools in Elberfeld in 1844. In particular the promotion of technical education and training has been singled out as indicative of the positive contribution of the German state to economic development. Technical education was clearly meant for application: it was symptomatic of a close connection between education and business, and may well have contributed to technological innovation (as has been argued in the case of Baden). In 1821 a technical school was created in Berlin. By 1850 Prussia had approximately 20 provincial trade schools (*Gewerbeschulen*) primarily serving local needs, and the 1850s and 1860s, in particular, witnessed a general expansion of technical training opportunities throughout Germany. Finally, there was a disproportional expansion of higher education, at least in terms of government funding, which represented a considerable subsidy for upper income families. During the early nineteenth century university enrolment increased substantially, although student numbers slumped during the 1830s and did not rise again until after 1870. At the same time, this period saw the creation of a number of specialized institutions – the forerunners of the technical high schools – which were primarily concerned with the application of science for practical and technological purposes. To this extent many German states, such as Prussia, had succeeded by the 1860s in creating a 'modern' education system which functioned relatively effectively even in the rapidly expanding urban communities of the Rhineland and the Ruhr.

However, although the importance of education was widely recognized throughout Germany during this period, noticeable differences persisted in terms of state educational policy and training provision. On the one hand, the overall level of state funding for schools and universities was already relatively high by the early 1860s: in Bavaria and Prussia it accounted for 18 per cent of total expenditure. On the other hand, per capita expenditure on higher education, science and technology varied considerably, with Baden, Württemberg and Bavaria achieving a greater level of provision than Saxony and Prussia throughout the 1850s and 1860s. Bavaria, in particular, appears to have underperformed in most aspects of primary education. The reform movement of the early nineteenth century was gradually emasculated by a conservative reaction. Although a comparatively favourable pupil–teacher ratio of 1:64 was recorded by 1860–1, Bavaria had the poorest school attendance rate of all German states. Indeed, it was only in the early 1870s that it finally passed the 80 per cent figure that Prussia had already achieved in the 1830s. It may well be the case that educational reforms in the period before 1871 followed a relatively similar pattern in most German states, reflecting a general process of institutional convergence, but the timing of legislation, as well as the extent of improved educational provision, remained very uneven. This was the case in relation to both teacher-training and technical education. Even in terms of school supervision and quality control, practice also continued to vary. There was substantial hostility in many German states, such as Bavaria, to any change in the confessional framework for primary and secondary education, but both Baden and Hesse-Darmstadt had successfully introduced non-confessional schools by the end of this period.

It is not surprising, therefore, that there should be some doubt over the precise contribution of the educational system to Germany's economic development in the pre-unification period. Certainly there was a noticeable increase in literacy rates and it is reasonable to infer that the cumulative impact of greater educational provision at virtually every level would have led to improvements in the quality of human capital as a factor of production. However, the actual extent of reform should not be exaggerated. Elementary education was largely provided in large, single classes with an emphasis on religious instruction and morality rather than practical training; the curriculum continued to reflect the standards of a pre-modern society and in states such as Bavaria it was only gradually modernized. Moreover, a considerable number of children below the age of 14 were only taught in half-day or holiday schools (*Halbtagsschulen* or *Feiertagsschulen*). Secondary education was also characterized by rigid compartmentalization: there were no significant changes to the curriculum between the 1830s and 1880s; science training in the grammar schools was still deficient and failed to meet the 'demands of the present'; recruitment remained class-based; and private funding for secondary education continued to play an important role. There was no significant correlation between technical high school enrolment and industrial production, even in the later nineteenth century, and certain aspects of technical training were subject to 'continuous academization'. Although the larger universities were already highly specialized by the early 1860s, it was only after this period that expenditure levels on higher education increased significantly. Indeed, despite the early development of a public education system in Germany, its net contribution to economic growth remains questionable, even in the late nineteenth century. In Prussia quality improvements in labour as a factor of production, according to a recent estimation, only contributed 2 per cent to the recorded rate of growth in total output between 1864 and 1911.

X   Conclusion

Many of the issues raised in this chapter cannot be viewed in isolation. Long-term processes of economic change and adjustment were evident well before the end of the eighteenth century, as well as after political unification (see below, Chapter 9). At the same time, there is clearly a need to rethink traditional explanatory models. Economic growth in the nineteenth century was to a large degree a regional phenomenon, and it is important to analyse the dualistic nature of development and its costs, as well as the impact of specific factors, within a regional context. The pattern of regional development, in turn, was an interdependent process which reflected the role of different economic, social and political factors.

In particular, Germany's economic development prior to unification in 1871 can only be understood within an appropriate political framework. The state was heavily involved in the industrialization process and in the promotion of economic growth, but any discussion of the precise role of the state and the impact of state policy needs to be refocused, given the continuing federal structure of the German state: the fragmentation of political power, the local impact of lobbyist groups, and the disproportional role of the federal state bureaucracy in formulating economic policy.

Such an approach, however, places in doubt the continued applicability of the Gerschenkronian paradigm as a means of explaining Germany's long-run development. Germany was not uniformly backward, even in a relative sense, at the end of the eighteenth century; economic growth was more continuous than previously thought, particularly in the earlier decades of the nineteenth century; and the impact of key factors, such as the banks, the *Zollverein*, railway development or educational provision, was more muted than previously imagined.

This reappraisal of economic development in the pre-unification period, however, has broader implications. In recent years the focus of a great deal of research on European economic development in the nineteenth century has been on the role of regions and the unevenness of economic growth. In the case of Germany, however, such an approach is even more relevant, because the long-run development process was directly affected by political forces and social institutions that continued to operate at the level of the federal state. Indeed, after 1871 (see below, Chapter 9) regional economic divergence became even more accentuated and political power, to a large extent, remained fragmented within the federal framework of the Bismarckian constitution.

Note:

1. On the basis of a detailed analysis of a number of European states in the nineteenth century, Alexander Gerschenkron put forward a number of hypotheses to explain the overall pattern of industrialization. According to the Gerschenkronian paradigm the relative backwardness of a country affected not only the rate of growth of industrial production, but the emphasis on producer rather than consumer industries. The more backward the country, the more active was the role of institutional factors, such as the banks or the state, and the greater the pressure on consumption levels in order to facilitate capital formation. For a fuller discussion of these issues, see Richard Sylla and Gianni Toniolo (eds.), *Patterns of European Industrialization. The Nineteenth Century.* (1991), pp. 1–28.

Select bibliography

Brose, E. D., *The Politics of Technological Change in Prussia* (1993).

Dumke, R. H., 'Tariffs and Market Structure: The German *Zollverein* as a Model for Economic Integration', in W. R. Lee, ed., *German Industry and German Industrialization. Essays in German Economic and Business History in the Nineteenth and Twentieth Centuries* (1991), pp. 77–115.

Henderson, W. O., *The Rise of German Industrial Power, 1834–1914.* (1975).

Lee, W. R., 'Germany', in Lee, ed., *European Demography and Economic Growth* (1979), pp. 144–95.

Olson, M., *The Rise and Decline of Nations. Economic Growth, Stagflation and Social Rigidities* (1982).

Tilly, R., 'Germany', in R. Sylla and G. Toniolo, eds., *Patterns of European Industrialization. The Nineteenth Century* (1991), pp. 175–96.

5
Cultural and intellectual trends

Karin Friedrich

Intellectual education is perfect in Germany, but everything there passes into theory ... the government is the real instructor of the people, and public education itself, however beneficial, may create men of letters, but not citizens, warriors, or statesmen. In Germany, a man who is not occupied with the comprehension of the whole universe has really nothing to do.[1]

This judgement on German higher education by Madame de Staël, the daughter of Louis Necker, Louis XVI's unfortunate finance minister, sums up the prevailing view on the unpolitical and escapist nature of intellectual life in nineteenth-century Germany, which regards early nineteenth-century Romantic Idealism as the first step toward the intellectual German *Sonderweg* ('special path') that led to the totalitarianism and irrationalism of the Nazi regime. Although this paradigm has been persuasively challenged in many areas of German social, economic and political history during the last decade, it still pervades many works on German cultural and intellectual history before and after the foundation of the Empire in 1871. The weakness and backwardness of the bourgeoisie, the main pillar of political reform in other European countries, has been blamed for the unpolitical, elitist and esoteric nature of most nineteenth-century German cultural and philosophical trends, which stood in stark contrast to Germany's rapid economic growth and the development of its natural and technical sciences.

The territorial divisions of Germany and a confusing diversity of intellectual, religious and artistic movements complicate the task of assessing the political and social achievements of German cultural life in the nineteenth century. Its main trends, which accompanied the social and intellectual changes from the end of the Holy Roman Empire to the foundation of the Kaiserreich under Prussian leadership show, however, that in no other area more than in the arts, literature and philosophy was the transformation of German society so clearly influenced and shaped by the middle classes.

What Thomas Nipperdey called the 'defeudalization' of the arts in Germany was a process guided by the effective improvement of education on the primary, secondary and university level. As Christopher Clark and Robert Lee show in preceding chapters (Chapters 3 and 4, above), the early introduction of compulsory elementary education and the growing diversity of school types contributed to an increase in literacy rates among the whole German population. It was the German bourgeoisie (*Bürgertum*) which benefited most from educational reforms. Yet there were distinct differences between the various parts of Germany and their governments' willingness to fund mass education. It is a frequently repeated myth that Prussia had introduced a system of compulsory education by the late eighteenth century. Austrian investment in elementary and secondary schooling under Maria Theresa and Joseph II by far exceeded Prussian financial efforts to improve the school system under Frederick II. But even in Prussia, school book production rose rapidly from the 1780s. From the point of view of the political authorities, however, education proved a double-edged sword. The encouragement of critical and independent thinking among the educated fitted ill with the unconstitutional government of the Restoration period and the repression of the 1848 revolution. The complexity of the German *Bürgertum* and its internal political and social divisions complicate the assessment of bourgeois cultural responses to the Restoration periods following 1815 as well as 1848. On the one hand, the quiet 'philistine' world of Biedermeier, to which many Germans turned as a result of political frustration and harsh repression, proved the most persistent of all German bourgeois art styles; on the other hand, its seemingly unpolitical nature often served as an efficient cover for satire and tentative political criticism without provoking the censor. Moreover, in the second half of the nineteenth century, Biedermeier and Realism triggered an elitist response from a new avant-garde, itself deeply rooted in the *Bürgertum*, which felt alienated from the established political and social order – possibly more so than in other countries. Thus the elitism and high abstraction of much of German art and philosophy, particularly in the last decades of the century, was indirectly the result of the involvement of the bourgeoisie, and not, as the *Sonderweg* theory suggests, its absence or weakness.

I The transformation of the German education system

When Madame de Staël published her famous work *De l'Allemagne* in 1813, wide-ranging military, administrative and educational reforms were in full swing in most German states. As part of these reforms, Berlin University had been founded in 1810. It seemed an odd moment for the Prussian king, facing occupation by Napoleon's armies at the time, to invest in an institution of higher learning. Yet the decision resulted from an intense debate about the purpose of scholarship and the relationship between science, research and teaching, which had preceded the Napoleonic wars.

Academic opinion was divided between governmental reformers such as Karl Freiherr vom Stein and Carl August von Hardenberg, who had deprived the universities of their old corporate status and favoured a utilitarian approach to the education of the administrative elite on the one hand, and supporters of Wilhelm von Humboldt's (1767–1835) neo-humanist concept of philosophical and scientific activity on the other. Humboldt's university was meant to combine teaching with research in an environment in which professors and students could form an intellectual and moral community, striving for the moral and material improvement of the human condition. 'Solitude and freedom' became the motto of the scholarly ideal of the post-Enlightenment period. Neo-humanists strove to educate morally responsible citizens, conscious of their political freedom, through intellectual pursuit for its own sake. This Idealist approach was opposed by reformers guided by the pedagogical ideas of the Swiss educator Johann Heinrich Pestalozzi (1746–1827), who saw more need to foster vocational and practical skills among the young in schools and academies which produced citizens 'useful' to the state. The difference between the two camps, however, has often been overemphasized. Although non-utilitarian in nature, Humboldt's concept of the university as an institution open to all talents was still influenced by Enlightenment ideas and driven by the political purpose of improving education firmly under the control of the state.

German patriots of the post-Napoleonic period, however, reacted with suspicion to Humboldt's classicist and universalist values. The Idealist philosopher Johann Gottlieb Fichte (1762–1814), whose historical work is explored by Stefan Berger (see his chapter 'The German Tradition of Historiography 1800–1995' in Fulbrook, ed., *German History since 1800* (1997), advocated a system of national education based on Johann Gottfried Herder's *Volksgeist* (national spirit), which was opposed to the 'emptiness of the Enlightenment'. The Romantic Lutheran theologian and philosopher Friedrich Schleiermacher (1768–1834), like Fichte, professor at Berlin University and a strong advocate of German cultural unity, argued that a Prussian university should play a more pragmatic role in the formation of the country's social and political elite. In 1810, a compromise was struck between Humboldt, who was head of the section for religion and public instruction in the Prussian Ministry of the Interior (a predecessor of the Ministry of Education), and the followers of Pestalozzi over the future shape of the reformed university in Berlin. The neo-humanist ideal of 'general human education' assured an emphasis on autonomous research, while a close pedagogical supervision sought to transform students into useful members of their community and loyal subjects of their monarch.

The universalism advocated by Humboldt, who was inspired by a social conscience shaped by the ideas of the French Revolution as well as the late eighteenth-century fascination with Greek antiquity, also prevailed in secondary and primary schools. A strict separation between vocational schools and general education at the *Gymnasium* prevented the early specialization of pupils destined by their talent for university. In 1812, university entrance was regulated in Prussia by an edict making the *Gymnasium* diploma, the *Abitur*, compulsory on the basis of a curriculum dictated by the ministries of education and culture in each state, many of which remodelled their requirements along Prussian lines. Candidates who passed the *Abitur* then had complete freedom of choice of any subject at any German university. The popularity of these reforms was reflected in the number of students entering German universities: between 1819 and 1830, enrolment more than doubled from 7,378 to 15,838 students, while general school attendance in Prussia rose from about 60 to over 90 per cent by 1864.[2] The multidisciplinary preparation of future university students and a generally meritocratic approach opened up some, albeit not unlimited, opportunities for social advancement beyond the university, into state service.

Examination regulations were accompanied by great improvements in the formation of future schoolmasters, for whom the obligation to study theology was replaced with a free choice of academic subjects. Neo-humanist ideals remained wedded to a strict control by the state and its department of culture over teacher-training. Teachers were employed by the government and became civil servants bound to obedience by an oath to their state. The overwhelmingly positive impression which elementary and higher education made on foreign observers in the first half of the nineteenth century suggests that German schooling was regarded as more liberal and modern than the educational system in countries with more liberal and parliamentary constitutions than the German states. The liberal Rhenish industrialist Friedrich Harkort (1793–1880), an admirer of the British parliament, condemned English schools as 'a barbarian colony rather than enlightened parts of a civilised Christian state', while the American John Quincy Adams observed that, in contrast to their American and English counterparts, Prussian teachers 'not merely load the memory of their pupils with words, but make things intelligible to their understanding; to habituate them to the use of their own reason'.[3]

After a promising start, however, the promotion of a secular, well-organized education system with rigorous teacher-training lost its impetus during the Restoration period, particularly after 1848. Undoubtedly, regional differences existed within Germany. Winfried Speitkamp has recently tried to diminish the importance of Prussia's leadership in political and educational reform: literacy and school attendance were not only poorer in the rural areas of Bavaria, where the reforms of the Montgelas ministry were reversed by the Catholic Church's reaffirmation of control over education in the 1820s, but also in Prussian provinces with a large Polish population. The latter usually fell foul of literacy tests which demanded writing and reading examinations in German, and not in their native (Polish) tongue, thus revealing the problematic nature of Prussian government statistics. As in Bavaria, teachers were soon regarded with suspicion. Frederick William IV blamed the revolution on the fostering of a 'rebellious spirit' in schools and universities, and attacked primary school-teachers for their supposed radicalism. The expulsion of teachers with republican preferences, the tightening of censorship, and the return to teacher-training dominated by religion under the regulations of the 1854 decree by Ferdinand Stiehl, then councillor in the Ministry of Education, once more reinforced the image of a strictly controlled, uninspiring school environment worthy of an absolutist, militaristic state. Philosophical and scientific pursuits were replaced by the mechanical memorization of Biblical texts and the Catechism. Low pay and the low social prestige of primary schoolteachers contributed to their sinking morale. The foundation of the German National Teachers' Association in 1861 slightly improved their fortunes and consequently the quality of elementary education. Nevertheless, in 1870, the narrow focus of German *Gymnasia* on the creation of an administrative elite, and the failure of the reforms to open up schooling for all social groups and classes in German society, was reflected in Harkort's criticism:

> Like the Hindu caste system, we too impress on the lower social classes the seal of lifelong servitude through the lack of education. Our learned schools do not relate to the people. Only the well-off can attend the more advanced schools and private institutes on account of their considerable costs.[4]

Except on the primary level, where boys and girls were educated together in village schools, female education lagged behind. From 1804, Bavaria provided the first college for female teachers, but until 1866 women were taught only 'practical' subjects, aimed at preparing girls for housework and motherhood. Education reformers and ministries considered 'noble womanhood' unsuited for higher education and intellectual pursuit; women's destiny was to lead a 'quiet and domestic life, unburdened by difficult mental work'. In 1837, the Berlin *Gymnasium* director Johann Heinrich Schulz wrote that teaching brought out in women the most 'pedantic, unattractive and nasty' character, prone to irrational reactions, while a man, even in rage, still kept his 'titanic and imposing authority'.[5] It was again in Berlin, however, that the first association for women teachers was founded in 1869, following the establishment of Louise Otto-Peters' General German Women's Association of 1865.

Not all social groups benefited from the tripartite system of primary schools, practical and vocational schools (*Realschule*) and the *Gymnasium*. The survival of high standards and a humanist orientation in the German *Gymnasium* were crucial to the development of a widening split between an intellectual meritocracy among the German bourgeoisie serving the state in civil and military offices, and an industrial, trade and craft-oriented German middle class educated in vocational and technical schools. Measured against the long-term growth of German industrialization, however, it seems that the persistence of neo-humanist ideals at least did not obstruct the development of the natural sciences and technical innovation in Germany.

II   Religious and philosophical trends

Despite the attempt of many German state governments to introduce complete control over school education, confessional schools and the influence of the Protestant and the Catholic churches on public education survived the reform period of the 1810s and gathered strength after the failed revolution of 1848. The reaction against the French Enlightenment and Revolution, as well as against Kantian rationalism and its emphasis on the critical abilities of human reason, has traditionally been held responsible for a religious revival that went hand in hand with the emotional appeal of German Romanticism.

Recently, however, Nicholas Riasanovsky has argued that far from being a mere condemnation of the Enlightenment, early German Romantic writers such as Novalis (Friedrich Leopold von Hardenberg, 1772–1801), Friedrich Schlegel (1772–1829) and Ludwig Tieck (1773–1853) were influenced by an Enlightenment-inspired pantheism which filled the religious vacuum left by the French Revolution. For intellectuals and the educated, secularized *Bürgertum*, Romantic art, music, philosophy and science took on religious qualities and replaced or complemented religion in the spiritual life of the nineteenth century. Novalis's belief that 'now on earth men must become Gods' was paralleled by Schlegel's plan to create a new human religion: 'God is I'.[6] Belief in salvation in this life instead of after death was taking root as there was, in the words of the poet Georg Büchner (1813–37), 'more of heaven on this side of the grave'. Thomas Nipperdey accurately pointed at the religious contents adopted by German cultural life in the first half of the nineteenth century: philosophy and the arts were transformed into the substitute religion of the post-Enlightenment era, which found expression in a cult of ultimate subjectivity that needed no church. True atheism, however, only took hold among a small intellectual avant-garde in the later nineteenth century, when the belief in the existence of a spiritual and transcendental realm was increasingly challenged by the rising natural and social sciences and the influence of materialist and nihilist philosophy.

The Christian faith even found vociferous defenders among the Romantic movement. The diatribe by the Protestant theologian Schleiermacher against Enlightenment intellectuals who 'disdain religion' set the Romantic tone against the rationalist definition of man and the 'paganism' of Weimar classical culture. Man could never be defined by reason alone. The religious emotionalism preached by the late eighteenth-century Pietists had emphasized the personal relationship between the individual and God. The Romantics went further and accepted their mystical, Romantic God as part of their human nature. Although Schleiermacher stressed that human longing for the infinite could be fulfilled before death, in this world, he was not a pantheist. Moreover, his Protestant devotion separated him as much from the more mystic branches of Romanticism, as from the strongly anti-Enlightenment Pietists in Prussia and Pomerania, and from the sceptics among Protestant theologians, such as Johann David Strauß, who questioned in his *Life of Jesus* (1835) the historical existence of Jesus Christ and tried to explain miracles with natural science.

Soon, however, Schleiermacher's Romantic theology was superseded by a secularized, rationalist religiosity among the Protestant *Bürgertum*. After 1848, the growing consensus within the German Protestant Church against political and social revolution forged an alliance between the Restoration governments and the orthodox Lutheran leadership in most Protestant states, especially in Prussia. Friedrich Julius Stahl (1802–61), the main ideologue of the Prussian state in the pre-March period (and paradoxically a baptized Jew from Bavaria), set the agenda in his work *The Christian State*, which justified divine-right rule with Luther's teaching of obedience towards secular powers and a national, state-dominated church. The changing focus of the popular Luther festivals between 1817 and 1863 closely mirrored the political changes in Germany during this period: in the early decades of the century, the depiction of Luther as a sympathetic fighter for religious and political freedom and national unity coincided with the hopes of the liberal movement of the *Vormärz* to win constitutionally guaranteed civic liberties and national unity. After 1848, however, Luther festivals started celebrating either a *bürgerlich* figure, in a cosy home with his wife and children, displaying the virtues of an unpolitical and obedient member of bourgeois society, or a useful representative of the *Bildungsbürger* establishment, with a doctorate and an academic post.

A similar process transformed German Catholicism, which in the first half of the century played a major role in the general religious revival that accompanied Romantic literature and philosophy. Several writers, such as Friedrich Schlegel and Adam Müller, converted to Catholicism in the early nineteenth century in search of the emotionality which they missed in orthodox Lutheranism. A favourite Romantic theme was the quest for an idealized image of the German Middle Ages.[7] It is no coincidence that the first Romantic novella was published in 1797 under the title *An Art-Loving Friar Pours Out His Heart*. The rediscovery of the Middle Ages and the Gothic as a 'typically German' art style also played a role in the Romantic project of completing the unfinished medieval cathedral in Cologne. The nationalist writer Joseph Görres (1776-1848), another convert to Catholicism, spoke of it as a symbol of national greatness uniting Germany not only politically but also across religious divides, as a 'home for all Germans'. Since Frederick William IV, however, personally oversaw the funding of its construction and, as the 'patriarch of the nation', became the protector and patron of the cathedral project, it lost its predominantly Catholic character. The 1842 and 1848 festivals that celebrated the continuation of building work on the cathedral were therefore not dominated by a religious but a national and dynastic agenda. These public events found the enthusiastic support of the liberal *Bildungsbürgertum* represented in the parliament of the Frankfurt Paulskirche. The presence of school classes, fraternities, associations and choir societies performing patriotic chorus works in front of the king, the assembled officialdom and the archbishop of Cologne, lent the cathedral festivals a popular tone, increasingly marginalizing the religious cause of the city's Catholic community.

Unlike Protestantism, and with the exception of the reformist splinter-groups of the *Deutschkatholiken* (German Catholics), the Catholic Church in Germany remained generally sceptical of patriotic and national activities.

The creation of political Catholicism and the ultramontane movement, analysed earlier by Clark (Chapter 3, above), centred around journals such as *Eos*, published in Munich, or *The Catholic* in Mainz, and in a social movement among artisans. In 1845 the Kolping Association (Adolf Kolping, 1813–65) for Catholic workers was founded, followed by the Pius Association and the Boniface Association in 1848 and 1849 respectively. After 1850, the growing strength of Catholicism was also reflected in the increase of the numbers of monasteries and convents: Bavaria had 27 monasteries in 1825, but 441 in 1864, which included charitable institutions connected with monastic establishments.

Romantic religion, and the subsequent pseudo-religious character of national festivals, was one response to the growing uncertainties of the industrial age; Romantic philosophy was another. The towering figure of German Idealism was Georg Wilhelm Friedrich Hegel (1770–1831), whose real significance for German intellectual development revealed itself only in the decades after his death, through the influence he exerted on such heterogeneous figures as Ludwig Feuerbach (1804–72), Karl Marx (1818–83), Arthur Schopenhauer (1788–1860) and Friedrich Nietzsche (1844–1900).

Hegel comprehended history as a dialectical process led by the 'world spirit', perfecting itself in several stages from the Orientals, the Greeks and the Romans to the Germans through a process of achieving ever higher levels of freedom. Hegel's ideas of political or constitutional freedom were not those of the liberals. In his *Phenomenology of the Spirit*, Hegel defined the condition of progress as 'reason that governs the world, and, therefore, in world history things have come to pass rationally'. The state was the embodiment of this worldly reason, the 'actually existing realized moral life', the 'divine idea as it exists on earth'. This and the formula that 'everything that is real is reasonable, and everything is reasonable because it exists', have often been criticized as a justification of the repressive institutions of the Prussian state.[8]

More important than Hegel's support for the authoritarian state, however, were the two main schools formed after Hegel's death, the 'Right Hegelians' and the 'Left Hegelians', of which the latter transformed Hegel's dialectical principle into a revolutionary theory. In Hegel's view of life, where all things real were determined by a dialectical process involving the human will as the highest expression of freedom and 'objective' institutions, the state and society, and not individual morality and a transcendental God, occupied the supreme place. Inspired by Hegel's philosophy, Bruno Bauer (1809–82) thus asked: 'why does hell concern us?' and formulated the atheist world-view further elaborated by Feuerbach and Marx. In rebellion against Hegel's 'world spirit', Feuerbach concluded that in a materialist world ('man is what he eats') God is a human invention, a mere projection of human desires and hopes. In his critique of the failure of the 1848 revolution, Marx called religion 'the opiate of the people', whose sedating effect prevented the proletariat from feeling the pain of its social misery: only if Christianity was got rid of could they be convinced of the necessity of popular revolution.

The writings of Marx and Feuerbach had little immediate impact. Atheism only began to affect German intellectual life more widely when the social and natural sciences, in particular anthropology and the theory of evolution, further undermined religious revelation as a source of certainties about the meaning of life. At the same time, the quest for more worldly knowledge itself adopted sometimes quasi-religious qualities: as the physician Rudolf Virchow wrote in 1865, 'science became our religion'. This development prepared a fertile ground for the success of Darwinism, while the wave of cultural pessimism and religious nihilism that followed the 'death of God' was embodied in the philosophy of Arthur Schopenhauer (1788–1860). He was convinced that all human life was built on the will to survive, a will that was in itself evil and destructive. Man could only reach moral superiority by liberating himself from this will in an individual and aesthetic act of art. With this apotheosis of Romantic and atheistic ideas, and his interest in non-Christian cultures and religions, Schopenhauer remains the thinker most closely conforming to the stereotype of German Romantic 'irrationalism' before Nietzsche.

III   Literature, music and the arts: Romanticism to Realism

The growing importance of speculative philosophy to the Romantics has often been attributed to the tendency in the German national and cultural character towards exaggeration, irreality and unpolitical abstraction: 'that peculiarly German sense of inwardness and remoteness from reality'.[9] Comparisons with other European Romantic movements and an interdisciplinary analysis have, however, led to the revision of this one-sided picture, decisively formed by the poet Heinrich Heine (1797–1856) and his caricature of German Romanticism, *The Romantic School* (1838).

The relationship between art and social, political and historical reality was more complex. The search for the infinite – as seen in the landscape paintings of Caspar David Friedrich (1774–1840) – the 'blue flower' of Romantic love, pantheism and the mysticism of natural philosophy with an ever more immanent God, the revival of medieval culture, the rediscovery of folklore in music and literature, the enchantment with deep, dark forests and sunny landscapes, the urge to travel the world, most aptly expressed in Joseph von Eichendorff's (1788–1857) poems and novellas – all these themes are also present in French, Russian and English Romanticism. The mutual inspiration of the English and Scottish Romantic movement led by Byron, Coleridge, Shelley, Carlyle and Scott, and German Romantics, such as E. T. A. Hoffmann (1776–1822), Schlegel and Friedrich Hölderlin (1770–1843), Novalis and Jean Paul (Johann Paul Friedrich Richter, 1763–1825), and the influences of German Romanticism on Balzac, Poe and Dostoevsky are well known.

Even though English and French Romantic literary heroes tend to be more politically active, this does not mean that German writers shunned political issues. Moreover, there was no political – liberal or conservative – consensus among them. First inspired by the French Revolution, but subsequently appalled by Napoleon's conquests, writers such as Fichte and Ernst Moritz Arndt (1769–1860), and poets such as Heinrich Kleist (1777–1811) and Theodor Körner (1791–1813), engaged in patriotic myths of the Germanic past and a pronounced Gallophobia. Other Romantics accepted a role in the political establishment: Schlegel became a supporter of Metternich's Restoration policy, Eichendorff was a councillor in the Prussian education ministry, and the Jacobin Joseph von Görres (1776–1848) turned into a Catholic defender of the Bavarian monarchy.

Without Idealism and Romanticism, the rebellious and highly politicized literary movement of Young Germany, would have been unthinkable. Emancipatory and socialist ideas, most prominently represented in the teaching of the utopian socialist Claude-Henri de Saint-Simon (1760–1825), deeply influenced the group of writers which gathered in the 1830s and 1840s around Karl Gutzkow (1811–78), Heinrich Laube (1806–84), Ludwig Börne (1786–1837), Nikolaus Lenau (1802–1850), and the two most gifted writers among them, Heine and Büchner. In contrast to the German literary establishment of the imperial period, the poets of Young Germany believed in modernization, which they associated with a parliamentary constitution for free citizens, the emancipation of women and a united German nation state. Literature and the arts were an inherently political enterprise for them, and they agreed with the two liberal authors of the 'Encyclopedia of Liberalism', the *Staatslexikon*, Karl Rotteck (1775–1840) and Karl Theodor Welcker (1784–1868), who stressed the political character of the arts: 'the constitution is the highest expression of order, and the development of the arts must be closely interwoven with the development of the constitution and with legislation'.[10]

The critical journalists and writers who in the early decades of the nineteenth century gathered in the literary salons of Bettina von Arnim, Henriette Herz, Rahel Varnhagen and Fanny Lewald actively contributed to this politicization of German literature. Ingeborg Drewitz concluded that it was the achievement of these Berlin salons to 'preserve the ideas of the Enlightenment into the industrial era'.[11] Literary and political circles, such as masonic lodges and the pre-March *Burschenschaft* movement among students, always remained highly exclusive and isolated from the majority of the population. This did not differ, however, from developments in other European countries. It was only with the advent of the patriotic Gymnasts' Movement, founded in 1811 and revived in 1842 by Friedrich Ludwig Jahn (1778–1852), male choirs and other patriotic associations, that less educated and lower social groups from among the German *Bürgertum* took a more active role in forming public opinion.[12]

The promotion of a popular cultural basis through these associations, however, did not guarantee the liberalization of German society. Ironically, the openly repressive nature of government policies targeting the rebels among the elite literary circles of the pre-March period triggered a greater literary and political interest from the *Bildungsbürgertum* than after the nominal introduction of freedom of expression during the post-1850 Restoration era. Of great importance here is censorship. In reaction to the liberal demands of the Hambach festival of 1832, the Central Office of Political Observation regularly confiscated the publications of representatives of the Young German movement. Pre-censorship applied to newspapers, periodicals and any works with fewer than 20 printed sheets. Clever distribution policies and the persistent cooperation of author, publisher, printer and bookseller, however, assured that an eager and attentive – albeit small – readership regularly received works that were confiscated shortly after publication. The policies were draconian enough to force Heine, who refused to compromise on a less confrontational style, into permanent exile in France from 1833. Torn between his German patriotism and the disgust with which he watched from abroad the failure of the German liberals to overcome the repressive policies conducted from Berlin and Vienna, Heine wrote partly with bitterness, partly with compassion, about the 'great fool that calls himself the German people'.

After 1850, however, new laws made it even harder for writers, publishers and booksellers to hoodwink their censors. State licences, money deposits, spies, denunciation, incarceration, police investigations and the control of proofs before printing led to widespread self-censorship and a diminishing willingness of publishers to run risks with politically sensitive publications. Even so, the political division of Germany helped to some degree to alleviate the harshness of repression. A group of scientists and scholars at the University of Göttingen (the famous 'Göttingen Seven'), who in 1837 resigned in protest against the *coup d'état* of the new king of Hanover, Ernst August II (who had unlawfully annulled the kingdom's liberal constitution by refusing to swear an oath to it), eventually found employment again at other German universities. Among the 'Göttingen Seven' was the historian and literary scholar Georg Gottfried Gervinus (1805–71), whose *History of German Literature* called for an end to Romanticism and for a more realistic and critical sense among the intelligentsia in assessing Germany's political future. Young Germany was not strong enough a force, according to Gervinus, to overcome the country's intellectual and artistic stagnation:

> Our literature has had its day and, if German life is not going to stand still, then we must entice its talents . . . to turn toward the real world and the State, where the new spirit waits to be poured into the new material.[13]

Like Heine, Gervinus attacked the intellectual apathy which he thought was increasingly taking hold of Germany's political and cultural life, after the critical elite, silenced by censorship and emigration, had run out of steam and were superseded by the art of the Biedermeier era – mocked by the Young Germans and members of the *Bildungsbürgertum* as a 'culture of Philistines'. Like all ideal-types, the concept of the *Bildungsbürgertum* – a bourgeoisie with the academic qualification of the *Abitur* or a university degree, and regarded as distinct from the middle classes in industrial and commercial professions – is only of limited value, as dividing lines between various groups in the middle classes were constantly shifting and must not be drawn too strictly. 'Herr Biedermeier', a *petit bourgeois* simpleton, was first invented by literary satire in the 1850s, but soon became associated with the frugal lifestyle of a bourgeoisie that retired into the private, domestic sphere, which for many seemed the only answer to the defeat suffered by the rebellious cultural elites of the pre-1848 period.

Biedermeier was fed from many sources: the anti-modernism, anti-industrialism and anti-urbanism of the small-town, apparently well-ordered world of the *Bürgertum* lay as much at the root of Biedermeier as the demonic, anti-modern side of Romantic emotionality. Both were aptly expressed in the poems of Eduard Mörike (1804–75) and Lenau – himself once a member of the Young Germany movement – and the novellas of Adalbert Stifter (1805–68). Wilhelm Riehl (1823–97), the founder of German ethnology, similarly railed against the 'cosmopolitan' revolutionaries of 1848, who catered to the corrupting influence of the urban, proletarian masses, instead of defending the peasantry, the natural stronghold of the German nation. Catholic writers such as Görres, Jeremias

Gotthelf (1797–1854) and Annette von Droste-Hülshoff (1797–1848) attacked the Young Germans for their worldly immorality, in particular their condemnation of conventional marriage and family values. Not all Biedermeier poets, however, withstood the tension between their desire to live in a 'wholesome old world' and the fundamental changes effected by the processes of urbanization and industrialization: Lenau went mad, Stifter killed himself, and Mörike died in embittered solitude.

In contrast to the literary products of the Young Germans whose reception always remained limited to a small circle, Biedermeier flourished, beyond literature, as a popular style of art. It provided furniture for the bourgeois German living room and paintings of harmonious families with pretty children. The mildly satirical pictures such as the 'Poor Poet', by the most famous Biedermeier artist, the Bavarian Carl Spitzweg (1808–85), enjoyed unbroken popularity among the German *Bürgertum* far into the imperial period. The style was often not without ambiguity. Using irony and satire, Wilhelm Busch (1822–1908) became the most celebrated Biedermeier caricaturist and writer through his work *Max and Moritz*, a moral tale about two badly behaved boys. The didactic focus of popular

Illustration 5.1   *The Poor Poet* by Carl Spitzweg (1839)

literature is also apparent in the most famous children's book of the period, Heinrich Hoffmann's *Struwelpeter*. Thus it was in the Biedermeier period that literature and the arts left the ivory tower of its classic and Romantic predecessors by adopting a more popular tone, while libraries, museums, concert halls, opera houses and theatres opened their doors to a wider public.

Royal operas and court theatres were either complemented or replaced by 'National Theatres', in Berlin (1807), Munich (1836) and the German Opera, built by Gottfried Semper 1841 in Dresden, where the middle classes gained access to the gallery and were no longer restricted to the stalls. In 1842, the French composer Hector Berlioz observed while travelling through Berlin that 'music is part of the air you breathe; you absorb it through the very pores of your skin. One meets it everywhere, in concert halls, church, theatre, in the streets, in the public gardens'.[14]

Ludwig van Beethoven's (1770–1827) idea of the new role music had to play in German *bürgerlich* society sharply differed from the almost exclusive function of court music or *Tafelmusik* in the eighteenth century. His furious protest 'I shall not play in front of such swines', addressing an audience at the Vienna court which continued with small-talk during one of his concerts, reflects a change in the role and identity of the artist as an autonomous self-conscious individual, rather than as a hireling of princes. Art itself was taking on a more autonomous nature and the function of a substitute religion, to be worshipped together with the genius who produced it and the nation which gave birth to such greatness, the German *Kulturnation* (cultural nation).

Programmes therefore increasingly focused on German works, such as Beethoven's *Fidelio*, and Carl Maria von Weber's opera *Der Freischütz*, premiered in 1821 in the Berlin Schauspielhaus, built by Karl Friedrich Schinkel 1818–21. The increasingly national character of music and dramatic art expressed itself most prominently in Richard Wagner's operas *Rienzi* (1842) and *Tannhäuser* (1845), both premiered in Dresden. National symbolism was also reflected in the transfer of Carl Maria von Weber's body from London to Dresden in 1844 to mark his significance for German culture.

Arnold Toynbee exaggerated when he wrote that in the nineteenth century 'when we say "music", we mean German music'. It is true, however, that music was not only the most abstract art and therefore closest to the emotional nature of the Romantic era, but it was at the same time the most universal and powerful art form. It transcended religious borders, social distinctions, dialects and mentalities within Germany and abroad. Apart from opera, the German *Lied* was a new musical genre which achieved international fame in the songs of Franz Schubert (1797–1828) and Robert Schumann (1810–56), and which followed the Romantic ideal by blending two forms of art: poetry and music. Interest among the *Bürgertum* in music associations, singing academies and public choir festivals, often with a patriotic and national sub-text that inspired the collection of large repertoires of folk songs, peaked in the revolutionary atmosphere of the 1840s. In the subsequent Restoration period, it was only the conscious retreat from political, anti-monarchical songs and theatre programmes that secured the survival of cultural associations.

The shift from a highly politicized cultural scene which enjoyed a short moment of almost unlimited freedom of expression in 1848, to the draconian restrictions during the Restoration period of the 1850s was sudden and extreme. If after the revolution, the gap between an elite and a mass audience narrowed, it happened at the cost of toning down radical political messages and liberal aspirations. It seemed after 1848 that German Realist writers such as Theodor Fontane (1819–98), Wilhelm Raabe (1831–1910) or Gustav Freytag (1816–95), could not live up to the great social and critical novels of their French and English counterparts, such as Charles Dickens, Honoré de Balzac and Gustave Flaubert. Nevertheless, a veritable reading revolution with a steady rise in literacy, a growing demand for local libraries from an increasingly sophisticated public, and an explosion in the number of periodicals, ranging from scientific and philosophical publications to satirical and fashion journals, accompanied the aftermath of the 1848 revolution.

As a typical product of the Restoration period, the magazine *Gartenlaube* introduced a new kind of journalism that was a far cry from the critical newspapers of the pre-March period and their constant battle against censorship and confiscation. Popularizing science, literature and art for the whole family, *Gartenlaube* reached an impressive weekly circulation of 100,000 in 1860; 15 years later, it sold 382,000 issues per week. In the years before unification, the production of cheaper paper, an improved postal service and the increase of leisure time as a result of shorter working hours created a new mass readership. Journals, encyclopedias and novels were the most popular reading materials consulted and borrowed from public libraries, whose numbers had already reached 2,000 by 1848. In 1867–8, in Berlin's 74 public libraries, almost 40 per cent of the regular users were craftsmen, 16 per cent *Gymnasium* pupils and students, 11 per cent workers, 9 per cent officials and clerks, 5 per cent teachers and 20 per cent women.[15] In the same year, the copyright laws were regulated, opening the way to allow the production of cheap editions of the German classics. Goethe's *Faust* sold 500,000 copies within a few days.

German rulers were aware of these trends and showed concern for a 'well-directed' popular education, in the words of King Ludwig I of Bavaria, the founder of Munich University, 'to ennoble the spirit and the habits of our people'. During the two decades before the political unification of Germany, one might therefore ask how successfully German art and literature asserted the claim of the German *Kulturnation* to intellectual and spiritual autonomy against the stifling control of the rulers and their governments.

IV   Towards a German national art and literature?

In the first half of the nineteenth century, the increasing importance of history as a scientific subject in its own right and the Romantics' rediscovery of the German past paved the way for the impact of historicism on all branches of German cultural and scientific life in the second half of the century. Nationalists discovered that not only history, whose supremacy Hegel had so firmly installed, but the history of German culture could be used to emphasize the superiority of a united German nation.[16] Historicism supported the idea of the organic individuality of nations and cultures and the need to judge them according to their values and ideals. Figures of such universal appeal as Friedrich Schiller therefore became the exclusive embodiment of German national culture: the festivals of 1859 that celebrated Schiller's 100th birthday no longer revered the image of the revolutionary hero, as during the pre-March period, but of the national poet, worshipped in altar-like monuments as 'saviour' and unifier of the German people. Popular demand for his public veneration even made the Prussian authorities, who had banned Schiller's works from schools only five years earlier, announce a literary prize in the poet's honour.

This 'nationalization' of culture was confirmed by the developments in other branches of cultural life after 1850. The foundation of German ethnography, national economy, cultural history and sociology contributed to the intellectual growing together of a German nation. The most important bases of this nation, except for a common statehood, however, were language and law. Although the Grimm brothers' efforts to trace and reconstruct a German literary tradition from the Middle Ages to modernity founded their fame as Romantic collectors of folk and children's tales, their work also resulted in the creation of the first comprehensive dictionary of the German language. Jacob Grimm's (1785–1863) study of Scandinavian language and linguistics inspired his interest in the newly emerging academic subject of *Germanistik* (German language and literature) during the 1840s. In 1846, the first conference of German philologists gathered in

Frankfurt am Main, and Jacob Grimm was elected president of the Congress of German Philology (*Germanistentag*). Heine's judgement of 1837 was shared by the German literary establishment after Wilhelm's and Jacob's deaths (in 1859 and 1863 respectively): 'Jacob Grimm's German grammar is a colossal work, a Gothic dome, where all German tribes raise their voices like a gigantic choir, each in its dialect'.[17]

At the same time, the rediscovery of Germanic legal traditions led to furious debates between the followers of Friedrich Karl von Savigny's (1779–1861) school of Roman law and those, like Karl Friedrich Eichhorn (1781–1854) and Georg Beseler (1809–88), who wanted to revive medieval customary law. Interest in the discovery of a medieval German heritage also guided the founders of the *Monumenta Germaniae Historica* (from 1819), the publication and annotated edition of historical sources which still continues today.

The invention of historical and national identity also dominated German architecture. In Munich, Leo von Klenze (1784–1864) was commissioned to build a Bavarian 'Hall of Fame', to honour Bavarian military heroes from the time of the Thirty Years War (1618–48). In Prussia, the king dedicated monuments to the soldiers who gave their blood in the Wars of Liberation against Napoleon. As Nipperdey emphasized, this gesture was understood and disliked by the people for what it was: an ill-chosen substitute for the promised but never granted liberal constitution. The tension between official, ruler-induced commemoration and a growing popular demand for national representation was never resolved, not even after unification.

More popular projects, which more genuinely expressed the idea of a German *Kulturnation* and which began to transcend the particularism of the German states, were the statues of 'great Germans' mushrooming in German cities and towns after the 1830s. In 1842, on the order of Ludwig I of Bavaria, the building of the Valhalla was accomplished. Situated on a hill overlooking the river Danube near Regensburg, the former imperial city which had housed the Diet of the Holy Roman Empire for centuries, the Valhalla was a temple erected in honour of the German heroes killed in the Napoleonic Wars. The whole nation was also represented in the monument of Arminius (17 BC–AD 21), the legendary hero who defeated the Roman legions of Quintilius Varus in the Teutoburg forest. Begun in 1841 and finished in the year of the declaration of the German Empire in 1871, it translated Arminius's victory over the Romans into a German victory over France. Similar popularity was achieved by the Luther monuments, which were financed by local Protestant communities and accompanied the festivals that transfigured the Saxon Reformer into a German hero who fought the dark forces of Rome and France, foreshadowing the *Kulturkampf*.

As an expression of secular, bourgeois culture, museums became sacred temples of the worship of the whole German nation and its achievements. Other public buildings also acquired an increasingly monumental character. The highest Bavarian court was built as a 'Palace of Justice', while post offices, town halls, schools and even public baths grew in size and ornament, sometimes much beyond their real importance. Political symbolism and splendour were no longer restricted to princely residences. Art and architecture were entering the public domain and public discussion.

Unlike many national monuments and festivals, German literature of the post-1850 period retained a predominantly provincial and inward-looking character. Before the works of Fontane, provincialism was the nature of the German literary scene: 'almost all [of Germany's] major writers in the period 1830–1890 were born and worked in the provinces'.[18] The reasons usually given for this situation are the same as for the thesis that Germany's liberal revolution failed in 1848: late industrialization and the lack of a national centre and capital such as Paris or London, due to the country's political fragmentation before 1871.

Recently, literary scholars and cultural historians outside Germany have generally started to acknowledge the great variety and spirit of experimentation, as well as the critical depth of German provincial literary and artistic production. The village novels of Berthold Auerbach (Moyses Baruch) deal with the problems of Jewish life in villages and small towns, while Paul Heyse (1830–1914), Friedrich Hebbel (1813–63) and Theodor Storm (1817–88) were masters of the novella with themes from their native environment – from the Bavarian mountains to the North Sea coast of Schleswig-Holstein. The discovery of tradition and the cult of the past did not exclusively focus on the nation as a whole, but regional culture also produced its version of cultural historicism. Germans were a nation of provincials – nowhere is this more obvious than in nineteenth-century German *Heimat*-literature.

Just as the German liberals in the 1860s became more moderate and recovered from the tempests of the 1848 revolution, the literary and artistic scene settled for a quieter and less provocative approach. The *Bildungsbürgertum* continued to push ideas of national and cultural unity, while more popular elements increasingly joined this German *Kulturnation*. As post-Romantic writers slowly reached beyond the horizon of their province, the moderately critical Realism of the 1860s did more for the popularization of art in Germany than the sharply critical, rebellious and highly abstract art of the pre-March period that preceded it, or the *fin-de-siècle* avant-garde that followed.

Notes:

1. Madame de Staël, 'Of the German universities', in *De l'Allemagne* (1813), pp. 171–2.
2. McClelland, C. E., *State, Society and University in Germany, 1700–1914* (1980), p. 157, and Thomas Nipperdey, *Deutsche Geschichte 1800–1866. Bürgerwelt und starker Staat* (Munich: Beck, 1983), p. 463.
3. Both quotes in Kenneth Barkin, 'Social Control and the Volksschule in Vormärz Prussia', *Central European History*, XVI (1983), pp. 47, 49.
4. Hahn, H.-J., *German Thought and Culture. From the Holy Roman Empire to the Present Day* (1995), p. 119.
5. Blochmann, Maria W., '*Laß dich gelüsten nach der Männer Weisheit und Bildung'. Frauenbildung als Emanzipationsgelüste 1800–1918* (1990), pp. 31–2.
6. Riasanovsky, Nicholas, *The Emergence of Romanticism* (1992), p. 73.
7. Klug, Matthias, *Rückwendung zum Mittelalter? Geschichtsbilder und historische Argumentation im politischen Katholizismus des Vormärz* (1995).
8. Voegelin, Eric, *Science, Politics and Gnosticism* (1968), p. 77; Russell, Bertrand, *History of Western Philosophy* (London: Unwin, 1974), p. 705.
9. Craig, Gordon, quoted by Peter Russell in *The Divided Mind. A Portrait of Modern German Culture* (1988), p. 74.
10. Rotteck, Karl, and Welcker, Karl Theodor, *Staatslexikon* (1840), vol. IX, p. 542.
11. Drewitz, Ingeborg, *Berliner Salons. Gesellschaft und Literatur zwischen Aufklärung und Industriezeitalter* (1965), p. 102.
12. Goltermann, Svenja, *Körper der Nation. Habitusformierung und die Politik des Turnens, 1860–1890* (1998), pp. 30–181.
13. Craig, Gordon A., *The Politics of the Unpolitical. German Writers and the Problem of Power, 1770–1871* (1995), p. 147.
14. Ringer, Alexander, ed., *The Early Romantic Era. Between Revolutions: 1789 and 1848* (1990), p. 109.
15. Glaser, Herrmann, *Deutsche Literatur–Eine Sozialgeschichte. Vom Nachmärz zur Gründerzeit: Realismus 1814–1880*, vol. vii (1982), p. 67.
16. See John Breuilly, 'The National Idea in Modern German History', in Fulbrook, ed., *German History since 1800* (1997).
17. Gerstner, Herrmann, *Brüder Grimm* (1973), p. 138.
18. Sagarra, Eda, *Tradition and Revolution. German Literature and Society 1830–1890* (1971), p. 73.

Select bibliography

Barkin, K., 'Social Control and the Volksschule in Vormärz Prussia', *Central European History*, XVI (1983), pp. 31–52.

Craig, G. A., *The Politics of the Unpolitical. German Writers and the Problem of Power, 1770-1871* (1995).

Engelhardt, D. V., 'Romanticism in Germany', in Roy Porter and Mikulas Teich, eds., *Romanticism in National Context* (1988), pp. 109–33.

Heafford, M., 'The Early History of the *Abitur* as an Administrative Device', *German History*, XXII (1995), pp. 285–304.

LaVopa, A., *Prussian Schoolteachers: Profession and Office, 1763–1848* (1980).

McClelland, C. E., *State, Society and University in Germany, 1700–1914* (1980).

Mosse, G. L., *The Nationalization of the Masses. Political Symbolism and Mass Movements in Germany from the Napoleonic Wars Through the Third Reich* (1975).

Nipperdey, T., *German History from Napoleon to Bismarck, 1800–1866*, transl. D. Nolan (1983).

Ringer, A., ed., *The Early Romantic Era, 1789–1848* (1990).

Sagarra, E., *Tradition and Revolution: German Literature and Society, 1830–1890* (1971).

Schleunes, K. A., *Schooling and Society. The Politics of Education in Prussia and Bavaria, 1750–1900* (1989).

Smith, W. D., *Politics and the Sciences of Culture in Germany, 1840–1920* (1991).

Speitkamp, W., 'Educational Reform in Germany between Revolution and Restoration', *German History*, XIX (1992), pp. 1–23.

Turner, R. S., 'The Bildungsbürgertum and the Learned Professions in Prussia, 1770–1830', *Social History*, XIII (1980), pp. 105–35.

6

The revolutions of 1848–1849 and the persistence of the old regime in Germany (1848–1850)

Wolfram Siemann

There is an anecdote about the Austrian Emperor Ferdinand I that penetrates right to the heart of Germany's problems in 1848. Ferdinand was not gifted with a brilliant mind, but at least Metternich had succeeded in instilling in him an immense revulsion towards any kind of representative body of the people. If it was only mentioned in conversation, Ferdinand felt threatened. This happened very frequently after the revolutionary unrest of 1848 had spread from France to Austria. His court physician was confronted with this sensitivity one day when the doctor told him innocently that he had an excellent constitution. The Emperor snapped, 'Why do you talk about constitution? Say nature, if you please!' This little story reflects a fundamental problem of the revolutionary era: the lack of readiness and maturity among the reigning elites to tolerate the achievements and changes the revolution brought in its wake.

At the beginning, the Prussian King Friedrich Wilhelm IV did not react as brusquely as his Austrian colleague: he promised, in March 1848, that Prussia would forthwith be one with the rest of Germany; he put on the black, red and gold national colours, ordered the troops to retreat from Berlin and seemed to accept national unification on a democratic basis. However, in November 1848 he confessed to the Bavarian ambassador, 'Now I can be honest again'; he had democratic newspapers and organizations banned and declared a state of siege in Berlin. A second question therefore arises: how far could monarchs, in so far as they were unwilling to bow to the revolution, still rely on the traditional pillars of their power: the police, the civil service and the army? This question addresses the issue of persistence of the old regime. It laid down the limits for a democratic development from the very beginning.

Another anecdote illustrates the contrasting levels of action. The speeches of the members of the Frankfurt parliament, meeting in the Paulskirche, were taken down in shorthand and published in the local press as soon as possible. This enabled constituents to see whether their member was doing a good job in Frankfurt. One member was asked during a stay in his home town why, in contrast to most of the other members, he was never mentioned in the papers. He answered, 'My good fellows, this isn't true. How often do you read "general murmur"! I'm always part of that.'

To sum it up more precisely: politics became, for the first time in Germany, the subject of free public debate; but the question remains whether the populace was mature enough for practical democracy. There still exists the idea of the impractical 'professors' parliament' at Frankfurt, the idealist liberal dreamers of 1848 with no sense for *Realpolitik*.

However, the German problems of 1848 cannot be properly judged without taking into account the European context. Recent research on the revolution emphasizes this, as the revolutions of 1848–9 were pan-European phenomena. In trying to view the deeper motives of all those revolutionary movements, four basic conditions have everywhere to be taken into account.

First, there were similar kinds of constitutional demands and there were several models to which people could appeal. One was the French *chartre constitutionelle* of 1814, which became exemplary for several constitutions in the separate German states, and then the *Deutsche Bundesakte* of 1815, the constitutional charter of Germany, which laid down that all the member states of the Confederation should proclaim a constitution which included consultative assemblies organized on the principle of the social estates (nobles, burghers, peasants). This constitutional principle derived its impact from the unfulfilled demands of the middle classes for sufficient political participation in states that drew their legitimation from monarchy, following the Restoration of 1815. Political struggle everywhere developed into struggle for a new order based on a written constitutional charter. Revolutionary struggle expressed itself as a struggle for law and constitution all over Europe – as a struggle for civil and political rights. This was already the case in the July revolution of 1830; it was even more so, though, in the initial phase of the 1848 revolution, which drew its first impulse not from France at all, but from Switzerland and Italy. The revision or the institution of a new constitution was always the issue precipitating unrest: after the *Sonderbundskrieg* (War of the Conferation of Seven Catholic Cantons) in November 1847, Switzerland, formerly a loose federation of separate states, constituted itself as a federal state with central powers and a federal capital in Bern. A further victory for the revolution was gained on 16 February 1848, at Palermo, when King Ferdinand II of Naples and Sicily issued a constitution. The breakdown of the July monarchy in France started with demonstrations in favour of electoral reform on 22 February 1848, and ended with the abdication of the king and the proclamation of a republic. In Germany, the so-called *Märzforderungen* (March demands) that were circulating at the beginning of the revolution, centred on constitutional demands: (1) arming the people under elected officers; (2) civil rights, especially unconditional freedom of the press and of assembly; (3) trial by jury, following the English (and French) examples; and (4) immediate institution of a national German parliament. In other words, a common denominator of all the European revolutions of 1848 was the fact that they were all constitutional movements at the same time. They ended with the proclamation of a constitution, first in the Swiss Confederation, Naples, Florence and Piedmont, later in Rome, Venice, Berlin and Vienna, and of course in Frankfurt.

The second basic condition was the European undercurrent of nationalism. The endeavour for national self-determination and independence was embodied in the German, Polish, Czech, Hungarian and Italian national movements. Among many nationalities the myth of the (unredeemed) nation grew and flourished during the first half of the nineteenth century, especially among the Greeks, Italians, Hungarians and Poles. Much of the oppositional propaganda in pre-1848 Germany included Germany as one of these nations. The roots of this nationalism could be found with the French Revolution of 1789, which constituted the primary example for a nation state with common national symbols. During the 'pre-March' period, the myth of the *Völkerfrühling* (spring of the peoples) developed under the Restoration systems. In the 1820s, it took the shape of philhellenism throughout Europe; in the 1830s, after the failure of the Warsaw uprising in November 1830, it manifested itself in a pro-Polish attitude.

These pre-revolutionary utopias gave considerable impact to the revolution in the spring of 1848; they soon faltered, however, when the possibility of integrating the nation into a common state began to manifest itself. The term 'eine Art Nationsanwärter' (a kind of aspirant nation) was appropriately applied by Hans Rothfels to characterize the nationalities of the nineteenth century: ethnic groups striving for more autonomy and struggling for political unity. Subsequently, whenever territorial sovereignty and the drawing of borders came into dispute, modern nationalism showed its destructive and belligerent power. The new nationality conflicts of 1848 and the following years were marked by the novel characteristic that both sides were convinced that they were in the right, trying to mobilize the entire nation: in Denmark for Holstein, in Poland for Posen, in Italy for Southern Tyrol. Revolution and war combined to form a dangerous compound, and the struggle for national unity grew into discord among the nations.

The third basic condition was the socioeconomic crisis of pre-industrial crafts; this stemmed from the effects of overpopulation and the beginnings of proletarianization in the cities and wide areas of the countryside (see Chapters 3 and 4, above). The common European factor was the final collapse of the old estate system, which had been the basis of the legal and social order governing everyday life. Pauperism, industrialization and the orientation of crafts and professions of all classes towards a market economy marked the long-term crisis of the traditional crafts. Importantly, with respect to these issues, the crisis of 1848–9 seemed to hark backwards: with Luddite unrest, anti-Semitism or the demand for guild protection of the craft, as opposed to the principle of freedom to practise a trade. This element especially reveals the ambiguous character of the 1848–9 movement, contradicting the interpretation of those events as an early stage of a history of progressive emancipation.

A fourth European dimension is manifested in the crop failures and subsequent famine and inflation of 1845 and 1846, culminating in 1847. Responses before the revolution grew to European dimensions: local unrest caused by famine spread in waves across countries on the one hand; on the other hand there was a growing tide of emigration in the second half of the 1840s, which have, after all, been called 'the hungry forties' (Theodore S. Hamerow). Suffering was worst in Ireland; but episodes of famine in many German regions – especially in Silesia – found much public resonance.

Demands for democracy, nationalist movements and the accumulated socioeconomic conflicts, combined to form a more general crisis, suddenly accelerating all political processes. Demands were speedily met that would have been punished as treason only a short time before. The escalating popular movement seemed so outrageous to some of its contemporary observers, 'crazy' even, that soon it was called 'the mad year' (*das tolle Jahr*).

The most recent research on the revolution has been following the manifold strivings and movements on a local, regional and broader level, and continues to do so. To guard against glib interpretations of the aims and driving forces in the revolution, its chances of success, and its reasons for final failure, historians have drawn attention to the 'complexity of 1848'. In hindsight, they find themselves faced with a revolution that failed because of the very diversity of the demands made of it.

To the contemporary observer, it might have appeared like this: the many-faceted combination of pent-up conflicts caused a gigantic surge of hope the moment it was unleashed. People believed that with fundamental reforms, new men and modern institutions, and a politics more sensitive to the popular mood, all the ills of the times could be cured at once. When hopes for the future are this high, disappointment will follow soon. Honeymoon and hangover were never far from each other. Questions about the 'complexity of 1848' cannot be answered by generalization. It is much more useful to get an overall view of the dynamics the revolution developed by distinguishing several levels of political action. What seemed like a single revolutionary process to contemporary observers can, by scientific analysis, be broken down to five separate levels. Thus it is much easier to explore the scope and the dynamics of democratic politics. Caricatures may help to illustrate these levels of action. It is the nature of caricatures to distort reality, so the cartoons at hand are, at the same time, documents of the public dispute that started to evolve in Germany in the year of the revolution.

I   Revolution at the grass-roots

This picture illuminates the first level of action: the revolution at the grass-roots. One can see its violent version in Illustration 6.1 showing the Vienna revolution in May 1848. The revolution at the grass-roots gave vent to spontaneous movements of the people. This happened on the barricades and at protest meetings in front of town halls and royal seats. Whole villages marched to the castles of their princes in southwestern Germany. One could see all social strata of the population there; one could even hear social revolutionary voices; the lower classes let out their pent-up rage.

The population was fundamentally concerned with politics as never before. Even contemporary observers were astonished at this process, like the *Breslauer Zeitung* which reported on 23 March 1848 that it was 'quite common to hear men from the lowest classes, even women, uttering clear and sensible opinions about political and social questions; just as if they had studied them for years'.

The more recent German research on the revolution has discovered, following Edward P. Thompson and Georges Rudé, social protest as a special driving force of revolution; the importance of peasant uprisings and

Illustration 6.1 Barricade-building in Vienna in May 1848: the revolution at the grass-roots

actions has become clear. Usually, the 1848–9 revolution is represented as a middle-class democratic revolution (*bürgerlich-demokratische Revolution*) but in fact, in its early phases around one-third of uprisings were agrarian in character. However, the farmers seldom pursued the same goals as the middle classes. They aimed to be free of their landlords but recognized the authority of the princes. Some understood freedom of the press not as freedom of the printed word, but as freedom from oppression by their landlords.

Another third of those participating in the revolution from below consisted of members of the urban lower classes: labourers, apprentices, journeymen, impoverished tradesmen, railroad and factory workers took part in the events; in April 1848, the public was agitated by a series of strikes, especially in factories and railroad construction sites.

In conclusion, one can note that peasants, tradesmen and workers, some two-thirds of those involved in the popular movements of early 1848, had been directly affected by social and economic crisis. In other words: those who carried the revolution from below belonged mostly to the lower orders, and were sharply distinct from the nobility and the middle classes.

If we take a look at the victims of the street fighting in Berlin, Frankfurt and Vienna, at those injured and killed, we see that most of them were also small tradesmen, journeymen and apprentices. They were simple people, townspeople. The crisis of the traditional trades that had lasted for decades – a structural crisis – found its visible outlet on the barricades. This crisis had already become evident in the early summer of 1847, when several uprisings caused by hunger had broken out throughout Germany. At this time, a Württemberg newspaper article had called the people mainly concerned 'in all places not at all those who really suffered hunger . . . the people acting throughout Germany are on the contrary run-down trades-men, journeymen, apprentices, women of the big cities [this because of the disturbances at the weekly markets] and so on'.

The role of women in revolution has been very much underestimated up till now. Illustration 6.1 even shows a woman building a barricade on the right-hand side. But one has to look further than the barricades to observe the role of women in the revolution. When asking about the space for political action for women which opened up with the revolution, we can be sure that working as an elected member of parliament in Frankfurt or in the state parliaments was most certainly not encompassed in it. However, women were very much present in the audience and actively tried to influence parliamentary decisions. They wrote press articles, letters to members of parliament or newspapers, took part in general assemblies, even spoke there in rare cases, and showed their political sympathies by wearing ribbons in the national colours, or even organizing petitions.

The most women could do within the institutional revolution was to organize themselves in their own associations. These women's societies, especially in the state of Württemberg and in the Rhine-Main area, in no way dealt exclusively with women's issues but were an active part of the political and national movement. Women donated jewellery and money for the German fleet, promoted 'ancient German' fashion in contrast to French fashion, which they now shunned, they organized lotteries to equip the citizens' militias, and organized help for the fleeing revolutionaries from Baden in the summer of 1849. Women did much of the work in German Catholic and Free Church communities, in which opposition to the orthodoxy of the two great denominations had brought together 150,000 people since 1845. These independent religious communities were an active part of political opposition, and women had equal rights here: they participated in their work at all levels, founded their own women's societies within the religious communities, and took part in educational and social work. Democratic and Free Church movements were closely connected in 1848–9.

So the people taking part in the revolution had many different goals, not only 'unity and freedom' like the liberal and democratic middle classes, as we read in general textbooks. The lower classes that carried the revolution reflected the decay of pre-industrial society; they aimed in many cases for the social conditions of the past: against free professions and freedom of movement, for the expulsion of strangers from town and state. A recently published book about social protest in the German states with the fitting title *Straße und Brot* ('Street and Bread') illustrates areas of life far removed from the parliaments. But in the second wave of the revolution in September 1848, and even more so in the revolution of May 1849, the former unity of the opposition was lost when the differences of interest within the grass-roots revolution came to light. This considerably weakened the revolutionary movement.

II   The political revolution

The grass-roots revolution opened the way for the second level of action: for a free press and a public organized into political parties.

Everywhere the governments of the princes had to concede freedom of the press and the free formation of political societies, for the first time in German history. Rapidly, a non-parliamentary political public developed. Rightly, it has emerged from the shadows into the light of research in recent years.

Obviously, the artist of Illustration 6.2 has a problem in depicting a society on its way to becoming an argumentative democracy. The picture shows the 'Reich-sweeping-mill'. It symbolizes public opinion, as is written on the funnel (*öffentliche Meinung*). The handle is operated by the *Deutsche Michel* a as personification of the whole German people. The picture deals with the call for re-elections under the impact of the September revolution. Michel works the mill as a sweeper. Below, as election returns, liberal and constitutional members emerge in an orderly and civilized manner. Above, on the left, republicans and democrats fly away; on the right conservatives and royalists are blown out.

In 1848, we stand at the very beginning of organized political parties in Germany. What criteria characterized these parties? They were freely formed organizations; they made up their opinions internally by majority votes; they submitted to a common programme and were open to anybody

Illustration 6.2   'Reich-sweeping-mill': the political revolution for free press and parties

of the same views. They aimed for votes in the coming elections, which they achieved quite effectively. It was not only the parliaments which proved their political competence in 1848; large parts of the urban population showed their own political maturity. It is amazing how quickly people became used to dealing with party rules.

As a new and special trait these parties were no longer just appendages of parliamentary factions or the result of state protection. They developed their own life and the variety of this party life has so far not been adequately assessed. Roughly, five political lines of thought can be distinguished: the conservatives, the constitutional liberals, the democrats, the political Catholics (*Pius-Vereine*) and the *Arbeitervereine* (workers' societies), organized nationally in the *Arbeiterverbrüderung* (workers' brotherhood).

So there was by no means just one homogenous mass of the socially discontented. Political life in the larger cities – especially in the southwest – had already been structured before the revolution. At Mannheim, for example, a reading society named '*Harmonie*' was a focal point where the opposition gathered. Public life came to the revolution already prepared; and it is not surprising that the earliest publicly expressed 'March demands' (*Märzforderungen*) came from Mannheim at the end of February.

Carola Lipp described the life experience of the middle-class political elite in a typical profile of a citizen from Württemberg. This interested and active citizen would have a high social status, would be a member of the crafts society (*Handwerkerverein*) to represent his economic interests, would sing in the *Liederkranz* (song circle) to express his musical interests, would join a political society in 1848, maintain public order as a member of the militia, go to general assemblies and festivals, would be informed about the hopes and dangers of the time from newspapers, might perhaps serve as an honorary member of the *Feuer-Rettungs-Compagnie* (a kind of early fire brigade) while most probably not joining the failed march of the Gymnasts Associations, which sought to save the Reich constitution against the Prussian troops in Baden and the Palatinate. His wife would be a member of a society that educated neglected children, while his daughter would participate in embroidering the citizenship flag in the *Jungfrauenverein* (maidens' society), and he himself would join a society to support out-of-work labourers. In 1849, he would win a seat in the local council.

This is to say: the revolution was deeply rooted in regional life via these societies, and the city became the centre of the revolution wherever the historical traditions of local self-government persisted.

The political societies found their voices in their own newspapers. The hitherto moderate tone of the press, enforced by censorship, was replaced by forceful polemics. The local newspaper of every town, city or region was suddenly dealing with national politics and the work of the Frankfurt National Assembly. It is an extremely arduous task to explore the jungle of the provincial press, and so far nobody has carried out an exhaustive analysis. Yet it is necessary to do so. The change in the local papers shows especially well how deep political interest began to reach in the year of the revolution. The newspapers show how the nobility, the clergy and the magistrates reacted, how active the local voters were and the variety of political parties. In addition, there were leaflets, placards, caricatures, handouts, organized petitions: the printed media were ubiquitous and so reached down to the grass-roots level of the revolution.

For the first time in Germany, there was freedom to express one's opinion publicly in the press and in political parties. Of course this expression was controversial and in no way unanimous. It is possible to say that this practical freedom was detrimental to the impetus of the revolution, just like the split between the liberals and the democrats. But was not the articulation of different interests necessary and unavoidable? Especially with regard to Prussia we are now well informed about conservative societies and their press; they did indeed weaken the revolution. On the other hand, there existed a central coordinating body of the democratic parties, the *Zentrale Märzverein*. It channelled the countless activities of regional revolutionary societies into what was called the campaign for the Imperial Constitution towards the end of the revolution. For a while, it strengthened the revolution.

All movements of the popular revolution, the press and the parties aimed for political influence; and this was seen to be concentrated in the state parliaments and the Frankfurt National Assembly.

III   The parliamentary revolution

So, we reach the third level of action: the elected bodies.

It is a fact frequently overlooked that in the year of the revolution there were elections not only in Frankfurt, Berlin and Vienna, but also in Munich, Stuttgart, Oldenburg, Bremen, Altenburg and so on – that is, everywhere where there were constitutions that had to be revised and made democratic. Much political energy was spent on this. It multiplied political activities and scattered them. At a local level, the old magistrates and mayors were sometimes driven out and a new local constitution was fought for, as well as a reduction of police power, and an extension of voting rights. Political energy was released and at the same time absorbed by German federalism.

This level – the elected bodies – was very much dominated by civil servants and the educated middle classes. Parliamentary parties developed, the members of which maintained close contact with their constituencies. The three levels of revolution at the grass-roots, press and societies, and the parliament were closely interconnected. A situation typical of new representative systems soon developed: the voters and those they had elected soon found themselves involved in an increasingly dangerous conflict. This conflict erupted in September when a revolutionary uproar threatened the continuation of the National Assembly. Not only later critics, but also some contemporary observers had a problem with the practices of the parliamentary system. Illustration 6.3   shows the members of the Frankfurt Parliament on a see-saw. Heinrich von Gagern, president of the parliament, tries to hold his balance on top. To the left, the left-wing members are quarrelling; Arnold Ruge is already falling backwards over a precipice. On the right the right-wing members are fighting. The caricaturist's sympathies are with the moderate middle.

Nowadays the negative judgements about the reputedly impractical 'parliament of professors' have been revised. We have learned to take the proceedings of the parliament and its parties seriously, and are able to appreciate the enormous and unusual achievements of the Frankfurt

Illustration 6.3   The Frankfurt Parliament on a seesaw: the parliamentary revolution

National Assembly and the parliaments of the separate regions. They were faced with the task of finding a mode of parliamentary proceedings out of nothing. The 1848 parliaments, especially the Frankfurt Assembly, had to act in the face of immense outside threats and pressures, yet they arrived at results and compromises in the same way as any other parliament. It is easy to imagine the parliaments breaking down from external pressure and internal fragmentation, yet they did not. The members were not experienced in parliamentary proceedings, even if they had been members of former state parliaments, yet they were able to work democratically even under the most extreme conditions. Past research has tended to criticize the conflicts and fragmentation; to acknowledge these as an innate part of a representative and democratic system is easier for us today than for the post-revolutionary observers used to an authoritarian system. Everything that shapes modern parliamentary life was in evidence even then: the influence of small but decisive minorities, politics working with changing majorities, with obstructive negative coalitions, tension between party discipline and the freedom of individual deputies, the influences from lobbies outside parliament and interest groups.

Even if nationalist feeling ran high in the German National Assembly, one could argue that a reasonable answer to the national question was proposed by the assembly. The aim of establishing a constitutional state within 'national' borders offered protection to national minorities and respected their languages and religions (Article 188 of the Imperial Constitution of 1849). A similar solution was proposed in the draft constitution drawn up by the Austrian parliament in Vienna for dealing with the problems of a multinational state. Neither of these constitutions were implemented but they suggested a way of achieving peaceful coexistence between several nationalities within a single state.

In 1848–9 the Frankfurt Assembly not only worked out a constitution for a unified Germany (which finally failed) but also engaged in concrete parliamentary politics. But how did democracy actually work in 1848? This question is asked more and more often nowadays. As the parliament achieved astonishing results there is no reason to deny its astonishing political maturity. But now the question arises as to why the constitution failed if all that was indeed so excellent. In this context we will have to consider the fact that the fate of the revolution as a whole was not exclusively, perhaps not even decisively, determined by voting in the Frankfurt Assembly.

IV   The governmental revolution

There were many more dimensions to the process. So we will now have to direct our attention to the fourth level of action: the ministries.

During the events of March the reigning monarchs were for a time disorientated and at a loss what to do. In Illustration 6.4 the caricaturist likens their actions to the random character of a game of roulette. The representatives of the European powers are shown waiting eagerly for the outcome. Where will the 'globe' come to rest – at progress, republic, equality, constitutional monarchy, anarchy, freedom or reform? On the left we see the Prussian King Friedrich Wilhelm IV, on the right Emperor Ferdinand I of Austria. In the background on the right the French King Louis Philippe is already leaving the game, having lost after the February revolution.

In fact the revolution almost everywhere stopped short of toppling the Princes. Parallel to the revolutionary events of March the reigning monarchs appointed commoners and liberal noblemen from opposition factions into their governments. These were the so-called March ministries, by means of which the monarchs seemingly gave power to the pre-March opposition. These reshuffles within governments seemed to provide evidence of the long-awaited breakthrough of the middle classes.

Mein Herr, machen Sie ihr Spiel fertig, während der Ball noch rollt!

Illustration 6.4   'Sir, finish your turn, while the ball is still rolling': the governmental revolution

It is necessary to view the events not only in the light of their outcome but also from the perspective of contemporary expectations. For the majority of the middle classes the institution of those March ministries must have had a calming effect, as they interpreted it as a promise from the monarchs for future parliamentary politics. The achievements appeared to be so vast that it was time to 'close down the revolution', as people put it. In fact the new governments concentrated their executive powers on achieving 'law and order' in the face of the continuing revolutionary uprisings. With this, they played exactly the part the monarchs had cast them in: to make the revolution lose its force.

This was certainly evident in Baden after the failure of the Hecker revolution in April 1848. The government of Baden had Gustav Struve and Karl Blind tried by jury as leaders of the revolution. The Württemberg government accused the Württemberg revolutionaries of treason and tightened the criminal law concerning political offences. Even during the revolution, counter-revolutionary politics began in the separate states.

As they did against individuals, so governments also took measures against political societies. As early as the 12 July 1848, the Württemberg government had a democratic society in Stuttgart (the *Kreisverein*) banned. Bavaria prohibited democratic associations on 12 August 1848; the government of Hesse-Darmstadt suppressed local unrest by means of the army and the police. Even the provisional central government instituted by the Frankfurt National Assembly had the same aims. We hear again and again that this central authority was nothing but a powerless phantom. After the September uprisings, on 3 October 1848, this alleged phantom addressed a decree to all German states ordering the institution of a political police. The regional governments were ordered to investigate the existing political societies, their tendencies, programmes, major decisions, number of members and influence among the people. The provisional government also asked about their connections with societies in other German states.

This state security decree demanded no less than the general surveillance of all political societies by the police. The central power instituted by the revolution thus undermined its own roots. The March ministries of many separate states did likewise. Already in autumn 1848 Hanover, Bavaria and Prussia began their surveillance records on political activities. The persecuting authorities of counter-revolution later used them to eradicate the remnants of the political societies.

V   Monarchy and counter-revolution

The central government even used troops to achieve law and order. They had been given the central command of the former *Deutsche Bund*. This leads to the fifth level of action: the pillars of traditional monarchist power.

Illustration 6.5, taken from the *Düsseldorfer Monatshefte*, is entitled 'Panorama of Europe in August 1849'. One could call it a pictorial piece of reactionary politics. We see the map of Europe, on which three large figures are shown. Two of them hold brooms, symbolizing reaction. The figure on the left, pointing to the ships leaving full of refugees, is Napoleon III who has almost entirely finished cleaning his country. The one in the middle with the spiked helmet is the Prussian king still sweeping. His broom points to southwest Germany, from where the revolutionaries are being swept away. They are gathering under a big hat resembling a liberty cap inscribed 'Helvetia'. Just at the edge of that cap we can see a gallows with a hanged man, reminiscent of the court-martials in Baden. In Frankfurt, nothing is left but a scarecrow which may be interpreted as the remnants of Imperial Administrator (a rough translation of *Reichsverweser*) and parliament. Small figures scurry between the feet of the Prussian king; they are the reigning

Illustration 6.5   Panorama of Europe in August 1849: monarchy and counter-revolution

monarchs. Two of them stand a little apart from the teeming mass of the very small ones: one at Stuttgart with the Württemberg antlers, one near Munich dressed in a beer stein (mug). In the east, we see the Austrians still fighting the Hungarians. Near Warsaw only a burnt-out candle remains from the failure of the Polish revolution. In Denmark the Dane dances, obviously triumphant because of Schleswig and Holstein. If one looks one also discovers the German navy, but in letters only, on the water of the Baltic sea – there is no trace of ships. And on the other side of the English channel there is Queen Victoria in a carriage, looking without much interest through her glasses at the European spring cleaning.

The revolution had 'stopped before the thrones', as the contemporary saying put it. And that meant the executive power remained with the monarchs. The noble officers, the common soldiers of the professional armies and the civil servants in the administration and the police force stood ready in the hour of counter-revolution. The part local officials, magistrates and militias played in this context is a subject of its own, and as yet little researched.

The army, in particular, was used against the revolution; for the first time in April in Baden, then on a smaller scale in several places, again in September 1848 at Frankfurt, and again in the summer of 1849. The last phase of revolutionary uprisings, after Friedrich Wilhelm IV had declined the imperial crown, erupted in parts of Prussia, Saxony, the Palatinate and Baden, threatening to spread to Bavarian territory on the right bank of the Rhine and to Württemberg.

The example of Baden shows that the revolution was successful when it was taken up by the troops. This happened temporarily in Vienna, during the militia uprisings in the Rhineland and Westphalia, but completely and effectively only in Baden after the Grand Duke had been driven out. The Baden revolutionaries succeeded when they were able to institute a State Assembly to work out a constitution, and a provisional republican government. They had won the support of the population and at least some of the pillars of power: officers, state officials and judges.

The counter-revolution approached from beyond the borders. The Grand Duke asked from exile in Mainz for the help of Prussian and Reich troops. By order of the provisional central government at Frankfurt, its Minister of War directed contingents from Hessen, Württemberg and Nassau to Baden. Troops from Bavaria, Württemberg and Austria also stood ready to intervene from the east and the south.

We still know far too little about this campaign for a Reich constitution, this last wave of the revolution. It came to a sad end at Rastatt on 23 July 1849 when the 5600 revolutionary fighters encircled in the fortress signed the surrender. In contrast to events in Saxony and the Palatinate, in Baden Prussian courts-martials bloodily liquidated the revolution. In addition, courts of war and civil judges sentenced another 1000 revolutionaries.

The decisive battle was not fought in Baden, but earlier and elsewhere; and the standing armies with their monarchs won. As yet very little is known about the role of the armies during the revolution. It was especially striking how seldom the professional armies took up the cause of the revolution. I tend to think they did not yet identify sufficiently with nationalist (in the positive sense) ideas. When Prussian soldiers shot Saxon guerrillas or Baden soldiers, they did not waste a thought on the fact that they were confronting Germans. During the revolution, soldiers only threatened to revolt when they were conscious of facing compatriots, but in 1848 that meant, in the eyes of the soldiers, Prussians, Saxons, Bavarians and so on, not Germans. The moment when the army started to side with the revolutionaries and protesters played an important part in the fact that there was virtually no bloodshed during the uprisings of 1989 in Dresden or in August 1991 in Moscow. Generals Windischgrätz and Radetzky, or Banus Jellacic, were successful in their fight for the Habsburg monarchy because they could use troops of different nationalities (Czechs and Croatians) against Germans in Prague or Vienna, against Hungarians in the east and against Italians in Upper Italy.

With all these factors we also have to consider the fact that the revolution of 1848–9 was part of a European movement that failed everywhere with the exception of Switzerland. The turning point in the European revolution was reached in other places much earlier than in Germany. In the summer and autumn of 1848 monarchist troops had suppressed the revolution in many European states: in Cracow, Posen, Prague, Paris and Upper Italy. In summer 1849 revolutionaries from other countries reached the German scene: the Russian officer Bakunin came in via Dresden; a Polish general led the forces in the Palatinate, supported by a Hungarian colonel; a Polish general commanded troops in Baden; legionaries came from France and Switzerland; Frenchmen, Swiss and Hungarians formed their own legions during the fight for the establishment of the Reich constitution. The traditional armies of the monarchies for the most part did not succumb to the challenge of the revolution, other than in Baden, in Vienna, or among the Prussian militia in the Rhineland and Westphalia. The regular troops were not ready to take up the cause of the revolution. In battles they always showed their superiority, supported by modern equipment. To put it more drastically: Prussian guns destroyed the national myth of the barricades.

The caricature above (Illustration 6.5) already interprets the revolution as only one part of the events which were happening throughout Europe. So the question as to what might have happened if Friedrich Wilhelm IV had accepted the imperial crown is completely futile. He would not have done it, as he was not a romantic, but a coolly calculating monarch very much conscious of his power, and to whom military force meant more than any constitution.

VI   Conclusion

In the light of the demise of East German socialism there is nowadays much emphasis on the fact that it was only a minority that effected the revolution. The same question may be asked concerning the events of 1848, pointing to a problem that could, on all five levels, be termed the locations of non-action, the calm zones of the revolution. We still know far too little about them. At the turning point towards counter-revolution those calm zones suddenly gained importance; those zones of political lull that had remained quiet during the revolution or that had become estranged from it in the early months: for example, the rural population. Strengthening loyalty to the monarchs, a feeling of tiredness towards the revolution and a passive 'protest against protest'; in a way the 'silent majority' gave strength to the old powers-that-be even before the impetus of the revolution faltered on the other levels of action. For example, when in October 1848 there were open uprisings on the streets of Vienna, Franz Joseph took flight and found a warm welcome at Innsbruck. In general, the most recent research on the revolution has shown that from the summer of 1848 onwards, conservatives and '*Kriegervereine*' (soldiers' societies) began to organize in order to fight the revolution; this was the case especially in Prussia and Austria, but also in Bavaria.

All in all, no single simple interpretation of the 1848–9 revolutions in Germany can be offered. Three central facts support this claim most emphatically:

- Those active in the revolution of 1848 were on all five levels unable to grasp the dynamics of the revolution as a whole. Their powers of judgement and decision were not up to it. There was no decisive centre of action.
- Those active in the events of 1848–9 did not have one single, clearly decided aim which they failed to achieve. The Reich constitution was one aim, but the revolution was about more than that.
- The roots of the revolution were ambiguous. On the one hand, it manifested a crisis of pre-industrial society, an answer to overpopulation, hunger, inflation, distress among the trades. It stimulated dreams of old times, of guilds, of a closed-in burgher mentality and work without machines. It awakened fear of class conflict which had hitherto been concealed through the restrictions on movement from one occuption to another. The revolution revealed that opposition to change lay deep within society; indeed, the revolution actually aroused such opposition to active resistance.

    On the other hand, the revolution was a crisis of political emancipation, which meant that new forms matured within society that were suitable for solving the problems of the future. Political parties, the press, the parliaments and the political societies were the new media of political emancipation. Under the domination of the pre-revolutionary elites they could only partially develop their possibilities. The bureaucratic-military bodies of the state and the old loyalties turned out to be stronger in the end. We should term the process a tentative and broken attempt at emancipation. The monarchist elites among the nobility did not see – in contrast to much earlier events in England – the chance that change within society offered them. Not one among the ruling monarchs of the larger German states was amenable to a constitutional compromise on the basis of 1848. This was amply proved during the bitter decade of reactionary politics that followed. The monarchs had been successful in deceiving their March ministers. They used them in the hour of their need; they dismissed them in the hour of reaction.

Only during the 1860s did the realization dawn among the reigning court elites that controversies in the sphere of public opinion and political parties did not endanger the state; on the contrary, press and parties could be seen and used as welcome allies of one's own politics. This, at least, was the approach taken by Bismarck. When he came to power in 1862, the memory of 1848–9 was still very much alive, much more so than is generally appreciated today. From this point of view, the revolution had not (yet) failed. The Prussian constitutional conflict, when an attempt to implant the parliamentary system into the largest German monarchy failed, can be seen as its late heritage.

The more we contemplate all those dimensions which are revealed when we view the different levels of action, the less able we are simply to state that the revolution failed utterly. The revolution gave the impetus to a long-term wave of modernization. National unity remained a real prospect, both experienced and recalled. The peasants remained victorious in any case: they were finally and irrevocably freed from their dependence on their landlords. The legal system had changed fundamentally at all levels. Political participation was established despite the subsequent reactionary Restoration. Prussia had become a constitutional state. The Frankfurt constitution remained exemplary for a hundred years, up to the time of the Parliamentary Council in 1948–9. The national revolution also had the effect of altering relations between the various German states in ways which are important for a study of Germany as a federal political system, although much more research is needed on this. To see the revolution simply as a failure would mean understating its meaning and importance in German history.

Select bibliography

Barclay, David E. *Frederick William IV and the Prussian Monarchy* (1995).
Dieter, Dowe, *et al.*, eds., *Europe in 1848: Revolution and Reform* (2000).
Langewiesche, D., 'Die deutsche Revolution von 1848/49 und die vorrevolutionäre Gesellschaft. Forschungsstand und Forschungsperspektiven'. Part II, *Archiv für Sozialgeschichte*, 31 (1991), pp. 331–443 (a critical general overview of research on the revolution carried out in the last decade, also excellent on specific points of specialism).

Sheehan, J., *German History, 1770–1866* (1989).

Siemann, W., *The German Revolution of 1848–49* (Eng. trs., 1998).

Siemann, W., *Vom Staatenbund zum Nationalstaat. Deutschland 1806–1871* (1995).

Sperber, J., *Rhineland Radicals. The Democratic Movement and the Revolution of 1848* (1991).

Sperber, J., *The European Revolutions, 1848–1851* (1994).

7

Revolution to unification

John Breuilly

The story of German unification has usually been told from the perspective of Bismarck and Prussia.[1] Other views were marginalized or dismissed as impractical. Subsequent historical emphases, for example in economic history, have often strengthened rather than challenged the accompanying sense of inevitability. For example, when John Maynard Keynes wrote that Germany was unified by 'coal and iron' rather than 'blood and iron', this made Prussia's rise to power appear even more irreversible than in older, politically oriented historical writing. Yet there have always been alternative views as well as views of alternatives, even if often ignored. Historians realized that in 1945 nation states can be unmade; in 1989–90 that they can be re-made. We have not yet lost our sense of surprise at that second unification. This sense needs to be projected into our understanding of the first unification.

I will argue that Bismarck was an 'outsider' and that the views on Prussia and the national question he propounded in the 1850s were unrealistic. However, the world rather than Bismarck's view of it changed rapidly between then and the mid-1860s. Now his realism became one of substance as well as tone. Under these changed conditions Bismarck's methods and objectives could be successfully put into practice, although the risk of failure remained high. This essay presents an argument; not all historians would agree with it; and it focuses on explaining unification rather than surveying the years between 1850 and 1871.

I Bismarck the outsider

Bismarck came to political prominence in 1847 when Frederick William IV summoned a United Diet. There was conflict over whether the crown should concede a written constitution. This was related to the previous king's promise of a constitution during the war against Napoleon. Royalists insisted Prussians had been animated by monarchical and religious loyalties; the liberal majority stressed the prospect of a constitution. Bismarck shocked both sides by declaring that Prussians did not care about such things but were preoccupied with material issues. His cynicism about political principles was already clear.

However, he was a monarchist, indeed in 1848 an outspoken reactionary. For him the revolution was the work of urban mobs and intellectuals, enjoying some success only because of the failure of nerve on the part of the king and his advisers. The rural population had no interest in the revolution. A recovery of nerve, a whiff of grapeshot and mobilizing the conservative majority would suffice to restore order.

The revolution was swiftly defeated, if not quite as Bismarck advocated. His reward for vigorous royalism was appointment as Prussian ambassador to the restored Diet of the German Confederation in 1851. This was a remarkable decision. Bismarck had attended university with a view to a career in the civil service but had soon abandoned that and retired to the life of a provincial squire. The constitutional and revolutionary politics of 1847–50 plucked him from obscurity. He became an ambassador without working his passage as bureaucrat or courtier and without training in the arts of diplomacy. He was an outsider and remained suspicious of court and bureaucracy all his life.

In the Diet Bismarck confronted Habsburg supremacy. In 1850 Austria had compelled Prussia to abandon a forward policy in northern and central Germany, in turn relinquishing her ambition of integrating non-German territories with the Confederation. The Confederation was restored and Austria intended to dominate it. Bismarck wanted to end Austrian primacy and regarded the Confederation as an absurdity. The other states had no independence and survived only by balancing Prussia against Austria. The most sensible arrangement would be two territorial spheres of influence dominated by Prussia and Austria. Quite where the boundary would be drawn, how Austria was to be persuaded to accept this 'solution', how the accompanying international complications were to be handled: these were matters to be settled according to circumstances. Bismarck's fixity of purpose was accompanied by flexibility of method. Some of his ideas dismayed principled conservatives, like agreements with Louis Napoleon and with nationalists opposed to the Habsburg dynasty.

II   The improbability of Prussian success, 1851–1862

No matter how flexible Bismarck's methods, they had no chance of success through the 1850s.

II.1   Population

The population of Prussia in 1850 was 16 million, that of the German part of the Habsburg Empire 17 million, with another 16 million in non-German parts. Prussia's population was increasing more quickly than Austria's but remained inferior. She lagged far behind Russia (70 million) and France (35 million), although in the latter case this was an improvement upon the 3:1 ratio of 1820. Population is not a direct indication of state power but it is the base on which that power rests.

II.2   Economy

Prussian economic growth was rapid in the 1850s and 1860s, involving the emergence of new industries associated with coal, and iron and steel production. Prussia's growth outstripped that of Austria, France and Russia but this should not be exaggerated. An attempt at calculating shares of world manufacturing output in 1860 yields the following percentages: Britain – 20, France – 8, Russia – 7, Prussia – 5, Austria – 4. These are very rough but if anything exaggerate Prussia's share by equating her with the subsequent Second Empire. (This is a constant irritation with pre-1871 'German' statistics.) Prussia in 1860 had about the same proportion of her labour force (20 per cent) in manufacturing industry as France. Austria and France were not economically stagnant; rather they were not as dynamic as Prussia.

This dynamism enabled Prussia to dominate the German customs union (*Zollverein*). After 1848 the *Zollverein* was used in conflicts between Prussia and Austria, with struggles over the entry of Hanover and the terms of a renewal of the Zollverein treaty for another 12 years. Prussia used her predominance to prevent Austria joining. Struggle over control of the *Zollverein* flared up again in the early 1860s. This demonstrated Prussian economic influence over other states. However, it is not clear how this might be translated into political domination, especially as most of those states supported Austria to counterbalance economic subordination.

A second advantage lay in qualitative features of Prussian growth. By 1860 Prussia produced more steel than France, Russia or Austria. Prussia in 1850 had a more extensive railway network than France, Russia or Austria and by 1860 this had increased in relation to Austria. Given the importance of new methods of transportation and weaponry in the wars of unification, these indicators of Prussian superiority were vital. Prussian military leadership proved better able to harness these achievements than their opponents.

Yet such advantages had not translated themselves into political and military power by 1860. Government expenditure was a lower proportion of GNP than Britain or Austria and about the same as France. In 1860 Prussian expenditure on her army (36 per cent) was a lower proportion of state expenditure than in France (39 per cent) or Austria (51 per cent). That is reflected in army sizes: Austria – 306,000; France – 608,000; Prussia – 201,000.

II.3   Diplomacy and war

One must also consider how states related to one another. After 1848–9 it appeared that the settlement of 1814–15 had been restored. Russia had played her part as 'policeman' of Europe, helping Austria repress the Hungarian rebellion. Britain pursued a policy of maintaining a peaceful status quo in Europe, though not prepared to intervene directly. The German Confederation was restored under Austrian leadership. The one significant difference was that France was now ruled by a Bonaparte who did not accept the 1814–15 settlement.

The Crimean War (1854–6) destroyed the old alliance against France. She fought with Britain against Russia. The result was to push Russia out of European affairs and cause a breakdown in Austro-Russian relations. Austria had adopted a policy of armed neutrality, but one biased against Russia because of concerns about southeast Europe. The war revealed the importance of steam-powered transport. In 1813–15 Russia marched troops across Europe as quickly as any other state. In the mid-1850s she could not send soldiers or equipment to the Crimea as quickly as Britain and France with their steamships.

A consequence of the weakening of Austria was the war of 1859–60 against France and Piedmont. France now pursued a forward policy in Europe, presenting herself as the champion of national movements against the dynastic status quo. Austria was left isolated. The rapid transport of soldiers to northern Italy and deployment of new weapons produced devastating results on the battlefield. Austria sued rapidly for peace at the cost of Lombardy, sparking off a process that led to an Italian kingdom by the end of 1860.

Bismarck urged Berlin to exploit these Austrian setbacks. The Prussian government, for conservative and pragmatic reasons, declined to act as he suggested. Neutrality was adopted during the Crimean War as Prussia had no wish to alienate the other powers. In 1859 it was considered impossible to ally with Bonapartist France against a fellow German dynasty. As the war took on a national character in Italy it inspired thoughts of something similar in Germany, but not direct action against Austria. Instead Prussia demanded parity with Austria as the price of support, in particular command of the army on the border with France. Austria refused such demands and Prussia remained neutral. Objectively Austria's position was weakened but she remained more populous and powerful than Prussia in 1860. Bismarck had been transferred to Russia by a government anxious to take him away from the sensitive post in Frankfurt.

II.4   Culture

The failure of the German National Assembly in 1848–9 demonstrated support for national unity but also how limited and divided that was and how formidable were the obstacles.[2] People were more concerned with other issues and did not see the relevance of a nation state to these. Catholics looked to Austria; Protestants to Prussia. Inhabitants of smaller states feared domination from either Vienna or Berlin. Democrats opposed an authoritarian nation state. Liberals wanted to preserve state powers but to harmonize arrangements so that people could enjoy common rights throughout Germany. Each viewpoint commanded minority support but was regarded with indifference or hostility by many more. Those who wanted unity were compelled by failure to be more realistic. Given the lack of popular support and the hostility of the Habsburg dynasty to strengthening national institutions, they looked to Prussia.

There was little scope for a national movement during the 1850s. Counter-revolution made open politics impossible. Governments restricted the scope for cultural activity which might have promoted a sense of national identity. Economic growth brought increased migration, urban growth and better communications which could have promoted national identity. But most migration was short-distance and within state boundaries. The emigration of many political activists to the USA depleted the ranks of a national movement. Amongst elites people were more drawn together at state than national level, for example through the operation of a Prussian constitution from December 1848.

Towards the end of the 1850s a relaxation of controls allowed more communication across state boundaries. State restrictions had not prevented the emergence of a national press dominated by liberals. Associations with a national commitment such as choral societies, sharp-shooting clubs, gymnastic and workers' educational associations had a larger membership and geographical spread than ever before. The extent of national feeling was vividly expressed at the centenary of Schiller's birth in November 1859. Many people participated throughout Germany and in German settlements in Europe and overseas to celebrate someone who, both in his life and art, was taken to embody the idea of cultural nationality as something transcendent, even religious. Yet this involved at most a few hundred thousand people. It is difficult to know how many were inspired by the message propagated by the educated nationalists who organized the celebrations. In any case, these nationalists had little idea of how to turn their ideas to political account. Nevertheless, the centre of gravity of this movement was in Protestant regions, concentrated in northern and central Germany, which could be regarded as favourable to Prussia.

So there was no massive national sentiment in favour of a Prussian forward policy in German in 1860. The war in Italy and the liberalization of domestic politics in Prussia with the accession of William to power (Regent 1858; King 1861) encouraged a national movement which looked to Prussia for leadership, expressed in the formation of the National Association (*Nationalverein*) in 1859. But the *Nationalverein* never exceeded 25,000 members and was politically divided. Admittedly it could appeal to the expanding cluster of cultural associations and operate through a network of elite organizations and liberal parties in various states. Nevertheless, this does not suggest huge support. Outside Prussia even nationalists who looked to Prussia for leadership wanted to see a liberalization of Prussian institutions first.

II.5   Crisis in Prussia

The optimism associated with the 'New Era' soon faded. William was acutely aware of military weakness which precluded any ambitious foreign policy. He had been alarmed by the decrepit nature of the army revealed by partial mobilization in 1859. He was determined to increase the size of the army and length of service. Prussia's army was, uniquely amongst the major powers, a conscript army based on short-term service (two and a half years), followed by two years in the line reserves and fourteen in the reserve army (Landwehr). Prussia did not call up all those liable to service. William wanted to increase the call-up rate; extend line service to three years, line reserve service to five years, followed by eleven years in the Landwehr which would be reduced to garrison and rear-line duties. The reforms would more than double the size of the regular army, greatly increase that of the reserves, involve a massive expansion in the number of officers, the formation of many new infantry and cavalry regiments and vastly increased expenditure.

The liberal majority of the Prussian lower house (the Landtag) could not accept this. Liberals recognized the need for a stronger army but objected to the thrust of the reforms, for example, marginalizing the Landwehr, especially if the army remained firmly under royal control without parliamentary influence.

William refused to compromise. Parliament refused to approve budgets. A series of elections produced ever-larger and more determined liberal majorities. By the autumn of 1862 William was contemplating abdication. Bismarck had recently been transferred from St Petersburg to Paris where he remained in close contact with conservative circles in Berlin concerned that the king ride out the storm. The Minister of War, Albert von Roon, advised William that one man had the nerve and ability to do this for him, a man who had vigorously, even recklessly, defended royal prerogatives against parliamentary presumption. Bismarck was called to Berlin and appointed Minister-President in September.

The odds against success, either in the domestic crisis or the realization of his expansionist dreams, were huge. Public and parliamentary opinion, much of it shaped by wealthy groups with access to major newspapers and periodicals, opposed his appointment. Without military reform Prussia remained the weakest of the major powers. National sentiment, itself weak and divided, rebuffed overtures from a man known only for his defence of Prussian dynasticism. Austria, after setbacks in 1859–60, had embarked on constitutional reform and was proposing changes in the German Confederation designed to enlist national support.

III The process of unification

Bismarck was appointed to solve the domestic crisis. He withdrew the pending budget but collected revenues, arguing that in the event of a stand-off between crown and parliament the executive must continue to run the country on the basis of laws already passed. Parliament rejected this novel theory ('the constitutional gap') but, as it also rejected extra-parliamentary resistance such as a tax boycott, Bismarck overrode that opposition. He tried to interfere with parliamentary immunity and to bribe or bully journalists to undermine liberal opponents. Bismarck probably wanted some compromise to end the crisis but the king and many conservatives would not countenance this.

The domestic crisis overshadowed all else. When Bismarck, addressing a parliamentary committee, made the speech containing the famous assertion that an effective German policy would have to be based on 'iron and blood' rather than parliamentary resolutions, he saw himself offering the liberals a realistic solution to the national question. However, liberals saw it as a threat to them and, given Bismarck's weak position, an empty one. His one major foreign policy move, support for Russian suppression of a Polish uprising in 1863, alienated liberal opinion. In 1863 Bismarck was confronted by an assertive German policy on Austria's part and had great difficulty persuading William not to attend a congress of German princes. Only the Schleswig-Holstein issue enabled Bismarck to escape from this unpromising situation.

III.1   The war against Denmark

Schleswig and Holstein were two duchies ruled in personal union by the Danish crown. Holstein was German-speaking and a member of the Confederation. Schleswig had German and Danish speakers and was not in the Confederation. Danish nationalists claimed Schleswig; German nationalists insisted on the indivisibility of the duchies. The succession of Christian IX to the Danish throne on the death of Frederick VII on 15 November 1863 did not automatically confer his succession to rule over the duchies as well. Christian IX signed a charter incorporating Schleswig into Denmark. German nationalists responded by demanding the title of Duke of Schleswig-Holstein be granted to Frederick, Duke of Augustenburg, who would bring both duchies into the Confederation.

The matter had been subject to international treaty since 1850. The major powers wanted the Treaty of London observed and were relieved when Austria and Prussia signalled this as their aim. The Danish government, under nationalist pressure, refused to comply with the treaty and in late 1863 the Confederation sent troops into Holstein. Denmark hoped for international support, if only because of concern about sea routes. British policy was undecided and unprepared for unilateral action. Napoleon was happy to let a crisis brew which he might exploit. Russia, though broadly pro-Danish, was unhappy with her nationalist intransigence and concerned to maintain good relations with Austria and Prussia as she suppressed the Polish insurrection.

Consequently there was no concerted international resistance when Prussian and Austrian troops invaded Schleswig at the end of January 1864, especially as their avowed aim was to enforce the terms of the Treaty of London, and they did not dispute Danish rights in Schleswig and Holstein or support the Augustenburg claim. No diplomatic advances were made during an armistice between April and June, the war was resumed and Denmark compelled to hand over the duchies to Austria and Prussia in October.

German national sentiment was marginalized once Austria and Prussia took control in January 1864. German nationalists were appalled at how Berlin and Vienna disavowed Augustenburg and treated the issue as a matter of treaties rather than national interest. Occasionally Austria or Prussia appealed to nationalism but in a cynical and self-serving way. For Austria the main advantage of sacrificing the good opinion of the national movement was that Prussia did so too. Vienna was happiest to pursue a policy of 'dualism' with Prussia which fitted with Confederal traditions and ensured dynastic control.

Unfortunately for Austria, Schleswig-Holstein was geographically remote and of no direct interest. Once the area was under joint Austro-Prussian control it was impossible for Austria to shape events. Austria sought support from Prussia on issues such as entry into the *Zollverein* and in Italy in exchange for giving Prussia a freer hand in Schleswig-Holstein. When that failed the leader of the dualist policy in Vienna, Rechberg, resigned in October 1864. Austria became more assertive and bid for nationalist support by taking up the Augustenburg cause. Opposition from Prussia made war appear likely but this was posponed by the Gastein Convention of August 1865 establishing separate military governments: Austria in Holstein, Prussia in Schleswig. Austria abandoned her constitutional experiment and the government made concessions to Hungarian demands for greater autonomy. Austria was clearing the decks for action in Germany.

It is doubtful whether Bismarck had any clear objective in November 1863. He could not afford to alienate the major powers and could only take an active position in defence of international treaty obligations in alliance with Austria. However, following military success Bismarck could contemplate annexation of the duchies. War removed treaty obligations. By keeping conditions for settlement vague or unacceptable to Denmark he ensured the continuation of military occupation. When forced to go along with the Augustenburg option once it was clear Danish authority would not be restored, he hedged it about with conditions which made it impossible for Frederick to accept. The result was *de facto* military occupation. The principal issue now was whether Bismarck was prepared to confront Austria and take direct control in the duchies. This appeared to be the case in early 1865 as Austria took up the Augustenburg cause. However, there was a powerful peace party in Berlin, including the Crown Prince. The King was proving difficult to persuade into war against a fellow German prince. There were problems raising war finance, especially given the constitutional crisis. Above all, it was not clear that the diplomatic and military balance of power favoured war. Prussia had secured no allies against Austria. The war against Denmark had proved a useful testing-ground for the military reforms and brought the Chief of the General Staff, Moltke, to the top. But many observers had been impressed with Austrian military effort. Moltke, though desirous of war with Austria, was realistic about the risks involved. In 1860 he had assumed a good chance of Habsburg success, the destruction of the defeated dynasty and major concessions to France and Russia by the victor.

Nevertheless, for Bismarck, a confrontation with Austria to settle issues in Germany was inevitable. The war against Denmark, the first military success since 1815, stimulated Prussian rather than German patriotism. Even some liberal nationalists began to see in a greater-Prussia policy a way forward. Bismarck had learnt that Britain and Russia were unlikely to interfere in crises in central Europe. He now had to ensure Austria's diplomatic isolation, secure alliances for Prussia and make the necessary financial and military preparations.

III.2   The war of 1866

The diplomatic key was France. After success in Europe in the 1850s Louis Napoleon had suffered setbacks in Mexico in the 1860s and his health was failing. The renewal of domestic opposition made success abroad important. His German policy was shaped by ideology and interest. He supported national movements, especially if he could tie them to France. This made it difficult to cooperate with the Habsburg Empire. His interests would be served by a breakdown of Austro-Prussian dualism which should provide opportunities for diplomatic and territorial profit.

Bismarck met with Napoleon at Biarritz in October 1865. Napoleon was difficult to pin down. He favoured some extension of Prussian influence in northern Germany. A weakening of Austria might help bring his Italian policy to completion. However, he had no wish to see Prussia become too powerful and pursued ideas of balancing this by the enlargement of some of the medium states. He was not averse to territorial gains; Belgium and the Rhinelands were vaguely mentioned. The policy was Bismarckian: no fixed plan but a determination to create and exploit favourable opportunities. It took little genius on Bismarck's part to secure Napoleon's good wishes.

Napoleon could help matters forward. Italian unification would only be complete with the removal of Papal authority in Rome and the recovery of Venetia. France backed the Papacy with soldiers and Catholic opinion in France made it impossible to abandon that policy. Venetia therefore became the principal objective. Prussia wanted Italian leverage against Austria and Italy had the same use for Prussia. In March 1866, with tensions mounting in Schleswig-Holstein, General Govone came to Berlin to secure an alliance against Austria. Both sides were suspicious that each would use the other to obtain concessions from Austria at their own expense. With Napoleon's support an agreement limited to three months stipulated that Italy would go to war with Austria if Prussia did. Prussia did not make the same commitment but agreed that, in the event of war, neither side would make peace until both had made territorial gains. This was to be Venetia for Italy and some unspecified equivalent for Prussia. Napoleon's calculation was made clear by a remark he made at the time:

> In this way [by means of the Prussian-Italian agreement] Italy will get Venice, and France will benefit by the conflict of the two powers whose alliance hems her in. Once the struggle has begun France can throw her weight into the balance and must obviously become the arbitrator and master of the situation.[3]

Napoleon also engaged in discussions with Austria and vaguely indicated the support he could offer in the event of war with Prussia. Ideas of enlarging states like Bavaria or Württemberg or even creating an independent Rhenish state attracted Napoleon. This should not offend national sentiments (indeed it was more in line with federalist views than Hohenzollern or Habsburg domination) and would secure client states for France. Austria agreed that Venetia would be ceded to Italy. Italy was in the fortunate position that both Prussia and Austria had promised her Venetia, but only after a war.

This commitment made it clear that Austria regarded maintenance of her position in Germany as the first priority. She was not prepared to negotiate division into territorial spheres of influence. Her preferred policy was dualism with Prussia. Although she flirted with more radical policies – support for Confederal reform, a direct imposition of Habsburg hegemony – these are best understood as departures from normal policy or ways of pressurizing Prussia into returning to dualism. Accordingly Austrian war aims in 1866 were less clear-cut than those of Prussia. Indeed, some in Austria regarded war as the most extreme method of compelling Prussia to return to dualism rather than as providing an alternative solution. This helps explain why all the medium German states (with the exception of Baden which abstained) voted in the Federal Diet in support of Austria in June 1866. Meanwhile the national movement was paralysed as German civil war approached.

Most contemporaries assumed an Austrian victory. The shift of power towards Prussia was taking place rapidly and was hardly appreciated. While Prussian military expenditure had doubled since 1860, Austria's had halved. The Italian alliance compelled Austria to divide her armies, sending 100,000 to the south, leaving 175,000 Austrian soldiers and 32,000 Saxons facing 250,000 Prussians in the north. The rapid collapse of the Hanoverian and Bavarian armies removed them from the equation.

The new capacities of mass mobilization were realized. Nearly half a million soldiers were transported to the battlefields of northern Bohemia, more than were present at the greatest of the Napoleonic battles fought at Leipzig in October 1813. The speed with which this was done was unprecedented. Prussia did best. One single-track railway ran north from Vienna into Bohemia; by contrast, Prussia used five lines to bring her troops southwards. Moltke adopted the novel and risky strategy of keeping his forces separate for faster movement, only concentrating them on the eve of battle. Consequently the Austrian commander, Benedek, was always on the defensive, reacting to situations created by Prussia. Even if there were moments when he could have counter-attacked to devastating effect, this defensive posture made it improbable that he would. Although Austrian artillery and cavalry matched that of Prussia, the new breech-loading rifle gave the infantry a decisive advantage against the Austrian doctrine of 'cold steel'. It was only possible to make and supply such a weapon with the new manufacturing technology now available and only Prussia with her well-educated and short-term conscript army could contemplate handling the problems of retraining and discipline involved.

III.3   Germany after Königgrätz

The Habsburg dynasty had no stomach for prolonged war after the first heavy defeat. Bismarck was anxious to accommodate this preference although he had to persuade William and Moltke not to continue the war, forcing the Habsburgs into renewed resistance and opening up possibilities of international interference. Austria suffered no territorial loss in Germany.

Hanover, the Electorate of Hesse and the Duchy of Nassau were less fortunate; they were annexed to Prussia, their princes deposed and, along with Schleswig and Holstein, transformed into Prussian provinces. The Free and Imperial City of Frankfurt am Main was also seized. A more extended territorial sphere of influence was established in the form of the North German Confederation comprising all the other German states north of the river Main. Bismarck brought the south German states into a secret military alliance. These states were also members of the *Zollverein*.

Bismarck recognized there was a limit to how much Prussia could absorb, even without diplomatic obstacles. In a memorandum written during the crisis of 1859 he had declared that Prussia should: 'march southwards with our entire army carrying frontier posts in our big packs. We can plant them either on the Bodensee or as far south as Protestantism is the dominant faith.'[4] The sense that Catholic populations would be difficult to absorb, whatever the common nationality, is clear. He even

Map 7.1 Germany and Austria–Hungary, 1867

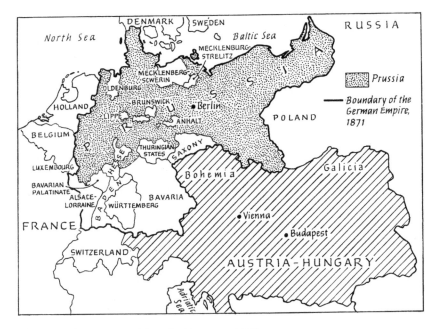

Map 7.2 Germany and Austria–Hungary, 1871

argued against taking part of Protestant Franconia from Bavaria because of the state loyalty that had been developed. This sensitivity to opinion expressed itself in two striking innovations in relation to Prussia and the North German Confederation.

In Prussia on the same day as the battle of Königgrätz (3 July), whose outcome was yet unknown, new Landtag elections were held. The liberal opposition was defeated by a surge of Prussian patriotism. Bismarck, basking in military triumph, returned to Berlin and a more compliant parliament. Surely royal prerogative would be asserted and parliament put in its place. Instead Bismarck introduced an Indemnity Bill. The government would put its measures to parliament for approval in the normal way; and parliament would not seek retribution for its treatment since 1862. It remained open to the government to resume non-parliamentary rule under the terms of the 'constitutional gap' doctrine. Nevertheless this was a symbolic concession to liberalism which angered conservatives. Bismarck believed that strong, stable government rested on the support of major social forces. These were never precisely defined but bourgeois liberals were clearly included. Bismarck's anti-liberal measures were not attempts to destroy liberalism but to force it into cooperation with him. Most liberal deputies accepted the olive branch, forming the National Liberal Party and leaving the oppositional minority in the Progressive Party.

Bismarck regarded this constitutionalism as the best way of integrating the new provinces. Hanoverians were not asked to exchange a Guelph for a Hohenzollern but subjection to a feeble and antiquated kingdom for citizenship in a poweful and modern constitutional monarchy. Although some (e.g., Hanover's Catholic minority) rejected the offer, the new provinces developed into powerful strongholds of National Liberalism.

Similar considerations informed Bismarck's policy in the North German Confederation. With war approaching in 1866 Bismarck declared that Prussia supported reform of the Confederation, including a popularly elected parliament. This seemed unlikely from a man ruling in defiance of his own parliament. Bismarck was, however, perfectly serious and the constitution drawn up for the North German Confederation included this provision. His intentions are not clear. Analysis of elections to the Landtag had suggested that liberals were not genuinely popular. Bismarck had long argued that the monarchy could be popular. The new parliament, the Reichstag, could be used as a counterbalance to the Prussian Landtag. Anyway, Bismarck did not appear to be risking much. The Reichstag had limited powers. The legislative initiative was in the hands of the Bundesrat whose president was the King of Prussia and which consisted of state delegations with sufficient Prussian votes to veto unwelcome measures.

The military component of the budget – over 90 per cent of Confederal expenditure – was exempt from parliamentary control. Nevertheless this was a bold move and laid the basis for the development of legitimate mass politics in Germany.

III.4   From North German Confederation to war with France

Bismarck had to integrate new Prussia into old Prussia, consolidate the North German Confederation and bring the south German states into his orbit. He also had to block revanchism in Austria and deal with French reactions to the unexpected outcome of 1866.

Agreement with the National Liberals was the key to the first two tasks. This party emerged as the largest in the Reichstag. An ambitious legislative programme was carried through including unifying measures in such matters as currency, weights and measures, commercial and labour relations law and common citizenship rights. Many constraints on a market economy were removed.

This was part of a burgeoning national movement which was Protestant, progressive and optimistic. The National Liberals believed history was on their side and that Bismarck was helping construct the modern state and society which would eventually sweep aside his kind of rule and values. Bismarck also emphasized the national and constitutional character of the Confederation to appeal to opinion in southern Germany and resist French claims to 'German' territory.

The bid for south German support included the formation of a customs parliament in which members of the Reichstag would be joined by popularly elected deputies from the south. The plan backfired. The elections provided Catholics, state loyalists and democrats with the opportunity to mobilize anti-Prussian sentiment. This unlikely alliance won a majority of seats. Strong anti-Prussian feeling continued to be expressed in south Germany up to 1870.

In Austria a new Chancellor, formerly Prime Minister of Saxony, Count Beust, aimed to regain influence in Germany. Under a new constitution of 1867 the Hungarian half of the empire was granted a large measure of autonomy on terms which benefited the Magyar majority. The Magyars opposed any ambitious German policy. This, plus financial crisis, the growing influence of Czechs in the western half of the Empire and a renewed concern with affairs in southeastern Europe, constrained Beust. He encouraged France in anti-Prussian policies but could offer little in return, especially if this might appear anti-German. While Prussian relations with Russia remained good, there was no help to be had there.

This left France isolated, especially as Britain regarded France as the major threat to European stability, a view strengthened by Napoleon's pursuit of profit from the new German arrangements. His government was unpopular at home and there was concern about the creation of a new power whose territories extended to the left bank of the Rhine. Ambitions about Belgium and the Rhinelands were set aside. By 1867 Napoleon was concentrating on Luxembourg which was bound in personal union with the Netherlands. The King of the Netherlands was prepared to sell Luxembourg to France but only with Prussian agreement. Once the matter became public, Bismarck used the storm of protest in Germany to insist that he could not give way.

Napoleon liberalized at home. The new, popular ministers who came into government in 1869–70 were more anti-Prussian than their predecessors. Military reforms expanded and improved the army. By 1870 France felt confident. Even if she began war alone she envisaged that other powers like Austria and Denmark could be drawn in.

Preparedness for war and sensitivity to further national affronts from Prussia were sparked off by news on 2 July 1870 that Prince Leopold, a member of the House of Hohenzollern, had been offered the Spanish crown. The French were sure this was another Prussian plot and demanded not only withdrawal of the candidacy but a clear undertaking that Prussia would never again engage in such a policy. The former was secured; the latter was used by Bismarck to justify a war in which France appeared the aggressor.

Did Bismarck plan for war with France? One cannot give definite answers about motives but can simply note various points. Bismarck's national policy in southern Germany was in disarray by early 1870. The idea of reviving the imperial title had foundered, partly on objections from the kings of Bavaria and Württemberg. Those governments faced crises over the issue of introducing Prussian-style military reforms. Moltke advised that the military balance of power would worsen. Prussia had further modernized her army after 1867. The extension of Prussia, the creation of the North German Confederation and the military alliance with the south German states meant Bismarck could call upon demographic resources roughly equal to those of France and the backing of a stronger economy. But the French were making military progress, had popular support for war against Prussia and might in the future secure alliances. There were good reasons, therefore, for settling issues through war with France. The Hohenzollern candidacy must be seen in this context. Bismarck denied knowing of the candidacy until just before it was made public. For many years historians were denied access to relevant documents. Once these were seen, after 1945, it was clear that Bismarck had lied. He had known of the matter from the outset and advised support for the candidacy.

It is going too far to say he did this to bring about war. As Bismarck pointed out, the French overreacted both in their judgement of the significance of a Hohenzollern on the Spanish throne and in demanding Prussian undertakings for the future. More likely is that Bismarck wanted another iron in the fire to be used if expedient and dropped if necessary. In July 1870 he decided to use it. Concern about continued French pressure, reversing slippage in the south German states and cutting the ground from under Austrian revanchism all led Bismarck to this policy.

The response of public opinion in Germany to the outbreak of war was gratifying. Strong anti-French sentiments were expressed. South German and Catholic soldiers fought as bravely as Protestants from the north. Yet we should not exaggerate. We know little about popular opinion which should not be confused with public opinion, in a press dominated by National Liberals. Common anti-French sentiment which led many hostile to Prussia and Bismarck to rally behind the national cause masked conflicting views about how Germany should be organized after the war.

The war began as in 1866, though on a more massive scale. German mobilisation was more rapid than that of France. In under three weeks over one million soldiers had reported for duty and nearly half a million had been moved to the French frontier, whereas the French had fewer than 250,000 soldiers in the army on the Rhine. France never recovered and was always on the back-foot, reacting to German moves. There were moments when action against divided German forces might have turned the tide but in the confusion of war it was expecting too much for such high-risk decisions to be taken. By early September the French had lost decisive battles and many soldiers. Although France continued to raise armies, they lacked the weapons, officers and experienced cadres lost in that first phase. War was no longer a matter of improvization, with chances of recovering from early setbacks, as in the revolutionary and Napoleonic period. War was about the capacity to send huge numbers of men with highly destructive fire-power quickly into the territory of the enemy and to smash that enemy before he was ready.

Where the war diverged from 1866 was in length and bitterness. This was a national, not a civil war. Bismarck was not concerned to save the Bonapartist state as he had been the Habsburg crown. He mistrusted French undertakings and thought only superior power would prevent a reversal of German triumph. Achieving that superiority included annexing Alsace-Lorraine and imposing a large indemnity. These objectives could be pursued at leisure as no other power was prepared to intervene.

Nevertheless, Bismarck did not seek the total military destruction of France as advocated by Moltke.

V The new German state

Once victory was secured Bismarck could turn his attention to the entry of the south German states into a national state. There was no question of annexation as in 1867. The constitution was founded upon treaties made separately with each of the states. State rights and differences were respected.[5]

The imperial title was assumed by the King of Prussia. The dynastic emphasis was expressed in the foundation ceremony at Versailles. The Emperor was surrounded by fellow German princes, army officers and high state officials. The nation, including its parliamentary representatives, watched from outside as the dynasties constructed a nation state which forcibly excluded Austrian Germans and included Danish, Polish and French speakers. The imperial state was a thin layer of government super-imposed on the states and heavily dependent on Prussia. The new state was reluctant to adopt national symbols. Manipulating the various conflicting institutions to secure his own power was Bismarck, the loner, the outsider, but surrounded with a nimbus of genius which raised him above the level of any other figure in Europe between 1815 and 1917.

This state has to be understood in terms of its sudden and violent creation. It was not the product of a steady convergence between power and culture, state institutions and national sentiments. As late as 1860 Prussia was in no position to challenge for dominance in Germany. Rapid changes in international relations, economic and technological perfor-mance, and the nature of war, opened up a brief window of opportunity for Prussia in the mid-1860s. It seems likely that Prussia would have soon lost these advantages, especially as other states came to appreciate their significance. The sentiment of nationality would have continued to grow in importance as this was a pan-European phenomenon and a central feature of modern society. However, there was no dominant political expression of that sentiment, neither territorial nor institutional. National feelings were ignored rather than exploited up to 1867 as a political genius, brought to leadership in Prussia through a domestic crisis, pursued with great flexibility objectives he had fixed upon a decade earlier. What had been impracticable then, now had become possible. Once the possible is made actual, the temptation is to make it appear inevitable. But there were always other possibilities. Germany was becoming more national but there was nothing preordained about how it became a national state.

Notes:

1. See Stefan Berger, 'The German Tradition of Historiography, 1800–1995' in Fulbrook, ed., *German History since 1800* (1997).
2. See Chapter 6 by Siemann, above, as well as my essay 'The National Idea in Modern German History' in Fulbrook, ed., *German History since 1800*, pp. 556–84.
3. Quoted in Heinrich Friedjung, *The Struggle for Supremacy in Germany 1859–1866* (1935; re-issued 1966), pp. 113–14.
4. Bismarck, *Gesammelte Werke* (1924–35), vol XIV, document 724, Bismarck to Gustav von Alvensleben, 23 April/5 May 1859.
5. For further details see the next chapter.

Select bibliography

E. Hobsbawn, *The Age of Capital* (1975) for European background. T. Hamerow, *The Social Foundations of German Unification 1858–1871*, 2 vols (1969, 1972) is compendious. J. Sheehan, *German History 1770–1866* (1989) is superb. G. Craig, *Germany 1866–1945* (1978) is strong on political and military history. For those who can read German the most recent work that focuses specifically on the two decades culminating in unification is Harm-Hinrich Brandt, *Deutsche Geschichte: Entscheidung über die Nation* (1999).

For European diplomacy, W. E. Mosse, *The European Great Powers and the German Question 1848–1871* (1958) is still useful. On war and diplomacy, see W. Carr, *The Wars of German Unification* (1991). For Austria, see F. R. Bridge, *The Habsburg Monarchy among the Great Powers 1815–1918* (1990). For France, see R. Magraw, *France 1815–1914: The Bourgeois Century* (1983).

On nationalism, see the survey by H. Schulze, *The Course of German Nationalism: From Frederick the Great to Bismarck 1763—1867* (1991). D. Düding, 'The Nineteenth-Century German Nationalist Movement as a Movement of Societies', in H. Schulze, ed., *Nation-building in Central Europe* (1987), pp.19–49 is useful.

For the wars, see G. Wawro, *The Austro-Prussian War: Austria's War with Prussia and Italy in 1866* (1996) and M. Howard, *The Franco-Prussian War: The German invasion of France, 1870–1871* (1961). For a broader approach, see D. Showalter, *Railroads and Rifles: Soldiers, Technology and the Unification of Germany* (1986).

For Prussia and Bismarck, see: L. Gall, *Bismarck: The White Revolutionary*, vol. I (1986); and O. Pflanze, *Bismarck and the Development of Germany*: vol. I: *The Period of Unification 1815–1871* (1990).

Kennedy, P., *The Rise and Fall of the Great Powers: Economic Change and Military Conflict from 1500 to 2000* (1988) and M. Mann, *The Sources of Social Power* vol. II: *The Rise of Classes and Nation-States, 1760–1914* (1993) place German unification into general and theoretical, if different, contexts.

I consider the subject at greater length in J. Breuilly, *The Formation of the First German Nation-State, 1800–1871* (1996) which includes references to further secondary literature in English and German.

Part II

1871–1918

Introduction to Part II: 1871–1918

The German Second Empire was proclaimed in the palace of Versailles in January 1871. The site is significant – stressing the dynastic nature of the new state and that it was the product of success in war. The same state ended its life in November 1918 with admission of defeat in war and a revolution in favour of a republic. Not surprisingly the centrality of war and monarchy in both the foundation and destruction of the first German nation-state have shaped much of the historical writing on the Second Empire. This similarity of beginning and end has in turn to be related to the tremendous changes that took place in Germany over this half century. There is also the problem of setting the history of Germany into a broader context, asking how much that history resembled the history of other societies and states, as well as considering the significance of interactions between Germany and other countries.

There are five chapters in this section. As with Part I there is a rough distinction between political, social and economic, and cultural and intellectual history.

Political history is the main concern of the two chapters by Lerman. In Chapter 8, on Bismarckian Germany, the focus is on the constitutional arrangements of the new state, the dominant position of Bismarck within these arrangements and the evolution of politics between 1871 and 1890. In Chapter 10, on Wilhelmine Germany, the concern is with the changing character of politics, especially the emergence of mass politics, the particular position Wilhelm II occupied within the political system, and the debate over German foreign policy, in particular in relation to the origins and outbreak of the First World War. In Chapter 12 Chickering takes the story of the Second Empire to its end, providing a sweeping analysis of the changes and strains to which state and society were subjected during the First World War. In Chapter 9 on social and economic history, Berghahn concentrates on the dynamic and changing character of Germany, in particular the rapid growth of population, towns and industry. Clearly this economic development and social change had important bearings on the emergence of mass politics and the capacity of the German state to bid for much greater influence in both Europe and the wider world. Finally, in Chapter 11 on the cultural history of the Second Empire, Jefferies draws attention to the great variety of styles and schools in art, architecture and other cultural fields, offering amongst other things an important corrective to one-dimensional representations of imperial German culture as reflecting authoritarian traditionalism or cultural pessimism and having little in common with other countries.

It is not possible to cover every aspect of the history of Germany in this period, one which is second only to that of the Third Reich in the amount of research and volume of publications it has attracted in recent decades. 'Germany' now comes to mean the territory of the Second Empire. Habsburg Germany tends to disappear from view, figuring only as the hapless ally of 1914 or the cultural hothouse of Vienna. Yet, given the increasing dominance of the national in politics, society and international relations, it is difficult to see how one could proceed otherwise. Popular culture is briefly addressed by Jefferies who considers the commercialization of culture, and by Berghahn who alludes to the rising expectations of ordinary Germans who experienced material improvements and could exercise more choice in such matters as where they lived and what job they did. However, there was no opportunity to look systematically at the subject of popular culture. The same point applies to the increased inter-penetration of state and society, for example in terms of the development of welfare and public health policies, although these are touched upon by Berghahn.

Interpretations of the Second Empire have been greatly influenced by the manner of its demise and the question of any continuities, similarities or connections between it and the Third Reich. At one extreme there is the view that 1871 had seen the creation of a very peculiar kind of state with a distinct authoritarian and nationalist character which, combined with increased political centralization, rapid industrial growth and military innovation, represented a threat to peace and progress, a threat which manifested itself in war in 1914 and again in 1939. At the other extreme is the view that Germany was but one national state and industrializing society amongst others, that the path towards war in 1914 was the product of multiple and conflicting policies of the European powers all together, and that the rise of Hitler to power and the outbreak of a second world war need to be seen in terms of pan-European developments peculiar to the post-1918 period. Neither extreme is sustainable. Good detailed historical study rather grapples with complexities which undermine such extreme positions. However, that has by no means led to consensus, as will become clear to the reader of these essays. The history of the first German state remains a lively and contested one.

8

Bismarckian Germany and the structure of the German Empire

Katharine A. Lerman

The nature of the German Empire, founded by Bismarck in 1871 after three victorious Prussian wars, is central to all debates on the continuities and peculiarities in modern German history. Most obviously the impact of the First World War and defeat, the fragility of parliamentary democracy in the Weimar Republic, and the origins of the Nazi dictatorship can scarcely be assessed without an understanding of German society and political culture in the decades before 1914. Indeed, it was largely a preoccupation with Germany's responsibility for the two world wars which stimulated a revival of interest from the late 1960s in the history of the Empire. Yet the extent to which Germany followed a special or peculiar course of develop-ment which differed in key aspects from the experience of her (essentially western) European neighbours also focuses attention on the kind of state which Bismarck created. For while Germany's dynamic economic and social growth in the second half of the nineteenth century appears to locate her securely in the mainstream of western European industrializing nations, liberal historians have generally not been so sanguine about the political legacy of Bismarckian Germany.

Historical debate on the nature of the *Kaiserreich* has inevitably been overshadowed by the violent circumstances surrounding its birth in 1871 and demise in 1918, as well as by a consciousness of Germany's catastrophic impact on the international state system in the first half of the twentieth century. Once celebrated as the triumphant culmination of nearly two centuries of Prussian history, the embodiment of human progress and the vindication of the Germans' previously disappointed aspirations for nationhood, after 1945 Bismarck's creation came to be assessed primarily in negative terms. The 'unification' of Germany was a revolution, imposed from above, which defied rather than fulfilled the aspirations of the revolutionaries of 1848. Bismarck's wars signified the partition of the German nation, allowing a state to emerge which was not liberal, national or united. The Germany of 1871 was artificial and unnatural, an 'exotic plant' (Röhl) which could only be sustained in a hothouse of patriotism and war. Prussia's conquest of Germany imposed an authoritarian and illiberal vision of German national identity which could not tolerate alternative conceptions of German nationhood and permanently excluded the religious and ethnic minorities within the Empire.

For all the refinements to our picture of the Empire brought about in recent years by social historians and others intent on showing that there was 'another Germany' before 1914, most historical writing on the subject has tended to share this teleological perspective. Despite occasional pleas that Germans should not be ashamed of Imperial Germany or its history (Mommsen), the need to explain, if not the origins of the Third Reich then at least Germany's role in precipitating the First World War, dominates the historiography of the period.

Structural interpretations have proliferated in history textbooks which recite a whole litany of political, social and economic problems afflicting Germany before 1914. These are mainly rooted in socioeconomic analyses but draw on a liberal critique of the Empire which is as old as the Empire itself. In the 1970s Hans-Ulrich Wehler achieved widespread acclaim for an interpretative synthesis which drew attention to the unevenness of German industrial development, the proliferation of social tensions and antagonisms, and the growth of an interventionist state intent on preserving the political and social status quo. He argued that Bismarck's Germany was a semi-absolutist, pseudo-constitutional military monarchy, underpinned from 1879 by a powerful coalition of conservative economic interests (above all the agrarian Junkers) which determined the parameters of political change in Germany until 1918 and beyond.

Wehler's rigidly systematized and bleak representation of the Empire was soon subjected to increasing scholarly criticism. Yet attempts to 'normalize' the history of the Empire and no longer see it as a 'site of pathology' (Eley) also encountered problems. In the 1980s Geoff Eley questioned the causal relationship often drawn between politics and economics in the Empire and drew attention to the dangers inherent in an all too simplistic economic and social reductionism. But, while he successfully challenged assumptions about what constituted a 'healthy' or 'normal' development for a state and broadened the discussion of the political realm to include previously discounted social groups, his argument that Bismarck's unification, in removing the obstacles to the development of industrial capitalism in Germany, signified a German variant of a 'bourgeois revolution', ultimately only led back to the political peculiarities which distinguished Germany's history from that of her neighbours. A recent new survey of Imperial Germany by Volker Berghahn has highlighted the methodological and thematic diversity of current historical writing on the Empire and richly confirms the more general shift of interest away from political and diplomatic history. Yet although its stated aim is to write 'a history of German society in all its aspects', the central question it poses is the familiar political one of why Germany went to war in 1914.

The Empire Bismarck created survived for 47 years, slightly longer than Germany was divided after the Second World War. For all the mutations that the idea and reality of 'Germany' have undergone since 1871 and despite the existence of substantial disaffected minorities in Imperial Germany, Bismarck's 'lesser German' unification was successful in achieving a national legitimacy which it was beyond the capacity of two world wars and 40 years of division to extinguish. Clearly, as the Third Reich recedes further into history and a new, reunited Germany is consolidated, a Germany which is smaller, more democratic and less threatening within the European state system than its predecessors, historians will ask new questions and find different avenues of investigation into the nature and development of the Bismarckian Reich.

I   The Imperial German political system

The political system of the Empire tends to defy classification, so much so that some historians have disputed whether it can be described as a 'system' at all. Bismarck himself adopted this approach, emphasizing that the strength of its constitutional arrangements would lie in their distance from 'principle, system and dogmatism' and preferring to leave much unclarified, to await resolution over time and in practice. The system was certainly complicated and unique (for only Meiji Japan adopted elements of the Bismarckian constitution) and it is possible to elevate different features of quite a delicate balance as being characteristic of the whole. This has encouraged historians to describe Imperial Germany variously as a military monarchy, a pseudo-constitutional state, a semi-constitutional state with parliamentary or plebiscitary additions, a Prusso-German semi-autocracy, and a pseudo-parliamentary regime. They have also invented a whole range of epithets to convey the senses in which the constitutional arrangements of

1871 were incomplete and unfinished (Schieder), represented a compromise (Nipperdey) or signified the deferment of hard political choices (Mommsen).

Historians have scarcely found it much easier to evaluate the functioning of the political system in practice. Notwithstanding the fact that all too often assumptions have crept into the debate, for example the expectation that Germany 'should' have developed into a parliamentary monarchy on the British model, its sheer originality as well as its rather improvised development from 1871 have led to conflicting interpretations of its progressive potential. For Wehler, it mattered little whether Germany was ruled by a 'Bonapartist semi-dictatorship' under Bismarck or subject to the 'polycratic chaos' which he saw as characterizing successive governments under Kaiser Wilhelm II; the essential framework remained the military monarchy with its sham constitutionalism and its entrenched 'pre-industrial' social supporters who successfully resisted political modernization before 1918. For others, the conflict between monarchical power and parliamentary pretensions in the Empire ensured that its political history would be more dynamic than Wehler's rigid construct, with its emasculated political parties and manipulative government strategies, could encompass – although even then opinions have diverged over whether Germany became a more monarchical or more parliamentary state after Bismarck's dismissal. Perhaps inevitably the very complexity, some might say fragmentation, of the political system has facilitated a great diversity of historical approaches and interpretations. Without an eye for the whole, the respective roles of the Kaiser and his court, the army, the Reich administration, the Prussian ministerial bureaucracy, the federal states and the political parties may be deemed more or less important solely according to the perspective of the viewer.

The constitution of 1871 essentially incorporated the main provisions of the constitution of the North German Confederation which was thrashed out between Bismarck and the National Liberals in the constituent Reichstag in 1867 and had always envisaged the eventual accession of the four southern states. It was certainly not a sham, grafted on to more traditional authoritarian structures with little more than a decorative function; and nor was it dreamed up by Bismarck without advice or consultation during a couple of days on holiday (as legend has it), although it unmistakably bore the imprint of his personality and aims. The constitution contained appeals to tradition and it aimed to accommodate the diversity of German experience, preserving Germany's federal structure and leaving the constitutions of the individual member states, most crucially that of Prussia – now enlarged by the annexation of Schleswig,

Holstein, Hanover, northern Hesse, Wiesbaden and Frankfurt – untouched. But it also sought to provide a framework for the consolidation of a new nation state under Prussian leadership and it created an entirely new political structure, with national institutions, which was subject to considerable unitary pressure. In this respect it differed quite markedly from the much looser German Confederation which had preceded it.

The letter of the constitution can be briefly summarized, although a problem faced by both contemporaries and historians is that the political system never functioned as the original document intended. Sovereignty was theoretically vested in a federal council or Bundesrat which was composed of delegates from the various state governments and represented the apparently voluntary alliance of the German princes. A national parliament, the Reichstag, was established which was elected by universal and equal male suffrage, a very radical and democratic suffrage by the standards of the time. Legislation had to be passed by both the Reichstag and the Bundesrat, which combined some of the functions of a legislative upper house with its executive role. The Prussian king became the German Kaiser or Emperor, an imperial monarch who headed the political executive and the military apparatus, controlled all personnel appointments and enjoyed specific prerogatives such as the right to declare war or martial law in an emergency (though these needed subsequent Bundesrat approval). According to Article 17 of the constitution, it was the duty of the Kaiser 'to prepare and publish the laws of the Empire and to supervise their execution', but his decrees and ordinances, issued in the name of the Empire, had to be countersigned by the Reich Chancellor before they became constitutionally valid. The Reich Chancellor was the sole Reich minister mentioned in the constitution and was appointed by the monarch. He presided over the Bundesrat and, on countersigning imperial orders, assumed 'responsibility' for them, a formulation which left much room for conflicting interpretations with respect to the Chancellor's relationship with the Reichstag.

While the Bundesrat was a bulwark of federalism in the new Empire, the existence of a powerful national figurehead and a national, representative parliament was intended to counterbalance centrifugal forces and limit the self-assertion or 'particularism' of the states. The constitutional provisions can be seen as creating a delicate equilibrium, with the key institutions keeping each other in check and the Reich chancellorship, an office which Bismarck occupied continuously from 1871 to 1890, located at the fulcrum of the political system. However, Bismarck had not originally conceived of the chancellorship as a very significant post and he had not planned to assume the office himself. It was parliamentary pressure which secured the

Chancellor's right of countersignature and his, albeit limited, legal responsibility before the Reichstag. These combined powers placed the Chancellor at the centre of the decision-making process and ensured that he would carry the main burden of coordinating the complex machinery of government.

Historians have tended to focus on the liberals' failure to achieve important concessions in 1867–71 such as a centralized Reich government with ministerial responsibility to parliament or effective parliamentary control over the military budget (which accounted for over 90 per cent of central government expenditure before 1890). Nevertheless it is questionable whether most liberals wanted the introduction of parliamentary government at this juncture (if at all) and they were very doubtful about the implications of universal male suffrage. Moreover, many of the most controversial decisions were of limited duration and there was every expectation that there would be further opportunities to revise them. The liberals were successful in modifying aspects of the original draft (for example the strengthening of the position of the Reich Chancellor and the Reichstag's increased budgetary powers) but Bismarck basically determined the parameters of what could be achieved in the wake of the Prussian military victories. Yet Bismarck, too, had an interest in securing the future collaboration of the more moderate liberals and he was pushed further than he originally wanted to go. No individual or party was entirely satisfied with the constitutional arrangements which were passed by big majorities in the Reichstag and Prussian Landtag, but most accepted them as a basis for future development. For liberals especially, the achievement of a united Germany with a central executive and representative institutions was a major advance and in theory at least there was scope for Reich legislation to amend the constitution and extend the competence of imperial institutions.

The features of the constitutional structure which have aroused the most controversy are those which impeded a further liberalization or the progressive 'parliamentarization' of the Empire. Some of these, such as the lack of parliamentary control over the composition of the executive or the extraordinary status of the military (at its core the Prussian army) outside the new constitution, were evident from the outset. Others, such as the enormous potential power of the Kaiser, only emerged later with the accession of Wilhelm II or, as in the case of the ultimately tortuous arrangements for financing the Empire, were compounded by subsequent political decisions which shifted the balance in favour of the states.

The peculiar position of the Bundesrat, which by virtue of its composition and procedure could never fulfil the role of an imperial government or even play a central role in the decision-making process, was correctly calculated by Bismarck to present a formidable barrier to the expansion of parliamentary power. With delegates bound to vote according to the instructions of the state governments they represented, the theoretical sovereignty of the 'allied governments' was purely fictional and, when it came to the details of legislation, all the advantages rested with the administration in Berlin. Yet its mere existence was a fundamental obstacle to the development of a Reich cabinet responsible to parliament and its secret sessions contributed to the frustration of Reichstag deputies who repeatedly found that they had no means of calling the real decision-makers in Prussia to account.

Prussia's role as the dominant state within the Empire is generally cited as the most important impediment to the progressive evolution of the political system after 1871. Even after unification, Prussia continued to be ruled on the basis of the very limited constitution of 1850, which had placed few restrictions on the king's autocratic power. The Prussian military victories and the resolution of the constitutional conflict may have revolutionized the party system to the government's advantage but there had been no significant change in the power relationships within Prussia. In the event of a renewed clash between the king and the Prussian Landtag, there was no guarantee that the government would not once again exploit the alleged 'gap' in the constitution and resort to arbitrary rule. In fact, with liberalism's decline from the late 1870s, the plutocratic three-class suffrage, which allowed the richest 15 per cent of the electorate to choose two-thirds of the seats, began to produce conservative parliamentary majorities in the Prussian House of Deputies, which further undermined the political pressure within Prussia for reform. The composition of the House of Deputies, as well as the even more reactionary, hereditary House of Lords, came to impose legislative constraints upon Prussian governments which were in practice sometimes more willing to countenance reform.

There was no sense in which the Empire could have existed independently of Prussia, yet the Empire's federal structure effectively shielded and protected Prussia's hegemony. The German Kaiser was always the Prussian king; his power of command (*Kommandogewalt*) over the army ensured that those who aspired to change the constitutional status quo always had to reckon with the possibility that the monarchy might sanction violence to defend its power. The Chancellor, too, was always the Prussian foreign minister and – with the exception of two brief interludes – Prussian minister-president; it was by virtue of the former position that he instructed Prussian votes in the Bundesrat. (When the incumbent briefly surrendered the premiership in 1872–3 and 1892–4 he found his power and the confidence of the states in his leadership severely curtailed.) Especially in the early years of the Empire, imperial legislation was drafted in the Prussian ministries and no laws were passed which had not been extensively discussed in the Prussian state ministry. As the Reich administration developed, too, it became inextricably interlocked with the Prussian ministerial bureaucracy; in terms of personnel and function their offices overlapped.

All the above features of the imperial German political system represented powerful barriers to constitutional change after 1871, and it is perhaps not surprising if most historians tend to be gloomy about the Empire's prospects for peaceful political reform and adaptation. Nevertheless, there is ample evidence that the Empire's political institutions were capable of evolution and development, even if the direction this took may not have conformed to existing political models and the overall effects were ambiguous.

The unitary pressures which were manifestly at work within the Empire are generally regarded as positive in their effects. Especially during the first decade of the Empire's existence, imperial institutions developed very rapidly and, facilitated by the dignified restraint of Wilhelm I as well as by the emotional appeal of 'Kaiser and Reich', the imperial monarchy gained popularity and respect. The urgent need for legislation to establish the economic and legal framework of the Empire ensured a significant role for the German Reichstag, despite its constitutional limitations, within the new polity. Its representative character, the relatively high election turnouts (especially in the nationalist elections of 1878 and 1887) and its public debates all helped it become a focus of German political life. The central Reich executive (or 'Reich leadership' as it came to be called) expanded dramatically under the authority of the Chancellor. By the late 1870s a series of Reich offices had been created, each under a state secretary who could deputize for the chancellor.

It can even be argued that the relationship between Prussia and the Reich became far less clear-cut in the context of the growing momentum of imperial institutions. For all the complaints about a Prussification of Germany, it became increasingly apparent (especially to conservatives) that the identity of 'old Prussia' had been significantly 'diluted' by its integration into the new Empire. Prussia could no longer be governed without consideration of the wider interests of the Reich and, as Bismarck increasingly adopted the practice of making his state secretaries Prussian ministers without portfolio, the Prussian government could no longer retain an exclusively Prussian character. By the 1890s it was not merely the case that non-Prussians sat in the ministry of state, but that a Bavarian Chancellor simultaneously became Prussian minister-president.

Yet immediately, of course, one must balance this perspective, for imperial institutions also evolved in ways which did little to further the cause of constitutional government. For example, the twin problems of defective civil–military coordination in the Empire and inadequate political control over the army grew steadily worse rather than better, even under Bismarck's chancellorship. The army effectively evaded political and parliamentary controls, and Bismarck himself was prepared to connive in this process by permitting the progressive emasculation of the office of Prussian war minister. (He preferred to see the minister's responsibilities carved up between several military agencies rather than bolster the authority of a potential rival.) Similarly the highly imperfect and provisional compromises which were struck in the attempt to ensure the Empire's financial solvency signified a growing entanglement between financial and constitutional issues to the detriment of both. Not only the federal governments but also state parliaments, elected according to indirect and very unequal suffrages, resisted efforts to transfer important powers of the purse to a democratically elected Reichstag with fewer scruples about taxing wealth and property. Finally, as the issue of the monarchical succession loomed ever larger, so did the growing significance of the Kaiser's court as a locus of political intrigue beyond the Chancellor's control. The political vitality of the army and the court attests to the continuing importance of the 'extra-constitutional' realm in the decision-making process.

Altogether it must be stated that the Bismarckian government system never functioned very smoothly, although it would doubtless be wrong to conflate the problems of the Bismarckian and Wilhelmine eras and assume its future was fixed by 1890. The constitutional and political structure of the Empire, in which not only Prussia but some 20 other states retained their monarchies, courts, governments, diplomats, parliaments (with upper and lower houses) and – in some cases – their own armies in peacetime, was bound to be highly complicated and unwieldy. As will be seen, Bismarck himself was never very happy with the new structures which were superimposed on the old. Moreover, the latent incompatibility between rival monarchical and parliamentary claims to power conditioned German political life throughout the Empire's existence.

II The role of Bismarck

Bismarck has remained the most controversial figure in modern German political history, with widely divergent assessments of his role and significance. Recent scholarly biographies of Bismarck have largely succeeded in demythologizing the 'great man' but have found it much more difficult to separate the man from his achievement. In so far as historians have tried to place the wars of 1864–71 and the Empire which emerged from them within a wider context of largely autonomous pressures for unification, they still run up against a series of problems pertaining to Bismarck's individuality and his responsibility for the political development of the Empire. For if the Empire was an artificial and anachronistic construction, this only attests further to Bismarck's successful manipulation of the national and liberal forces of his day, as well as to his ability to stem the tide of change after 1871. Whether German unification amounted to a limited 'revolution from above' or a 'bourgeois revolution' which signified the breakthrough of industrial capitalism in Germany, Bismarck emerges as the brilliant and shrewd tactician who succeeded in postponing the problem of political modernization for 60 years. Even Wehler was forced to concede that the traditional or pre-industrial forces in German society possessed in Bismarck a 'political potential *sui generis*'.[1] Once applauded as the architect of German unification, Bismarck is now much more likely to be judged critically as a man whose aims and methods imposed a massive burden on Germany's social and political development. Yet his exceptional status is not in doubt. Whether his legacy was positive or negative, historians cannot escape his dominating presence in the history of Germany and Europe from 1862 to 1890 (and beyond).

Bismarck's role within the imperial German political system after 1871 was so fundamental and decisive that he is widely seen as having instituted a 'chancellor dictatorship'. For some, this dictatorship is defined chiefly in terms of his personal power and authority within the executive and his largely unchallenged role in determining policy. Others have argued that this interpretation is too 'personalistic', preferring to shift the focus from Bismarck's style of rule within the executive to the social functions of his 'Bonapartist dictatorship', a concept they see as combining the more traditional and authoritarian features of his government with more charismatic or plebiscitary elements.

Bismarck's role in German unification undoubtedly ensured him a pre-eminent position in Prussia and the Empire after 1871. It also furthered a process, already underway during the constitutional conflict of the 1860s, whereby government and decision-making became increasingly associated with one man (especially in the eyes of his critics) and the main political division during the subsequent years he remained in office was between his supporters and opponents, those who affirmed the creation of the Bismarckian national state and those who rejected it. Yet if Bismarck appeared to place the monarchy in the political shade, enjoying many of the prerogatives of autocratic power within the executive and becoming, in the words of Wilhelm I, 'more necessary than I am',[2] there continued to be important practical and theoretical limitations to his position. Bismarck himself was all too aware of the potential scope at the Kaiser's court and within the army for independent decision-making and, of course, he needed a parliamentary majority for the passage of legislation and approval of the budget. Ultimately the monarch's power of appointment rendered the imperial Chancellor as much a royal servant as a Reich minister. By 1890, when it was clear that Bismarck had no alternative basis of political support, Kaiser Wilhelm II felt free simply to dismiss him.

Between 1871 and 1890 Bismarck came to exert a tight grip over all aspects of policy in the Empire and Prussia. Buoyed up by his outstanding achievement in restructuring the map of central Europe in 1866–71, it was inevitable that, as Reich Chancellor and Prussian Foreign Minister, he enjoyed a virtual autonomy in the sphere of foreign policy. He could be confident that, provided he could assert his will over the Kaiser and discipline the diplomatic service into complete subordination, there would be no questioning of his diplomatic wisdom and skill. Only at the very end of his chancellorship was there mounting disquiet within ruling circles over his conduct of foreign policy and, in particular, his efforts to maintain Russia's friendship. With respect to domestic affairs Bismarck's authority was, initially at least, subject to more significant constraints. His position was limited not only by the collegial structure of the Prussian government (which he deliberately avoided in the Reich) and the theoretical sovereignty of the states rather than the imperial executive, but also by more practical considerations such as the availability of personnel, the nature of the party constellation and a degree of uncertainty about how the new constitutional system would function in practice. Yet Bismarck's interest in consolidating imperial institutions after 1871 never deflected him from the goal of consolidating his personal power. His frequent improvisation and experimentation with the political arrangements within the Empire – resigning and reassuming offices, creating new institutions or resurrecting old ones, adjusting the balance between Reich and Prussian institutions first one way and then the other – was motivated as much by self-interest as by a desire to ensure smooth and stable government.

Bismarck's frequent tinkering with the political machinery of his new creation suggests a dissatisfaction with the system and his place within it which is hard to reconcile with the concept of dictatorship. Indeed, even confining the perspective to the executive, it is clear that power relationships in the first two decades of the Empire's existence were more fluid than is often suggested. The basis of Bismarck's power underwent perceptible shifts between 1871 and 1890 for, although the confidence of the Kaiser underpinned his position, his dependence on the monarchy waxed and waned according to the degree to which he could command the political support of parliaments, colleagues and states. For example, faced with a hostile Reichstag majority between 1881 and 1886, he found that he was more dependent on Wilhelm I's support than at any time since the constitutional conflict of the 1860s – a realization which cannot have enhanced his sense of security, as his predicament coincided with growing fears about the succession and suspicions of proliferating intrigues at court. Similarly, though his authority over the Prussian ministerial bureaucracy was undisputed by the 1880s, the task of achieving a consensus among the federal states became more difficult after the political changes of 1878–9 when they no longer felt threatened by the unitary implications of his collaboration with the liberals in the Reichstag. Bismarck increasingly had to resort to bullying tactics to preserve a superficial harmony and unanimity in the Bundesrat; from 1888, with Wilhelm II beginning to play a more active role in decision-making, the lesser states found again that they had more freedom to espouse alternative policy proposals.

Bismarck rapidly established his undisputed leadership over the imperial executive. He soon dismantled the single, centralized Reich Chancellor's office which, under Rudolf Delbrück, had accumulated extensive power over imperial domestic affairs, and he preferred to institute a more decentralized imperial executive which, however, remained firmly under his personal control. While the state secretary of the foreign office enjoyed direct access to the chancellor, the state secretaries of the five main departments responsible for domestic affairs from 1878 communicated with him through a small personal secretariat, the Reich Chancellery, which was located in his residence in Berlin's Wilhelmstrasse. There was no form of collective government in the Reich and nothing which resembled an imperial cabinet. The new system ensured there would be a minimum of political discussion and consultation between the Chancellor's subordinates and that all final decisions would rest with Bismarck.

In Prussia, Bismarck's position from 1871 was secure but not unassailable. Despite the parliamentary collaboration with the liberals for much of the decade, Bismarck had to work with Prussian ministers who had had no qualms in fighting the constitutional conflict alongside him and opposed, for example, the reform of Prussian local government and abolition of Junker police powers in 1872. At the same time he came to resent a loss of freedom of manoeuvre which resulted not only from the need to work with a liberal parliamentary majority but also from what he perceived to be the stranglehold which liberal ministers had over the Prussian Ministry of State. Recent work has shown how Bismarck's ideas, even in the early

1870s, to institute extensive social welfare reforms ran aground when ministers with key portfolios such as trade resisted any kind of state intervention in the economy. The desire to subordinate the Prussian Ministry to his leadership was an important motive in Bismarck's anti-socialist offensive and break with the National Liberal Party in 1878. Only after the ministerial changes of the summer of 1879 (which, incidentally, paid little heed to the apparent change of political direction) did Bismarck finally establish his undisputed authority over the Ministry of State. From 1880 he also personally headed the Prussian Ministry of Trade, which meant that he was well placed to spearhead the new social insurance legislation.

Bismarck's success in taming and disciplining Prussian ministers reduced them to a status comparable with the state secretaries in the imperial executive. Bismarck had never found it easy to work with other people and he had always been intolerant of criticism and dissent. These traits were magnified once his political ascendancy was secured so that any kind of opposition or constructive questioning was effectively eliminated. Bismarck was frequently contemptuous of colleagues whom he variously criticized, even in the Reichstag, for being too independent, lacking in creativity or spineless. The task of finding men of calibre who had the personal and political skills to work with the Minister-President became increasingly difficult as time went on. In 1878 nine men refused the Ministry of Finance before one was persuaded to take over the post. Bismarck's hold over an ageing Wilhelm I meant that he could remove inconvenient colleagues in the 1880s, particularly those, like Botho Eulenburg, the Minister of the Interior, whom he suspected in 1881 of 'wanting to govern'.[3] His reluctance to initiate subordinates into his thought processes, his mistrust of potential rivals, and his conviction that naming a successor was the political equivalent of being dead, encouraged him to rely more and more on his son, Herbert, who was State Secretary of the Foreign Office from 1886.

Bismarck achieved a dictatorial position within the Reich and Prussian executives, but he was persistently thwarted in his efforts to control the course of Germany's political development. The heterogeneity of German society, Germany's dynamic economic and demographic growth, and the unwieldiness of the new constitutional arrangements all precluded the possibility that he could shape the peacetime domestic development of the Empire in the same way as he had forged its international status. As early as 1872 there were complaints within government circles that the 'Iron Chancellor', denied the conditions of conflict and war, lacked the requisite qualities and skills to promote the constructive evolution of imperial domestic politics. By the end of the decade

Bismarck was widely perceived to be no longer the man he was, all too willing to set himself ambitious political and social goals which could never be achieved in the short time and with the limited means he now had at his disposal.

III   Political developments during Bismarck's chancellorship

It has become customary to divide Bismarckian domestic politics into two quite distinct liberal and conservative eras, punctuated by Bismarck's break with the National Liberal Party in 1878 and his adoption of economic protectionism in 1879. Between 1867 and 1878 Bismarck continued the collaboration with the moderate liberal movement which had begun with the passage of the Indemnity Bill in 1866. During this period many important laws were passed which established the administrative and legal framework of the new Empire, and facilitated the creation of a national economy. At the same time the so-called *Kulturkampf* or 'struggle for civilization' against the substantial Catholic minority and its political representative, the Centre Party, was prosecuted with particular vigour by the Prussian government and its liberal allies, although it affected the lesser German states and impacted upon Reich legislation too.

In 1878, however, Bismarck deliberately sought a confrontation with his erstwhile political friends, introducing an unacceptable anti-socialist bill into the Reichstag and precipitating new elections. The new Reichstag subsequently approved a revised anti-socialist bill and, in 1879, a conservative–Centre majority passed a tariff law which signified the abandonment of economic liberalism. Thereafter, it is argued, government policies shifted markedly to the right in the 1880s, while Bismarck effectively consolidated his authoritarian or 'Bonapartist' dictatorship. The tariff levels were raised in 1885 so that German agriculture was afforded a similar degree of protection to that of industry, and the grain tariffs were increased again in 1887. The government continued to repress social democracy and pursued much more overtly nationalistic policies against the ethnic minorities within the Empire, above all the three million or so Prussian Poles. At the same time the state intervened more and more directly in economic and social life, not least instituting a comprehensive system of state social insurance provision which was a forerunner of its kind.

There is no doubt that the economic and political climate was very different in the 1880s from what it had been in the years immediately following political unification. The economic crash and subsequent slowdown in economic growth from 1873 helped to produce a crisis of confidence in economic liberalism by the late 1870s which manifested itself in heightened fears and insecurities among all social groups. Traditional practice as well as current anxiety ensured that many of those who felt most threatened by the vagaries of the market or the ferocity of foreign competition looked to the government to protect their interests and alleviate their distress. The growth of new social and economic problems inevitably cut across traditional political alignments, producing tensions and conflicts within political parties which were still in the main only loosely organized on the basis of ideological affinities, for example a shared view about dynastic, clerical or constitutional issues, and did not necessarily represent similar economic interests. Inevitably, too, new political and social conflicts offered fresh opportunities for manoeuvre to a government which had no organic relationship with the political parties in the Reichstag and which, in claiming to stand above party or sectional interests, naturally favoured authoritarian solutions to the nation's problems.

Nevertheless there are several reasons for questioning whether dividing Bismarck's chancellorship into two separate eras, each characterized with reference to conventional political categories of liberalism and conservatism, facilitates an understanding of political developments between 1871 and 1890. The dichotomy tends to arise from a focus on parliamentary politics, the relationships within and between the political parties, and the shifting basis of the government's parliamentary support, although, as we have seen, the parliaments and the political parties played a very specific and subordinate role in the political system as a whole. Moreover, even with respect to party politics, the situation in the 1870s and 1880s can be better understood with reference to the events of the previous decade than in conventional political terms. For German unification did not immediately create political unity, and confessional, regional and ethnic loyalties often remained more important in determining political alignments in the first decades of the Empire than day-to-day political, economic and social issues.

Most obviously, the passions aroused by the *Kulturkampf* can scarcely be appreciated if viewed solely in the context of a liberal campaign against clerical obscurantism or the progress of the secularizing state. Rather, in targeting Catholics and minorities within the Empire, the *Kulturkampf* was widely understood by contemporaries to be a war against the internal opponents of the lesser German unification, those whose territories had been defeated or annexed in 1866–71 and who regretted the exclusion of Catholic Austria. In this sense German political life after 1871 essentially represented the continuing struggle to achieve the national state. This struggle was admittedly waged by different means from the military campaigns of 1864–71 but it appeared no less urgent to supporters of the national idea in the light of the centrifugal pressures within the new Empire and widespread fears that what had been achieved so dramatically could just as easily be undone. Even 20 years after unification ruling circles in Berlin still harboured an almost paranoid anxiety that the Empire might yet dissolve into its constituent parts. Party political alignments in the Bismarckian era inevitably reflected the fundamental division between those who affirmed what Bismarck had achieved and those who rejected it. Arguably, so long as Bismarck remained at the helm, there was no way in which it could be otherwise. Events of the 1860s, as well as the personality and style of the Chancellor, conspired to make one of the central issues of Bismarckian politics the question whether one was for or against Bismarck.

The apparent discontinuities between the more liberal and progressive 1870s and the more conservative and authoritarian 1880s have tended to focus the historiographical debate over the past 20 years on the scope and significance of the 'great change' or *Wende* in 1878–9. Some historians such as Helmut Böhme have argued that the change of course in imperial domestic politics at the end of the 1870s was so fundamental and extensive that it amounted to a 'refounding' of the Empire on a conservative basis. Bismarck, they maintain, exploited the spectre of socialist revolution and the popular clamour for economic protectionism in the late 1870s to forge a new coalition of government support based on the most powerful economic interest groups in Imperial Germany, the so-called alliance of 'iron and rye'. This coalition between heavy industry and large-scale agriculture then underpinned the Empire's domestic development until 1918, thwarting the gradual evolution of parliamentary democracy and ensuring a rigid adherence to the social and political status quo.

From 1879, it is widely claimed, Bismarckian politics are best under-stood as a form of *Sammlungspolitik* or the 'rallying' of all conservative and national forces which supported the state. Anti-liberal in origin (though this animus against liberalism was later superseded by the fear of revolutionary socialism) *Sammlungspolitik* was reinforced by manipulative strategies to stabilize the existing order. These included the targeting of political enemies and minorities as a means of 'secondary integration', as well as 'social imperialist' strategies to divert popular attention away from the need for political reform. While Bismarck's 'social imperialism' did not extend beyond a sudden interest in colonial acquisitions in the mid-1880s and the exploitation of war scares for election purposes, his successors were ultimately prepared to embrace naval armaments and world war to shore up the monarchy and prevent social and political modernization.

The idea that the Empire was 'refounded' in 1878–9 and that the decisions taken during these years somehow determined the domestic development of Germany for several decades to come has been subject to growing scholarly criticism on a number of counts. It has been argued that the thesis (which largely derived from the study of economic policy) exaggerated the importance of economic issues generally and the tariff legislation in particular. It oversimplified the relationship between politics and economics in the Empire and obscured the diversity and complexity of the economic interest groups which stood to gain or lose from government policies. Historians of both the Bismarckian and Wilhelmine eras have questioned the applicability of the *Sammlungspolitik* model to the specific years or policies they have studied, doubting whether the alliance of 'iron and rye' was as solid or durable as has been suggested and whether government was any more stable as a result. Too much emphasis has been placed on government manipulation and design, too little on more pragmatic considerations or autonomous developments which influenced imperial German decision-making. More generally, the assumption of a fundamental incompatibility between economic protectionism and the development of liberal or democratic politics has been contested, especially in the light of contemporary experience.

Recent research has confirmed that the turning point of 1878–9 was not as sudden, dramatic or consequential as is often supposed. Otto Pflanze, for example, has painstakingly shown how the decisions of 1878–9, far from signifying the existence of a Bismarckian 'grand strategy' to shift German politics to the right, arose out of a number of related but uncoordinated issues which preoccupied Bismarck from quite early in the 1870s. Among Bismarck's prime domestic concerns were: the need to solve the Empire's financial constitution in a way which made it more independent of both the states and the Reichstag; his wish to reform the tax system in Prussia and the Reich in a way which would lift the burden of direct taxation from the lower classes and place more emphasis on indirect taxation; and his desire to take steps to alleviate the 'social question', above all by instituting a comprehensive system of social insurance. With respect to these issues Bismarck's motives were never purely or even predominantly manipulative (even his social insurance schemes were motivated as much by his peculiar brand of Christian pietism as by the need to ensure the loyalty of the working man to the state). But they were broadly conservative, shaped as much by his social background and his essentially limited personal experience as by a genuine understanding of society's problems.

The preoccupation with the great *Wende* and the government's manipulation has distorted the longer-term origins of the change of course and led to an underestimation of the significance of forces which were largely evolutionary or beyond the government's control. The effect has been to turn Bismarck, not for the first time, into an all-powerful tiger who was forever willing to change his political stripes if it suited his Machiavellian purposes. The extent to which Bismarck pursued similar goals throughout his chancellorship has also been obscured by a tendency to focus exclusively on the parliamentary arena and judge his policies solely on the basis of what eventually reached the statute books. Significant elements of Bismarck's wider political plans never got further than the Prussian Ministry of State or the Bundesrat before they encountered opposition or were demonstrated to be impractical.

Seen in its proper context, the tariff, for example, was scarcely central to Bismarck's plans in 1879. Never committed to economic liberalism, Bismarck adopted protectionism rather belatedly and opportunistically in 1879 in the belief that it would bring economic and political advantages. But he was far more interested in other measures, such as the nationalization of the railways or the creation of a lucrative government monopoly on brandy or tobacco, as a means of raising revenue. Nor should the tariff's role in cementing the alleged *Sammlung* be overstressed. Although agriculture was always favoured by Bismarck's policies, the preferential treatment of heavy industry in 1879 has to be offset against the effects of some of his other proposals, for example his plans to regulate the private insurance market or tax stock market transactions, which would have imposed new financial burdens on German industry. Employers were concerned about many aspects of the government's social and fiscal policies in the 1880s, and customs tariff policy was arguably the one significant area in which agrarian and industrial interests could cooperate effectively. In 1884, Bismarck terrified industrialists when he controversially referred in a Reichstag speech to the 'right to work'. Bismarck frequently equated agrarian interests with the national interest, but he was never as considerate of the needs of industry and business as is often suggested.

From the perspective of parliamentary politics, too, there was a high degree of consistency, both in terms of Bismarck's parliamentary aims and the political aspirations of the parties, which is often overlooked. Throughout his chancellorship Bismarck was determined to prevent any extension of parliamentary power, a stance which soon led to tensions with the more left-wing National Liberals who remained committed to further constitutional change. The confrontation of 1878 was long in the making, as by the middle of the decade Bismarck sought a means of severing the left-wing from the party and facilitating the party's drift to the right. This never meant that he expected to be able to govern without the liberals or the middle classes they represented. Bismarck may have perceived even in the 1870s that, having lost their monopoly on the national idea and compromised their liberal ideals in the *Kulturkampf*, liberals could no longer claim to represent the majority of those classes whose support he deemed essential for the monarchy. But he remained convinced that the National Liberals represented the most dynamic and (outside Prussia) the most national forces in German society. He never seriously entertained the possibility that liberal parliamentary support could be permanently replaced by a coalition of conservative, clerical and particularist forces. Indeed, far from wishing to replace the National Liberals by the Centre as a party of government (as is sometimes suggested) Bismarck seems to have hoped that the easing of the *Kulturkampf* would weaken political Catholicism and hasten the progressive dissolution of the Centre Party. This in turn would have facilitated the integration or reintegration of Catholics into the mainstream liberal and conservative parties.

Bismarck's collaboration with the liberals in the 1870s was never very smooth, but the effects of his confrontation with them in 1878–9 on the party constellation scarcely suited his political purposes better in the longer term. After the party split in 1880, the National Liberals continued to support the government, albeit with a much greater degree of subservience than they had had to suffer previously. Yet the Chancellor scarcely had greater flexibility in terms of party coalitions. Having resented his parliamentary dependence on the liberals in the 1870s and regretted the loss of the freedom he had enjoyed in the years of the constitutional struggle, Bismarck wanted the possibility of an alternative parliamentary coalition, such as was presented to him by the conservative and Centre support for protectionism in 1879. Yet he had no illusions about governing with the Centre which was to remain on most matters implacably opposed to government policies throughout the 1880s. Nor did Reichstag elections (with the sole exception of the election in 1887) produce more conservative or compliant Reichstags. In the early 1880s it was the left liberals (and the Centre) who appeared to have gained most from the blow Bismarck dealt the National Liberals, and neither a conservative–Centre coalition nor a conservative–National Liberal coalition could command a parliamentary majority. Bismarck was never so isolated in terms of political support as he was between 1881 and 1886, and during these years he was literally forced to make a virtue out of 'government above the parties', scratching together *ad hoc* majorities according to the issue.

Inevitably, too, after a succession of defeats, he came to realize that there was little point introducing legislation into the Reichstag which had no chance of being accepted. In 1881 even the National Liberal leader,

Bassermann, chided Bismarck for his (all too often half-baked and insufficiently considered) reform proposals and insisted that a breathing space was necessary after the legislative frenzy of the 1870s. The pace of legislative initiatives slackened and the Reichstag's role diminished in importance. Stagnation rather than conservative stability characterized the politics of the 1880s. In 1887 Bismarck achieved a notable electoral victory at a time of international crisis when the so-called Kartell (an electoral coalition of the two conservative parties and the National Liberals) defeated the opposition parties for the first time since 1878. Yet in practice even the Kartell could not provide a very stable or reliable basis of parliamentary support for the government, and Bismarck soon had reasons of his own to seek its destruction.

Above all, an examination of Bismarck's relations with the parliaments between 1871 and 1890 indicates the persistent, constant problem which arose from rival monarchical and parliamentary claims to power, compounded by the lack of any organic relationship between the executive and the legislature. Bismarck could rail against an electorate which did not understand his reform plans and reduce the number of occasions on which he appeared in the parliaments (he went five years without even speaking in the Prussian House of Deputies). But the government needed parliamentary support if it was to govern constitutionally. If the Reichstag denied it such support, the only recourse was to dissolve it and call new elections. Bismarck was prepared to use all the means at the government's disposal to swing the popular mood in elections or secure the passage of contentious legislation, above all army bills. He resorted to dramatic posturing and short-term expedients, such as the exploitation of the international crisis which was successful in the elections of 1887. But, faced with oppositional Reichstags between 1881 and 1887, he increasingly came to question the role of parliament itself. He harboured deep reservations about the consequences of universal suffrage; and he explored the possibility of bypassing the parliaments by such means as creating Prussian and Reich economic councils, organized on corporatist lines. He also threatened on many occasions to change the constitution by force, to impose a new franchise on the Reichstag or suppress it altogether, although ultimately a sense of realism prevailed until the last months of his chancellorship.

In exploring Bismarckian politics, historians have tended to focus on the exceptional situations, the government's apparent victories over the parties (in 1866–7, 1878–9, and 1887) as evidence of Bismarck's successful manipulation. The imperial German political parties have also attracted their share of the blame for political developments during Bismarck's chancellorship, having been variously accused of ideological rigidity, subversive materialism, negative campaigning, cringing conformity, an inability to transcend the representation of specific social milieux and an opportunistic willingness to change their political priorities under the impact of economic change and the rise of organized socialism. The parties, it seems, resigned themselves to political impotence and hindered the emergence of a progressive coalition dedicated to political reform. Nevertheless, despite the relative dearth of recent historical studies of Bismarckian high politics (excluding Bismarck biographies), especially in the 1880s, what is striking is how troublesome the party political situation was for Bismarck and how the routine of parliamentary life gave him so little cause for satisfaction. The 'Iron Chancellor', who expected unquestioned authority within the executive and popular gratitude for the scale of his past achievements, could not accept the representative character of a German Reichstag which seemed perpetually intent on criticizing and thwarting his plans. Unable to implement the domestic reforms he believed were necessary, chiefly because of the hostility of the parties, the states or both, Bismarck's predicament was exacerbated because, as he was only too aware, he lacked a secure power base.

In the 1880s, if not earlier, the crucial context of Bismarckian high politics was the imminence of the monarchical succession. By 1881, when the left liberals gained the most seats in the Reichstag elections, Bismarck's chancellorship already appeared increasingly conditional. Despite Bismarck's efforts to bolster his personal authority and preserve his position, the growing likelihood of a change of Kaiser cast a huge question-mark over his political future. Wilhelm I, who had been born in 1797, clearly could not survive for much longer and change, whether under his reputedly liberal son, Friedrich, or his youthful grandson, Wilhelm, would have to come. In this situation the political parties could largely afford to bide their time, confident that sooner or later there had to be an era after Bismarck in which the decisive contest over the distribution of power in the new state could be fought on a much more level playing field.

No one in Prussia or the Empire could have anticipated that Bismarck would remain in power for nearly 30 years or come to enjoy such an unassailable position under Wilhelm I. As Lothar Gall has pointed out, at virtually every moment during his long career, his fall appeared imminent and likely. However, despite his indomitable personality, his spectacular successes between 1864 and 1871, and his formidable reputation, Bismarck never enjoyed political popularity or trust. He was always regarded as an exceptional individual whose chancellorship, too, represented a transitional phase before the establishment of new, more 'normal' conditions. In a sense, irrespective of the Empire's constitutional and political imperfections, Bismarck's confrontational style and his perennial threats to revise a constitution over which he claimed a monopoly, it was impossible for the new political system to stabilize as long as Bismarck remained at the helm. This was increasingly perceived by all those who came into contact with ruling circles in Berlin. It helps to explain the stagnation of imperial domestic politics by the middle of the 1880s and the dimensions of the protracted succession crisis from 1888. Above all, it accounts for the predominant mood of stunned relief which followed Bismarck's dismissal in March 1890.

Notes:

1. Wehler, Hans-Ulrich, *The German Empire 1871–1918* (1985) p. 27.
2. Pflanze, Otto, *Bismarck and the Development of Germany*, vol. 2, *The Period of Consolidation 1871–1880* (1990), p. 507.
3. Pflanze, Otto, *Bismarck and the Development of Germany*, vol. 3, *The Period of Fortification 1880–1898* (1990) p. 37.

Select bibliography

Berghahn, Volker, *Imperial Germany 1871–1914. Economy, Society, Culture and Politics* (1994).

Blackbourn, David, and Eley, Geoff, *The Peculiarities of German History* (1984).

Böhme, Helmut, *Deutschlands Weg zur Grossmacht. Studien zum Verhältnis von Wirtschaft und Staat während der Reichsgründungszeit 1848–1881* (1969).

Eley, Geoff, *From Unification to Nazism* (1986).

Engelberg, Ernst, *Bismarck*, 2 vols. (1985 and 1990).

Gall, Lothar, *Bismarck. The White Revolutionary*, 2 vols. (1986).

Langewiesche, Dieter, *Liberalism in Germany* (2000).

Mommsen, Wolfgang J., *Imperial Germany 1867–1918. Politics, Culture and Society in an Authoritarian State* (1995).

Pflanze, Otto, *Bismarck and the Development of Germany*, 3 vols. (1990).

Pflanze, Otto, ed., *Innenpolitische Probleme des Bismarck-Reiches* (1983).

Nipperdey, Thomas, *Deutsche Geschichte 1866-1918*, vol. 2: *Machtstaat vor der Demokratie* (1993).

Röhl, J. C. G., *Germany without Bismarck. The Crisis of Government in the Second Reich 1890–1900* (1967).

Schieder, Theodor, *Das deutsche Kaiserreich von 1871 als Nationalstaat* (1961).

Sheehan, James F., *German Liberalism in the Nineteenth Century* (1978).

Wehler, Hans-Ulrich, *Das Deutsche Kaiserreich 1871–1918* (1973); *The German Empire 1871–1918* (1985).

9

Demographic growth, industrialization and social change

Volker Berghahn

Population growth, urbanization and industrialization represented long-term processes that did not start with the founding of the German Empire in 1871 (see Chapter 4, above). What can be said at a most general level, however, is that all three developments experienced a further acceleration in the late nineteenth century.

This is true, to begin with, of demographic change. In 1864 some 39.4 million people lived in the area of central Europe that was to become united under Prussian leadership six years later, by which time the population had increased to just around 41 million. About 24.6 million of the inhabitants of the new German Empire were Prussians, followed by 4.8 million Bavarians, 2.5 million Saxons, 1.8 million Württembergians and 1.5 million Badeners, with the rest distributed among the smaller states. Some 1.6 million people lived in Alsace-Lorraine, annexed after the defeat of France. By 1913 no less than another 27 million people had been added to the 1871 figure, and the total would have reached over 30 million, if the around three million Germans were included who emigrated overseas between 1871 and 1911. In percentage terms the overall increase was more than 58 per cent.

In trying to explain this veritable population explosion, the baby boom of the optimistic years around the time of the founding of the Empire clearly constitutes a major factor, and birth rates continued to be relatively high in the decades thereafter. It was only in 1912 that lower-class parents, following the earlier middle-class lead, began to limit family size. An increase in life expectancy and a decline in mortality rates were the other major factors in the demographic equation. In 1870 life expectancy from birth averaged no more than 35.6 years for men and 38.5 years for women. After the turn of the century another ten years had been added (44.8 years for men and 48.3 years for women).

For a long time infant mortality remained almost level (and hence contributed relatively little to the demographic explosion). Between 1870 and 1880 no fewer than 211 of every 1,000 legitimately born babies in towns and cities died within the first year; the figure for the rural areas was somewhat lower at 183. Infant mortality reached a shocking 403 per 1,000 for children born out of wedlock (312 per 1,000 births in the countryside). All these figures barely improved until the turn of the century, after which survival rates for infants rose markedly. By 1914 the number of infant deaths among city-dwellers had dropped to 147 per 1,000 births (159 per 1,000 in rural areas). The picture for illegitimate children looked bleaker still: 261 deaths per 1,000 births in towns and cities and 287 per 1,000 in the countryside.

The many millions, young and old, who grew up in the new Empire were not evenly distributed throughout the land. Indeed, the demographic explosion is directly connected with the phenomenon of urbanization and *Landflucht* (flight from the rural areas). Again the processes that were at work here had set in before 1871, but the growth of towns and cities thereafter can only be described as staggering, as Table 9.1 demonstrates.

Table 9.1 Growth of some major cities, 1850–1910 (000s)

City	1850	1871	1880	1900	1910
Berlin	412	826	1,122	1,889	2,071
Hamburg	175	290	490	706	931
Munich	107	169	230	500	596
Leipzig	63	107	149	456	679
Dresden	97	177	221	396	548
Cologne	97	129	145	373	517
Breslau	111	208	273	423	512
Frankfurt/Main	65	91	137	289	415
Düsseldorf	27	69	95	214	359
Nuremberg	54	83	100	261	333
Hanover	28	88	123	236	302
Essen	9	52	57	119	295
Chemnitz	34	68	95	207	288
Duisburg	9	31	41	93	229
Dortmund	11	44	67	143	214
Kiel	16	32	44	108	212
Mannheim	24	40	53	141	194

Put in percentage terms, cities like Dortmund, Essen and Kiel grew between 400 and 500 per cent between 1871 and 1910. Many others doubled and trebled in size. It was only to a certain extent that these growth rates were the result of high birth rates and rising life expectancies as well as declining infant mortality rates later on. Probably more significant were the additions as a result of internal migration. The set of global figures in Table 9.2 provides a first indication of the huge population movements from the rural to the urban areas that occurred during the imperial period.

Table 9.2   Gains and losses through internal migration by region, 1907 (000s)

Region	Residents (total)	Natives/ Staying	Natives/ Left	Newcomers	Gains/ Losses
Eastern Germany	12,066.2	11,708.1	2,326.7	358.1	−1,968.6
Berlin, Brandenburg	5,585.2	3,936.1	445.5	1,649.2	+1,203.7
Northwest Germany	6,881.9	6.106.8	495.7	775.1	+279.4
Central Germany	9,719.7	9,001.9	891.4	717.8	−173.6
Hesse	3,371.1	2,954.9	348.1	416.2	+68.1
Western Germany	10,171.1	9,080.6	449.4	1,090.5	+64.1
Southern Germany	12,580.5	12,200.0	431.4	380.5	−50.9

Many of these men and women were long-distance migrants, especially from the eastern provinces of Prussia to the urban centres of central Germany and of the Rhine–Ruhr region. However, further research may well show that short-distance migrants were even more important – people who had grown up in the vicinity of the major urban centres. A good number of them retained their ties with their families back in the villages of the region, and some of them even lived the life of commuters on a daily or seasonal basis, especially at harvest time. These migrants are of considerable interest to the historian of popular culture, since it may be assumed that they did not immediately shed their earlier lifestyles and merely assimilated to city culture in the broad sense.

Here are some illuminating figures: at the time of the founding of the Empire, around 64 per cent of the population lived in small communities with under 2,000 inhabitants. By 1910 this figure had declined to 40 per cent. Meanwhile the share of towns with over 50,000 people had gone up from 8.9 per cent in 1870 to 26.7 per cent in 1910. Cities of over 100,000 inhabitants saw the most dramatic shift from 4.8 per cent in 1870 to 21.3 percent in 1910. Still, it would be wrong to suggest that pre-1914 Germany consisted mainly of big cities. In 1910 just over one quarter of the population continued to live in provincial towns of between 2,000 and 20,000 inhabitants, and in numerical terms the rural population added up to 21 million. However, in the meantime, so many millions had joined the stream of internal migrants, long- or short-distance, that over half of the population had left their place of birth and started a new life elsewhere, mostly in the urban parts of the Reich.

Finally, movements within cities must not be overlooked. Although precise statistics are difficult to come by, people frequently changed their abode within the same community, especially among the lower classes. Young unmarried migrants tended to live a particularly unsteady life, having to rely on lodgings with families in often incredibly cramped conditions. If there was a row, they would move out, often overnight. Nor is it too difficult to see that the huge demand for housing in the cities led to rapid rent increases, frequently putting the cost of an apartment beyond the reach of a low-income occupant family. So, something cheaper had to be found in a hurry. Frequent moves were also triggered by unemployment or job changes. Given the low wage levels, many workers would not hesitate, in times of prosperity, to switch to another factory up the road that offered more money. Indeed the search for improved material conditions and a 'better life' lay at the heart of most of the population movement. It is at this point that demographic change and urbanization intersect with industrialization.

There has been some debate as to whether the shift from an economy based on agriculture to one based on industrial production was as dramatic as had been assumed, and Hartmut Kaelble has offered comparisons with other countries like Denmark, which – he argues – experienced a more momentous industrial revolution. Whatever the relativities in international perspective may be, here it suffices to emphasize that the changeover was momentous enough to produce major social dislocations, but also to generate, at least from the 1890s onwards, a new prosperity and a general improvement in material and cultural conditions.

If we take the share of agriculture in the gross national product (GNP), this sector of the economy remained in the lead with 35-40 per cent until the 1880s. Industry's share then stood at 30–35 per cent. Just before the First World War, agriculture had fallen back to 25 per cent, with industry now in the lead (45 per cent), followed by the commercial and service sector at 30 per cent. This means that agriculture remained important in the national economy and, thanks to the population explosion, in fact witnessed an expansion of its production.

That there was still money to be made in agriculture is also reflected in the increased use of sophisticated machinery like tractors and steam threshers to achieve productivity gains. And yet these gains could not overcome a broader structural handicap that inexorably caused agriculture to fall behind the other sectors in the long run: industry as well as the tertiary sector were simply more productive. This was the part of the economy where new riches were accumulated. At the time of the founding of the Empire in 1870–1, the industrial sector achieved annual growth rates of 4.5 per cent. This rate declined to around 3 per cent during the 'great depression' between 1873 and 1896, before returning to averages of 4.5 per cent in the decades up to the First World War.

The production of coal and pig iron may serve as a more specific indicator of industrial expansion. In the 1880s, Germany produced some 47 million tons of coal per annum. By 1913 this figure had grown four-fold to 191 million tons. In 1870–4 pig iron production had reached an annual average of 1.6 million tons. Between 1910 and 1913 the average was 14.8 million tons. In the early years, much of Germany's iron and steel production was consumed by railway building and, even though the expansion of the network saw a marked slowdown thereafter, by 1910 the system had none the less grown to 61,000 kilometres from its 1870 starting point of about 19,000 kilometres.

Late nineteenth-century Germany greatly benefited from the rapid expansion of electrical engineering and chemicals. These were the new industries based on scientific breakthroughs and technological innovation that complemented the older industries of the first industrial revolution like coal, iron and textiles. In fact, it has been argued that the first and the second industrial revolutions occurred in Germany virtually at the same time, as the new industries experienced their most spectacular growth. In chemicals and pharmaceuticals in particular, Germany had by 1900 achieved a leading position in the world. By 1914 it had also outpaced Britain, the first industrial nation, in steel production.

That money was to be made in industry is also reflected in optimistic investment rates which hovered around the 43 per cent mark between 1905 and 1913, with agriculture's rate trailing well behind at about 11 per cent. Tax returns similarly tell of new riches that were being created. In 1895 the Prussian Inland Revenue counted 3,429 taxpayers with a declared wealth of 1–2 million marks. Another 1,827 even declared over 2 million marks. By 1907 these figures had nearly doubled to 5,916 and 3,425 respectively. The disposable incomes of these individuals, most of whom were in industry or finance, must be held against the national average of wages and salaries which then stood at 834 marks per annum. The fact that this average had risen from 506 marks per annum in 1870 and was to reach 1,163 marks per annum in 1913 indicates that, even if the material benefits of industrialization continued to be very unevenly distributed, there was at least some improvement in living standards also among the mass of the population who had virtually no assets and relied on their weekly wage packets. Thus miners, who had earned around 767 marks per annum in 1870, took home 1,496 marks per annum by 1913. Metal workers reached slightly higher wage levels from the mid-1890s onwards. Meanwhile white-collar employees, for example at the Maschinenfabrik Esslingen in southwest Germany, received 1,871 marks per annum in 1871 and 3,753 marks per annum in 1912. To be sure, these increases look less impressive when the inflation rate is factored in. Still, and with slight variations in scholars' calculations, real wages grew by 30 per cent and more.

With agriculture clearly doing less well than industry, wage levels remained correspondingly lower here. On the large estates that were typical of the regions east of the river Elbe, the demand for land labourers remained high, but low returns, often exacerbated by inefficient management of the estates, made pay rises difficult, even if the lords had wanted to offer incentives to keep their labourers from wandering westward. Wage pressures could be relieved to some extent by the importation of cheap Polish migrant seasonal workers from the western parts of Russia, especially during harvest time. Unionization was prohibited. Given these conditions, many were no longer prepared to put up with often depressing living and housing conditions. They left for the city to find a job in better-paying industry. Another motive for leaving, especially among young land labourers and servants, was the patriarchal conditions on the large estates. The lords had been able to uphold their disciplinary and policing powers into the modern period and used them to curb freedom of movement. Leisure time was also strictly limited and regulated. Nor was there much to do after a long workday and city life became very alluring in this respect as well.

In other parts of the country, especially in the west, south and south-west the small family farm predominated. But fewer and fewer of them generated enough income to provide for all children. And so, like the land labourers in the east, the younger sons and daughters among them joined the trek to the cities in search of a better-paid job and a freer life. Some of them, as has been mentioned, continued to commute; most of them tried to establish a permanent base for themselves in the city, living as lodgers with other working-class families or, once married, looking for a small apartment in one of the large *Mietskasernen* ('rental garrisons') that mushroomed in the urban centres.

These were therefore the deeper causes of the massive internal migrations and the *Landflucht*: the hope for a better material life and the wish to escape from the traditionalist and restrictive conditions of the village or the estate. Even if factory discipline was very strict, at least one had a bit more money in one's pocket and disposal of leisure time was much freer. This story of socioeconomic change is also reflected in the age structure. By and large, the elderly stayed behind in agriculture; the young, men and women, moved to the cities where they had been told life was more exciting. What they discovered was that wages were barely above the poverty line. On the estates, meals and accommodation had often been free. Now a considerable percentage of the weekly income went into paying rent. To make ends meet, many families had to take in lodgers, and single beds were frequently shared between two or three people. Sanitary facilities were primitive, and illness, whenever it happened, was a disaster for the whole family. Ups and downs in the economy occasionally triggered higher unemployment rates. It was in such times that parents had to make further cuts in an already tight food budget. In the long run, to be sure, nutritional standards improved, but the main effect of this was that working-class families were able to put enough food on the table and no-one went hungry. Once or twice a week they might even be able to afford meat, with pork consumption, including sausage, quadrupling between 1850 and 1910.

It could be argued that a land labourer who moved to one of the new industrial centres, whatever the continued hardships he or she experienced (including a 10–12 hour daily work schedule six days week) was achieving some upward mobility by becoming an unskilled or semi-skilled industrial worker. Over time he might even rise to the position of skilled worker with better pay. Women, though, hardly ever got that far, while men, trying to move further upwards, soon hit a glass ceiling that the middle classes had erected. Nor, by and large, was it possible in Imperial Germany to gain upward mobility through marriage. Most workers married women of working-class or peasant background. Given the elitism of the educational system, intergenerational mobility also remained low, no matter how strongly working-class parents encouraged their children to improve their socioeconomic status by acquiring better qualifications.

In short, most blue-collar workers found that a clear line existed between them and the middle classes higher up the social scale. If urban societies had been highly differentiated and stratified even before the industrial revolution, the advent of the factory and the expansion of public administration produced new *Mittelstand* groups alongside the old *Mittelstand* of craftsmen, shopkeepers, teachers, petty civil servants and others. The number of university-trained professionals also increased, with people in traditional urban occupations like lawyers and doctors being complemented by technicians, lab scientists and financial and marketing experts. Most of the upward (and downward) mobility in Imperial Germany occurred within this broad middle stratum, though often over two generations. The son of a primary schoolteacher might become a 'professor' in a *Gymnasium*; the son of a small craftsman might expand his father's workshop into a prosperous factory.

Those who were hoping to become part of the upper middle class found that the hurdles of social acceptance became higher. The craftsman's son who had become a successful entrepreneur did not necessarily gain access to the more exclusive circles in which private bankers, tycoons or higher civil servants would move, even if his accumulated wealth put him into the same income bracket. Though an individual's position in the marketplace provided a rough gauge for the system of social stratification, less tangible factors than income have to be added when we try to understand interactions among the middle classes. This is also true of relationships between the upper middle class and the nobility. Urbanization and industrialization had eroded, but had not been able to destroy the latter's position as the First Estate. The survival of the monarchical principle and of so many princely courts in central Europe after 1871 perpetuated its position. As a result historians had long assumed that the aristocracy provided the social and cultural model that the upper middle class tried to emulate. More recent research indicates that this 'feudalisation' process was much more limited than had been postulated. Most wealthy entrepreneurs or professionals, it appears, developed their own identity and pride in what they represented. A few, but by no means all, craved to be given a noble title or to be accepted into the social world of the landowning aristocracy. The dominant pattern was one of social separateness rather than merger or intermarriage, although this did not prevent cooperation at the level of politics whenever there was a coincidence of interests.

Before we deal with the question of whether the social differentiations and inequalities discussed so far amount to a society that was stratified by social class, we must ask if there were other categories that divided or united people in larger collectives. Clearly gender is one such category (for discussion of its importance see Ute Frevert, 'Gender in German History' in Fulbrook, ed., *German History since 1800* (1997), pp. 512–38). Religious denomination would appear to be another to be considered in this chapter.

With a few vacillations, the denominational balance remained roughly the same in Imperial Germany: Over 62 per cent of the population were Protestants, some 36 per cent were Catholics. The percentage of Jews actually declined, though this group experienced a numerical increase from 512,000 to 615,000 between 1871 and 1910. Jews shared the fate of other ethnic minorities of finding themselves in an ambiguous position. On the one hand, the removal of all legal discrimination opened up unprecedented

opportunities to achieve social and economic success. Jews were disproportionately successful in the professions, in business, in the arts and in
intellectual life more generally. On the other hand, their achievements
fanned old prejudices against them among the Christian population. Anti-
Semitism proliferated from the 1880s onwards and resulted in renewed,
more selective discrimination. Thus it became virtually impossible to rise to
higher positions in the civil service, the judiciary and the armed forces.
Jewish scholars, however gifted and prolific, found it difficult to obtain
professorships. Jews were also excluded from social clubs and associations.
Many of them fought the drawing of such lines, some by joining the Central
Association for German Citizens of the Jewish Faith whose name gave its
aims away. Others became members of the Zionist movement which
believed that equality without having to abandon their cultural identity was
possible only in a Jewish national state.

Jewish protestations did little to undermine Christian prejudice.
Catholics rejected their Jewish fellow citizens for religious reasons as the
alleged 'murderers of Christ'. Economic anti-Semitism charged Jews with
usury and greed. And socially they continued to run up against the hauteur
of the upper middle classes and the nobility which refused to socialize with
'those upstarts'. All this is meant to say that anti-Semitism cut across the
above-mentioned lines of social stratification. It erected barriers of cultural
and religious prejudice that were not directly related to economic status.

The same point applies in principle to the treatment of Catholics by the
Protestant majority. Again, on the one hand, Catholics benefited from the
expanding opportunities in education and business; on the other, they were
held back in their advance. To some extent this 'backwardness' was self-
imposed and due to the fact that Catholics, unlike many Protestants (and
in this respect also Jews), remained more firmly rooted in their traditional
provincial milieux in which the church continued to wield a powerful
ideological influence. Thus Catholicism remained suspicious of the many
manifestations of modernity, of urbanization and industrialization, of
liberalism and the emergence of a more secular society. Even before the
founding of the Reich this had led many Protestant liberals to view
Catholicism as an obscurantist faith, under the thumb of the 'ultramontane' Vatican, that impeded socioeconomic and constitutional progress.

It is out of this sense that the Protestant majority joined forces with Reich
Chancellor Bismarck after 1871 to launch the *Kulturkampf* against the
Catholics. The latter were turned into 'enemies of the Reich', their institu-
tions, above all the religious orders, were subjected to open persecution.
Although Bismarck had his own reasons for unleashing this struggle (and
for abandoning it a few years later), it deepened the denominational divide.

Faced with ostracism, Catholics ventured even more cautiously outside the traditional milieu and fell behind Protestants. To be a Catholic remained a serious handicap when it came to promotion in the civil service, and not just in predominantly Protestant Prussia. Even in Bavaria, where the majority of the population was Catholic, the higher civil service was run by Protestants. The problem of denominationalism is most strikingly reflected in higher education where the share of Catholic students was disproportionately smaller. The contrast was less marked in the business world, especially in the Rhineland. Nevertheless, the crucial point to be remembered here is that it made a difference in society and the economy whether a person was Protestant, Catholic or Jewish, just as gender differences counted and women were disadvantaged *vis-à-vis* men with respect to jobs, social rights and legal position.

However, in the long run neither denomination nor gender proved as powerful a category of social inequality and stratification as that of social class. Certainly if being Catholic still counted for much in the 1870s, by 1913 it had become overlaid by criteria of class and status. One of the most telling indicators of the notion that Imperial Germany turned increasingly into a class society is to be found in the realm of political behaviour. Partly under the impact of the *Kulturkampf*, the Centre Party had become the party of Catholics, providing a political and ideological home to Catholic workers from the Ruhr industrial region, to Rhenish Catholic bankers, to Bavarian Catholic peasants and to Catholic landowners from Silesia. By 1912, however, this tie had loosened somewhat and Catholic workers now increasingly voted for social democracy which explicitly presented itself as a working-class party and explained the world in terms of class and rising class conflict.

Clearly, not merely millions of Protestant industrial workers, but also Catholic ones saw their daily experience more closely reflected in the interpretations of society that the socialists provided than what they were told by their anti-socialist priests. With political behaviour, social consciousness also shifted towards the importance of class as the determining feature of society. In their quest for a better life, for greater equality and upward mobility, industrial workers and their families had time and again come up against a strict divide. Conversely the middle classes, feeling threatened by the 'masses below', united to confine them permanently to a ghetto – physically, in terms of residential patterns and socially, by denying them access to channels of upward mobility. In doing so they enlisted the help of the state, first by having the government proscribe the working-class movement and later, from 1890, after the anti-socialist laws had lapsed, by police harassment and vigorous prosecution in the courts.

Perceptions and misperceptions of reality can be as powerful in shaping historical developments as reality itself. The point is that for millions of German industrial workers perceptions came to coincide with their actual daily experiences and the realities of their lives. Consequently they began to raise their voices against the discriminations and blatant injustices, and in the age of universal suffrage gave expression to their grievances at the polls by voting in growing numbers for the Social Democrats who excoriated the monarchical class state with its rigid hierarchies and its immobilism. By 1912 the SPD had become the largest party in the Reichstag, attracting some 4.2 million votes (34.8 per cent) and gaining 110 seats.

From the perspective of the 1990s it is not easy to appreciate the full extent to which the repressive organs of the state were used to contain the perceived threat from the working-class movement. However, police surveillance, outrageous court decisions and army orders to be prepared for a violent coup against the socialists and the trade unions were not the only ways in which the state intervened in the lives of the 'dangerous classes'. Its approach amounted rather to a more or less judicious use of carrot and stick *vis-à-vis* industrial workers and of subsidies for the rest. Thus, while the government gave massive help to the 'ailing' agrarians, left behind economically by industry, by erecting protectionist tariffs against foreign competitors, as well as to industry and commerce at home (for example, through support of research) and abroad (for example, through diplomatic and naval protection), Bismarck began to use the powers of the state to introduce social welfare programmes.

The creation of a universal workers' accident insurance was so obviously advantageous to the employers as well, removing the imponderabilities of suits for negligence by injured workers, that it enjoyed broad support. Bismarck's old age pension and health insurance schemes were more controversial, and not just because of their costs. However, in the end the Reich Chancellor's argument prevailed that if workers were given a pension they would stay away from radical parties. In the long run the introduction of welfare state policies may not have worked as intended. The organization of the working class did not decline. Instead it witnessed a seemingly unstoppable rise. What these policies may have done was to strengthen the hands of the moderates within the working-class movement who advocated a gradual transformation of existing socioeconomic and constitutional conditions against the radicals who talked of a violent overthrow. At the same time, state welfarism could not prevent the progressive polarization of national politics prior to 1914.

This applied, to begin with, to industrial relations. Although there were a few branches of industry that slowly moved towards a recognition of trade unions and wage bargaining, most employers' associations continued to pursue a hard line *vis-à-vis* the organized working class. Denied what they believed to be fair material demands, workers increasingly went on strike, to which the employers routinely responded with lock-outs. There were some very bitter labour conflicts in which the police and army promptly sided with the employers and the 'scabs' who were brought in. Overall, 1906 was the first really bad year, with 3,480 strikes and lock-outs. The last years of peace before 1914 saw a fresh wave of labour conflicts involving even larger numbers of workers. In the meantime the willingness of the majority parties and the Reich as well as Federal state authorities to make power-political concessions to the 'masses' also diminished. Indeed, in the eyes of the monarchical government as well as the middle classes and conservative agrarians the idea of constitutional reform in the direction of parliamentarism was so unacceptable that they used every means at their disposal to block a change in the status quo.

It was only in 1917, when the war was going badly, that the Reichstag gained a few additional powers of decision-making and that a promise of constitutional reform was held out, to be realized once victory had been won. Just making this promise for the future cost Chancellor Theobald von Bethmann Hollweg his job, because it was rejected by the powerful military leadership under Hindenburg and Ludendorff and the political forces backing them. The Kaiser was forced to renege on his famous Easter Message. A little more than a year later, Ludendorff went to see the monarch to tell him that the war had been lost militarily. State Secretary Hintze now came up with a cunning scheme. He proposed what amounted to a constitutional revolution: a new Reich government was to be appointed with the approval of the majority in the Reichstag. Germany, for all practical purposes, had become a constitutional monarchy with the Kaiser divested of his many supreme executive powers. The Social Democrats in parliament were among those who supported this solution that had been so persistently denied in previous years. Nor was it difficult to recognize the purpose of Hintze's move: in the hour of defeat the blame was to be shifted away from those who were in fact responsible both for unleashing the First World War and for prolonging it.

However, the 'revolution from above' of October 1918 could not stop the 'revolution from below' that brought the collapse of the Bismarckian Empire from breaking out a month later. At the same time, the political and constitutional revolution that occurred in November 1918 cannot be understood without appreciating the socioeconomic changes of the previous years. If the war had been over by Christmas 1914, as so many confidently expected when it broke out in the summer, the Wilhelmine class state would probably have been stabilized. Yet, as the war turned total and required the mobilization of all resources, the masses began to bear not only the brunt of the sacrifices in lives at the front, but also of the decline in living standards at home. Whereas the scarcity of food due to the Allied blockade benefited agriculture handsomely, and armaments-related industries were profitably producing goods for military victory round the clock, the working classes saw their economic position deteriorate. After 1916 the middle classes also began to feel the pinch. Still, at least they had valuables and savings that they could deploy on the black market to barter food for their families. What in the long run would hit them worse was that they had bought government bonds in support of the war effort, redeemable with attractive additional interest earnings after victory. It was only after the defeat that nemesis hit them: their bond certificates quickly became worthless scraps of paper. They had been virtually expropriated.

For the majority of the population the advent of total war therefore meant socioeconomic change for the worse, not to mention the demographic and psychological impact of the unprecedented blood-letting in the trenches. Social tension rose. By 1917 the government had to cope with food riots and massive strikes. The earlier consciousness of living in a class society and the increased tensions now escalated into open class conflict. Even if the October Revolution of 1918 had succeeded, there is little doubt that German society and its once prosperous industrial economy would have emerged completely changed from the experience of war and defeat.

Select bibliography

Demography, urbanization and economic change

Bade, K.-J., *Population, Labour and Migration in 19th- and 20th-Century Germany* (1987).
Bry, G., *Wages in Germany, 1871–1914* (1960).
Desai, A. V., *Real Wages in Germany, 1971-1914* (1968).
Henderson, W. O., *The Rise of German Industrial Power, 1834–1914* (1975).
Knodel, J., *The Decline of Fertility in Germany, 1871–1939* (1974).
Lee, W. R., ed., *Industrialisation and Industrial Growth in Germany* (1986).
Stolper, G., *The German Economy from 1870 to the Present* (1967).
Witt, P.-Chr., ed., *Wealth and Taxation in Central Europe* (1987).

Society and political mobilization

Augustine, D., *Patricians and Parvenus* (1994).
Bigler, R. M., *The Politics of German Protestantism* (1972).
Dahrendorf, R., *Democracy and Society in Germany* (1968).

10

Wilhelmine Germany

Katharine A. Lerman

The transition from the 'Bismarckian' era, dominated by the consequences of political unification and the need to consolidate a national state, to the 'Wilhelmine' era, where the political agenda was shaped by the rise of a new kind of popular politics and the desire to secure Germany's place as a world power, represented a significant caesura in the lives of most subjects of the *Kaiserreich*. The changes in the political landscape from the late 1880s obviously reflected the rapid transformation of Germany's economy and society, as well as a shifting cultural climate under the impact of new intellectual currents (or the popularization of older ones) and ideological challenges. Many of these changes were not unique to Germany but had a wider European resonance. Yet for contemporaries the departure of the conservative 'founder of the Reich' in 1890 and the advent of the brashly self-assertive young Kaiser, Wilhelm II, appeared to symbolize the changed mood. From 1890 German politics reflected not only the fears and insecurities which accompanied unprecedented social change, but also the inflated expectations, overweening self-confidence and optimism about the future which were engendered by a growing consciousness of Germany's military and economic dynamism. This juxtaposition of anxiety with hubris and ambition is often remarked upon with respect to Wilhelmine Germany. But it makes the task of interpreting the direction of German policy before the First World War and, in particular, Germany's responsibility for that war particularly difficult for historians.

I The rise of mass politics

The decade of the 1890s has been seen by some historians as the crucial period when the masses made their dramatic and explosive entry into German politics. Geoff Eley has written of the 'decomposition' of the

Bismarckian system of politics after 1890, linking this not so much to the political consequences of Bismarck's dismissal as to the growth of new political and social forces, and the fragmentation and decline of German liberalism. As the electorate expanded and became more politicized, it is argued that the older pattern of politics, which had pertained during the Bismarck era and depended on a significant proportion of the German population remaining outside the political process, was replaced by a new form of popular politics which was better adapted to the needs of a modern industrial society. Political parties, which had formerly functioned success-fully as loose associations of prestigious notables who came together mainly to win elections, were now challenged by demands from new social groups for mass representation and participation. To survive in the political environment of the 1890s political parties had to become better organized, campaign more intensively during elections, and develop new strategies for mobilizing mass support.

Obviously the rise of mass politics was not a phenomenon confined to Germany. Across Europe, politics reflected the impact of industrialization and urbanization, improvements in education and literacy, the rise of the popular press, and the growing strength of civil society, as witnessed, for example, in the proliferation of voluntary associations and other organiza-tions which sought to shape the contours of public life independently from the state. In most European countries, too, the growth of state intervention was bound to trigger some kind of popular response, especially from those who perceived that their interests were ignored or disadvantaged by state initiatives. Nevertheless, despite wider European trends, the breakthrough of the masses may be seen as particularly significant and consequential in the German context. The rapid pace of German industrialization, the authoritarian features of the Bismarckian political system, and the early introduction of universal male suffrage in 1867 were all peculiar to the German situation, serving to make the process of adjustment to the new political conditions particularly painful and traumatic for the established political parties. The rise of new political issues after Bismarck's departure in 1890, from commercial and fiscal policies to armaments and imperial-ism, as well as the severity of the structural crisis which affected German agriculture in the 1890s, contributed to the process of political mobiliza-tion, encouraging new forms of organization and popular protest among those who had previously lacked a political voice. Finally, the large number of nationalist associations and economic interest groups, which came into being after 1890 to address these issues, helped to develop new techniques of political agitation and a more demagogic political style, even if they never achieved the status of mass movements.

The most visible evidence for the impact of new social forces on German politics in the 1890s is undoubtedly furnished by the history of the German Social Democratic Party or SPD, whose membership and electoral support increased in leaps and bounds after the lapse of Bismarck's anti-socialist legislation in 1890 and whose strong presence on the left made itself felt across the entire political spectrum in Germany. Radicalized by 12 years of persecution and committed to defend the interests of the industrial proletariat, the party gained 19.7 per cent of the vote (35 out of 397 seats) in the Reichstag elections of February 1890 and attracted more votes than any other party. By 1912 over a third of the German electorate was prepared to vote for a party which had resisted all internal challenges and adhered rigorously to orthodox Marxism as its official ideology from 1891. Despite the electoral system's in-built bias against the party's urban voters (because constituency boundaries were never redrawn to reflect patterns of internal migration), the party gained 110 seats in the elections of 1912 and was the biggest party in the Reichstag on the eve of the First World War. In Prussia, however, the three-class suffrage ensured that it did not gain representation in the Landtag until 1908 (when it achieved 23 per cent of the vote but only eight out of a total of 433 seats). States such as Saxony and the city of Hamburg even adopted more restrictive franchises in order to thwart SPD majorities.

The SPD was the first German political party to develop into a highly organized, centralized, democratically structured and increasingly bureaucratic mass party. Its electoral success at national level (it only lost seats – but not votes – in the 'Hottentot elections' of 1907 which led it to rethink its strategy) was matched by a steady growth in its membership during the Wilhelmine era, so that by 1914 it had over one million members. The party offered its members a wide range of social and cultural activities from choral societies to cycling excursions, and has been seen as creating an entire 'sub-culture' in Wilhelmine Germany. Perhaps most importantly the party's supporters were sustained by an optimistic and all-inclusive ideology of progress which guaranteed that the future would belong to them.

The growth of the socialist movement was mirrored by the increasing strength of trade unionism in Germany before the First World War. Although the majority of German workers were not members of a trade union by 1914, socialist, liberal and Christian trade union organizations vied with each other to attract working-class support. The Free Trade Unions, affiliated to the SPD, were by far the most successful, developing from quite small and elitist organizations of activists in the 1890s to a formidable movement with nearly three million members by 1913. The

General Commission under Karl Legien which directed the Free Trade Unions was able to exert considerable pressure on the political leadership of the SPD, for example opposing the use of the mass strike as a political weapon (which was urged by Rosa Luxemburg and the extreme left of the party under the impact of the Russian revolution of 1905) since it might provoke the authorities into military repression.

The political impact of the growth of the industrial working class has received much attention within the context of an historiography which is not only interested in understanding the role of the SPD in Wilhelmine politics but also in charting the early history of a movement which assumed major political importance in the later stages of the First World War and during the 'German revolution' of 1918–19. Nevertheless, while the growth of mass politics in the 1890s and early 1900s undeniably benefited the SPD, the debate among Wilhelmine historians concerning the politicization of the masses and the significance of the 1890s has tended to focus more on the role of popular forces in reshaping German conservatism and the right than on the incontrovertible evidence of mass mobilization by the left.

A marked feature of the Wilhelmine political landscape was the proliferation of nationalist associations such as the Pan-German League (1891), the Society for the Eastern Marches (1894), the Navy League (1898), the Imperial League against Social Democracy (1904) and the Army League (1912). While the membership of the Pan-German League never exceeded 23,000, the Navy League, bolstered by government support and the social prestige of prominent supporters, attracted 331,000 members on the eve of the First World War. These associations used to be seen as signifying an anti-democratic pluralism which served to bypass parliament and ultimately benefited the government. But detailed studies have shown that they were not pliant instruments of government policy, even if their goals sometimes overlapped. Their direct political influence has also often been exaggerated, although the Imperial League Against Social Democracy played a significant role in the Reichstag elections of 1907 and the high-profile propaganda of the Navy and Army Leagues helped to create the political climate in which successive navy bills and the army bills of 1912–13 were passed. The nationalist associations were quite prepared to criticize the government if it suited their political purposes (as during the Second Moroccan Crisis of 1911 when they expected substantial colonial gains in Africa after the despatch of the German gunboat *Panther* to Agadir) and they certainly were significant in generating a more radical and demagogic style of politics. But how far their mobilization of popular support extended beyond specific issues and created a new kind of populist politics which challenged the hegemony of traditional elites is debatable. Middle-aged bureaucrats, military men, professionals and businessmen figured prominently in the associations which, as a recent study of the Army League by Marilyn Coetzee has confirmed, were not ideologically committed to demolishing traditional patterns of political behaviour and whose membership often declined rapidly once the immediate objectives were achieved. The claim that they served to mobilize a new social constituency among the *Mittelstand* or petty bourgeoisie is at best unproven.

Probably more important in mobilizing large numbers of people who had previously remained outside the political process was the Agrarian League. The formation of the Agrarian League in 1893, largely in response to the commercial policies of the 'New Course' under Chancellor Leo von Caprivi, played a significant role in mobilizing rural interests behind the campaign for agricultural protectionism and became particularly influential in Prussia east of the Elbe. The mainly Catholic farmers' and peasants' associations fulfilled a similar role in the south and west of Germany. Recent research by David Blackbourn, Ian Farr and others has emphasized how the new agrarian radicalism in the 1890s was neither manufactured nor manipulated by the prominent Junkers in the Agrarian League for their own exclusive purposes (see the articles by Ian Farr and Hans Jürgen Puhle in *Peasants and Lords* edited by Robert G. Moeller; and the articles by Ian Farr, David Blackbourn and Geoff Eley in *Society and Politics in Wilhelmine Germany* edited by Richard J. Evans). Rather, it represented a genuine rural populism whose origins lay in local peasant grievances and the increasing economic insecurity of independent producers and craftsmen. If all the political parties, including the SPD in southern Germany, attempted to garner support from this new rural constituency in the 1890s, the outcome – the eventual realignment of the right – was by no means certain. The revolt of the *Mittelstand* initially played into the hands of the anti-Semitic splinter parties. Anti-Semitic deputies commanded 16 seats in the Reichstag in 1893 and their disappearance after 1900 is generally attributed to the incorporation of their anti-Semitic ideology into mainstream political conservatism. Ultimately those parties which succeeded in gaining or regaining the support of a disaffected peasantry were forced to change and adapt their programmes as a consequence. The Conservative Party emerged from its trials in the 1890s unswervingly committed to protectionism, anti-Semitism and anti-socialism. The Centre, too, despite support from Catholic workers in urban areas, found itself having to cater increasingly to the needs of its predominantly peasant and *Mittelstand* constituency, a development which helps to explain its political shift to the right, at least until 1912–13.

The argument that the German masses became politicized in the 1890s is in many respects a compelling one but needs considerable qualification. Local and regional studies have highlighted the extreme volatility of rural politics in the 1890s and indicated that all the Bismarckian parties had difficulties adjusting to the new conditions. Nevertheless, if the established political parties found they had to become better organized and develop new means of mobilizing popular support, this appears to have been a response to a *decline* in popular participation in national elections rather than to the sudden entry of the masses into German politics. It has been pointed out that the turnout in the three Reichstag elections during the 1890s was lower than in the previous election of 1887 or the subsequent election of 1903. Turnout increased markedly over the whole period of the *Kaiserreich* from 51 per cent in 1871 to a remarkable 85 per cent in 1912, but there is no evidence that the decade of the 1890s was a particular watershed in this respect. Indeed, it is clear that the *Kulturkampf* of the 1870s was far more important in mobilizing the Catholic electorate (approximately one-third of the German population) than any of the 'modern' techniques developed by the parties or pressure groups after 1890. Not only the liberal parties but also the Conservatives and Centre were losing support in the 1890s; the activities of the Agrarian League and the Catholic peasant associations were attempts to counter this trend rather than mobilize new sources of support. The elections of 1898, which took place at the end of these allegedly crucial years of politicization, were also apparently the dullest on record, notwithstanding the calls of the Prussian Finance Minister, Miquel, for a *Sammlung* (rallying) of those parties which supported the state. Undoubtedly the masses were becoming progressively more politicized and involved in the political process, but the growth of mass politics, in Germany and elsewhere, appears to have been a longer, slower process rather than the notion of a sudden explosive 'entry' suggests.

Conclusions about the significance of the 1890s have often been too sweeping or based on partial and incomplete evidence. The Conservatives did develop a more modern party structure, but there were inevitable tensions within a political party which was hostile to democracy. If they ultimately capitalized on agrarian discontent, this was not self-evident in the 1890s. The Conservatives' share of the vote actually declined from 15.2 per cent in 1887 to 9.2 per cent in 1912, virtually halving the number of their seats in the Reichstag from 80 to 43. The Centre managed to regain its wavering peasant support but it never developed into a modern political party with membership contributions (like the SPD) or a clearly defined structure; rather, it remained a party reliant on committees of notables and

Catholic associations, as well as priests and the church hierarchy during elections. Finally, too much emphasis has been placed on the decline of German liberalism during the 1890s, apparently squeezed between the rise of organized labour and the new agrarian radicalism which benefited the Centre and the right. Yet, taking the two wings of liberalism together, their share of the national vote remained quite constant throughout the Wilhelmine period, and the left-liberals clearly succeeded in picking up support among new, expanding social groups such as teachers and white collar workers. If the National Liberals lost Reichstag seats, this often reflected the distribution of its electorate across constituencies and its shortage of 'safe seats'; by 1912 both the National Liberals and the newly reunited left-liberal Progressive People's Party had to win most of their seats in the 'run-off' elections held between the two main contenders in constituencies where no one party had achieved an overall majority. It is true that the liberals developed an organized party structure later than the Conservatives (from 1904–5), that they could not rely on economic or Catholic organizations to mobilize popular support for them, and that they remained much more committed to the kind of elitist, notable politics which continued to bring them such success in municipal elections where the democratic franchise did not apply. Yet it would be a mistake to write off their national electoral support because they, like their main competitors, lost ground in the 1890s. The problems of the liberals had a longer gestation (they can be traced back at least to the introduction of universal suffrage in 1867 and the impact of the depression from 1873) and were not primarily attributable to an alleged failure to adapt to new conditions in the 1890s.

Altogether there has been a tendency to classify the Wilhelmine political parties too rigidly in terms of sociocultural milieu, for example Catholic, agrarian–conservative, Protestant–bourgeois and Protestant-working class, and to make assumptions about the popular support of parties on the basis of their membership, the concerns of their activists or the political strategies of their representatives in parliament. Jonathan Sperber's research on voting behaviour in the *Kaiserreich* indicates that the boundaries between such milieux were far more fluid than generally assumed and that voters could shift their allegiance between parties – not least the Conservatives and the SPD – which were previously considered completely antithetical. Men who were mobilized to vote conservative or liberal on a nationalist issue, for example in the elections of 1887 or 1907, might vote differently in an election, such as that of 1903, which revolved chiefly around the issue of the price of bread in the wake of the new tariff law. If a party's share of the popular vote remained fairly constant over the imperial era, this did not necessarily mean that its social constituency remained stable or unchanged.

Perhaps the most interesting conclusion of Sperber's recent work on electoral behaviour concerns the popular support of the apparently proletarian SPD. Sperber challenges traditional assumptions by suggesting that only about 51 per cent of the party's voters in 1912 can be categorized as emanating from the (mainly Protestant) working class; the remaining 49 per cent appear to have been from the middle classes, again chiefly Protestant bourgeois but also secularized Catholics. Again, this may not be so surprising if it is remembered that one in three voters opted for the SPD in 1912 and that it gained over 75 per cent of the vote in a city like Berlin. If the SPD can claim credentials as a 'people's party' before 1914, gloomy assessments that it must have reached 'saturation point' in terms of its potential vote by 1912 appear wide of the mark. Its broader social appeal is also confirmed by the success of its mass peace rallies in 1911–12 which clearly attracted middle-class support. The electoral pact between the SPD and the Progressive People's Party for the run-off elections in 1912 may also not have been so unpopular with the supporters of both parties as some historians have assumed.

Altogether much has been written about the nature of the Wilhelmine political parties, but there clearly remains more to be learnt about their relations with each other in the contemporary context. It is understandable that historians have looked to the parties and nationalist associations of the Wilhelmine period to illuminate such issues as the social constituency of Nazism or the origins of *Lebensraum* (living space) ideology. It is undeniably important, too, to understand why it was that the SPD split during the First World War and how the later 'Weimar coalition' of Centre, left liberals and moderate socialists came into being. Nevertheless the danger of an overly teleological perpective can be that countervailing tendencies are all too often overlooked or ignored. In terms of its popular support, the SPD was not the same party in 1912 that it was in 1890; nor were the liberals (who also attracted working-class and Catholic support) so doomed as often supposed. Similarly, local studies can be invaluable in pointing to the shifting nature of political identities, the difficulties in forging internal party compromises and the variable factors which accounted for a party's support. To be a National Liberal voter in Hanover did not mean the same thing as being a National Liberal supporter in Württemberg or the Rhineland. But there is also a danger in extrapolating too much from local studies about national trends.

Finally, it must be stated that all the interest in the Wilhelmine political parties and nationalist associations cannot overcome one vital qualification concerning their political importance before 1914. Within the imperial German political system they could play only a very specific and prescribed role. However significant for the future, the development of the parties and the politicization of the masses could exert no more than an influence on the course of imperial domestic and foreign policy before 1914. To understand Wilhelmine high politics it is thus necessary to shift attention away from the trappings of democracy and the nascent populism at local level to the corridors of the bureaucracy in Berlin and the machinations at the Kaiser's court. However, at this level, too, there is lively controversy about the responsibility for German policy and considerable disagreement about how the political system was evolving.

II   Wilhelmine government and the role of Kaiser Wilhelm II

Discussion of imperial domestic politics between 1890 and 1914 is inevitably overshadowed by the outbreak of the First World War and the issue of political responsibility. Bismarck's departure in 1890 and the embarkation of Germany's rulers on a new course which eventually embraced military and naval expansion, imperialism and war, focus attention on the nature of German decision-making processes. Yet the gulf between the written and real constitutions, the interplay between different power factors and the rapid growth of new political and social forces to challenge the established authorities all leave much scope for conflicting interpretations of Germany's political development between 1890 and 1914. The more extreme assertions of 20 years ago – that government policy after Bismarck was determined by the anonymous forces of an authoritarian polycracy (Wehler), that the real ruler in Berlin from 1897 was Kaiser Wilhelm II (Röhl) or that the Reich by the early 1890s was a virtually ungovernable entity (Mommsen) – may now have been abandoned or heavily qualified, but important differences of perspective and methodology remain. The assumption is now quite widespread in the historiography that the German political system was in a state of crisis before 1914, whether that crisis is defined as 'permanent' from 1890 (Wehler), 'latent' (Mommsen) or 'stable' (Nipperdey). But not all historians accept that such a crisis existed, let alone that the decisions of July 1914 were a response to the domestic impasse.

   The debate about Kaiser Wilhelm II's 'personal rule' highlights some of the difficulties in interpreting German policy and decision-making before 1914, and points to the shortcomings of the political system as a whole. Kaiser Wilhelm II provided an essential element of continuity in German high politics from 1888 to 1918, yet there is little consensus among historians about the significance of his role. To a certain extent the debate rehearses some of the arguments which assume greater urgency later with respect to Hitler's position in the Third Reich. It reflects different kinds of historical explanation and familiar disputes about the importance of individual motivations and decisions within wider historical structures and processes. Yet it also reflects different frames of reference and different ambitions. The historian whose main interest is in high politics and the oligarchy at the top will obviously reach different conclusions from a historian who defines the regime more broadly, and is interested in the exercise of *Herrschaft* (power and authority) throughout society or the impact of Reich laws across a range of economic and social, public and private spheres. Similarly a chosen methodology may brilliantly expose the inadequacy of Germany's decision-making structures or the inferior quality of its government before 1914, but be quite inadequate if the aim is more ambitious and directed towards understanding the political, economic and social structures which supported German aggression in the first half of the twentieth century.

Neither contemporaries nor historians have doubted Wilhelm II's desire to rule personally. Encouraged as a young man to uphold Prussian auto-cratic traditions as a counterweight to the liberal tendencies of his parents, Wilhelm was convinced of his divine right to rule and wholly unwilling to play the modest role within the political system which his grandfather, Wilhelm I, had accepted. Within less than two years of his accession to the throne in June 1888, he had accumulated sufficient authority and prestige to force Bismarck's resignation. Convinced that he alone made German policy, that the task of ministers was to execute his orders and that his country 'must follow me wherever I go', Wilhelm was an irascible and unpredictable man who rarely tolerated contradiction. Among those who came into contact with the young monarch in the early 1890s, admirers praised his 'splendid qualities' and 'individuality' while his detractors lamented his 'immaturity', 'eccentricity' and 'psychic imbalance'.

Bismarck's departure plunged Germany into a protracted period of constitutional crisis which eventually clarified the extent to which the political settlement of 1867–71 had vested extensive powers in the imperial and Prussian monarchy. As King of Prussia, Wilhelm enjoyed prerogatives which had scarcely changed since the era of Friedrich Wilhelm IV, and in the 1890s he reinforced his position as 'the *de facto* minister-president' of Prussia by frequently presiding over meetings of the Prussian Ministry of State as 'crown councils'. In the Reich the constitution explicitly granted the Kaiser sovereignty in matters of foreign policy, the right to declare war and conclude peace, control of all personnel appointments in the administration (including the Reich Chancellor), the right to dissolve the Reichstag, and personal command over the army and navy. It was above all Wilhelm's power of appointment which prevented the evolution of a more collective system of government after Bismarck's resignation, a development which was particularly fateful given that none of Bismarck's successors as Chancellor could expect to enjoy comparable power and prestige within the executive. The Kaiser was able to remove ministers who proved too independent-minded or recalcitrant one by one, replacing them with men who knew that they owed their positions and allegiance exclusively to the crown.

In the 1890s Bismarck's successors struggled to maintain their authority in the face of a concerted drive by the Kaiser and his close friends to establish his 'personal rule'. But neither General Leo von Caprivi (1890–94) nor the ageing Prince Chlodwig zu Hohenlohe-Schillingsfürst (1894–1900) were able to prevent the progressive emasculation of the 'responsible government' which was simultaneously subjected to remorseless monarchical pressure, humiliating parliamentary defeats and damaging attacks by the bitterly critical 'Bismarck *fronde*'. From 1897 Hohenlohe was scarcely more than a 'straw Chancellor' and was effectively excluded from key areas of decision-making. New ministers such as Bülow and Tirpitz, the State Secretaries at the Foreign and Navy Offices, enjoyed Wilhelm II's confidence and wielded more influence than the Chancellor. While the Kaiser intervened more and more directly in political affairs, the 'responsible government' lacked all cohesion and departments went their own way.

This 'departmental anarchy' only ceased in October 1900 when Bernhard von Bülow became Reich Chancellor. A diplomat whose rapid promotion in the 1890s owed most to the influence of the Kaiser's best friend, Count Philipp zu Eulenburg, Bülow had promised in 1896 to institute 'personal rule in the good sense'[1] and he made his confidential relationship with the Kaiser the pivot of his government. By identifying himself closely with the Kaiser's will and making the retention of Wilhelm's trust his highest priority, Bülow effectively silenced ministerial opposition and restored the authority of the Chancellor. But the new stability after 1900 was achieved at a high price. First, Bülow had no interest in strengthening collegiate government, promoting a sense of collective responsibility or even encouraging the circulation of information throughout the executive. Preferring more secretive methods and relying on a few close advisers, he alienated his colleagues and subordinates by presenting them with *faits accomplis* and he remained indifferent to the work of the ministerial bureaucracy unless it threatened to give rise to political complications. Departments and individuals thus continued to enjoy considerable administrative autonomy and their work was neither coordinated nor subjected to rigorous political control. Second, although, for example, Bülow's self-chosen role as the 'king's minister' was successful in the short term in discouraging Wilhelm II's direct interventions in political matters, it did nothing to dispel the monarch's conviction of his 'personal rule'. Once difficulties began to accumulate in foreign and domestic policy from 1905–6, Bülow found he had few reserves on which he could draw when the Kaiser concluded he needed to intervene more directly himself. For example, at a critical juncture in the First Moroccan Crisis of 1905-6 (when Wilhelm II's landing at Tangiers and treatment of the Sultan of Morocco as an independent sovereign provoked a major crisis in Franco-German relations and much talk of war before an international conference was convened at Algeciras in early 1906) the Kaiser insisted on appointing a new favourite, Heinrich von Tschirschky, as State Secretary of the Foreign Office. While Bülow was obliged to preserve a semblance of harmony with Tschirschky, there were soon rumours of a 'Tschirschky circle' and a 'Bülow camp', with Tschirschky privately criticizing the Chancellor's laziness and his lack of a single 'productive, positive idea' in foreign policy, and Bülow seeking to undermine Tschirschky's position with the Kaiser by spreading press reports of the State Secretary's close association with the Bismarcks.[2]

It was above all the *Daily Telegraph* affair of November 1908 which focused public attention on the consequences of the Kaiser's 'personal rule' (a contemporary term). The storm over the publication of Wilhelm's naive and ill-considered remarks in the British newspaper (the Kaiser claimed, for example, that he had helped draw up the British plan of campaign in the Boer War) constituted the most serious domestic crisis in his reign before 1914, for a time precipitating united and unprecedented condemnation from the Chancellor, the Prussian Ministry of State, the Bundesrat, the Reichstag and the press, and calling the future of the monarchy itself into question. Nevertheless, the opportunity was lost to extract constitutional guarantees from the Kaiser against a repetition of such events. Despite accumulating an impressive array of support, Bülow was content merely to secure verbal assurances from Wilhelm, effectively transforming the political crisis into a personal one between Kaiser and Chancellor and ensuring that its only lasting consequence would be Wilhelm's determination to dismiss him as soon as politically possible.

The debate on the Kaiser's 'personal rule' exercised contemporaries and has produced little consensus among historians since. The Kaiser himself felt utterly betrayed by his Chancellor in 1908, convinced that in cooperating closely with Bülow he had fulfilled the role of a constitutional monarch since 1900 and that there had been no question of 'an autocratic regime which circumnavigated the Reich Chancellor'.[3] Historians, too, have been reluctant to interpret the interventions of 'Wilhelm the sudden' as constituting evidence of monarchical rule in Germany before the First World War. For many, 'personalistic explanations' of German decision-making before 1914 smack too much of the 'great man' theory of history and leave no scope for the evolution of more modern and anonymous processes of negotiation between different coalitions of interests. For others, the thesis of 'personal rule' ignores the significance of bureaucratic power in Wilhelmine Germany and in particular the extent to which the imperial bureaucracy succeeded, irrespective of the Kaiser's will, in playing an obstructive, preventive or ameliorative role in the decision-making process. Finally, historians have pointed to the defects in Wilhelm II's personality which made him an ineffectual and incompetent ruler. The Kaiser, it seems, was too weak, erratic, unpredictable, superficial, restless and peripatetic, to exert much of an influence on Berlin politics. His life was an endless whirl of state occasions, social events, military manoeuvres, court ceremonies, parades, cruises, foreign visits and hunting trips. Not bureaucratic by nature (but then neither was Bismarck or Hitler), he disliked routine work and never commanded the details of government policy.

Ironically it has often been those historians most critical of the thesis of the Kaiser's 'personal rule' (such as Mommsen and Wehler) who have been inclined to adopt virtually impossible criteria as a measure of the role of human agency in history, seeking to isolate Wilhelm from the wider institutional structure and ignore all the given constraints on the exercise of monarchical power. In searching for evidence of mature thought and a clarity of aims on Wilhelm's part, for consistency of purpose and a determined will to pursue matters to their conclusion, for concrete and unambiguous results of Wilhelm's actions, they have too often adopted the language and methodology of human intention and consequence which they purport to disdain. Clearly there is evidence of the Kaiser's direct involvement in decision-making from his decisive support for naval armaments, through his interest in specific areas of domestic legislation, such as social policy or the measures against the Poles in Prussia's eastern provinces, to his very frequent interventions in diplomacy and foreign policy. Moreover, if personal convictions are widely seen to have played a role in explaining the policies of Tirpitz, Miquel or Posadowsky (the conscientious State Secretary of the Reich Office of Interior responsible for much of the social legislation of the Wilhelmine era), it is quite ridiculous to deny the political importance of Wilhelm II's personality.

The tendency to define 'personal rule' as Wilhelm II's 'unconstitutional interference' (Mommsen) has proved particularly unhelpful. Much more fruitful has been new research into monarchical structures or 'the kingship mechanism' (Elias) in Wilhelmine Germany, so that even Wehler, who once dismissed the Kaiser as 'a weak figure atop a clay pedestal'[4] has revised his earlier assessment. There is now widespread agreement about the political significance of Wilhelm's powers of appointment and patronage, the effects of which reverberated throughout the entire bureaucracy as ministers, state secretaries and officials found that their influence waxed and waned in accordance with the favour and goodwill bestowed on them by the Kaiser. One state secretary later remarked that 'given the nature of the ruler, it was completely insignificant who was minister at any one time', for men who had no support in the parliaments or among the people had few means of opposing the monarch if they were determined to keep their privileges.[5]

The ultimate dependence of the entire internal administration on the Kaiser for their careers must be seen as an important qualification to any suggestions that real power resided with the 'independent bureaucratic government' (Mommsen) in Imperial Germany. Despite the growing professionalization, *esprit de corps* and self-interest of the bureaucracy and irrespective of its increasing impact on everyday life, the bureaucrats who staffed the Prussian ministries and Reich offices were essentially lawyers by training and (as was frequently lamented before 1914) many lacked even elementary political skills. A recent study of the 'social policy' of Berlepsch, the Prussian Minister of Trade in the early 1890s, concluded that it could not meet expectations because he took a bureaucratic rather than a political route to reform, simply trying to implement the Kaiser's February Decrees of 1890. Most of the men in the bureaucratic elite could not provide political leadership, a problem which was exacerbated because the Prussian Ministry of State was a very heterogeneous body, variously composed of bureaucrats, diplomats, generals, admirals and even ex-parliamentarians, who had all been appointed at different times for different reasons and shared none of the similarity of outlook characteristic of a modern party cabinet. On the two isolated occasions when the Chancellor and Prussian Ministry of State collectively confronted the Kaiser and insisted on the removal of a 'king's minister', namely the Köller crisis of 1895 and the Podbielski crisis of 1906, their victory soon proved a pyrrhic one since the Kaiser never forgave those who manoeuvred him into a position of constraint. In the Reich, unlike in Prussia, there was not even the semblance of a collective body before June 1914 when the very first conference of the heads of the Reich departments was held on the initiative of the State Secretary of Interior, Clemens von Delbrück.

Recent work on the Kaiser's court and entourage by John Röhl and Isabel Hull has ensured that Wilhelm can no longer be seen as an isolated individual but as operating within his own elevated and distinct power sphere. The Kaiser's court not only constituted the pinnacle of an elaborate social hierarchy in which the members of the civilian government generally occupied a very inferior position, but it was also fundamental to the real constitution of Wilhelmine Germany, linked to the state apparatus and military command posts through the influence of the Kaiser's civil, military and naval cabinets and serving also as an important communications network within the ruling elite. The size of the Kaiser's court expanded dramatically under Wilhelm II. It employed some 3,500 people at the turn of the century and also proved very costly to maintain, receiving 22.2 million marks from state resources in 1910. The precedence given according to birth, status and military rank, the pomp and ceremony, the invitations to balls and festivities, the honours, titles, orders and decorations bestowed by the monarch were all overt and visible symbols of the existence of a flourishing 'court culture' in Wilhelmine Germany. The position of the ruling elite cannot be understood without reference to its political and social dependence on the monarchy as an institution; nor can the mentality of those in high office be appreciated without reference to traditions of deference and the influence of monarchism as an ideology. Germany's monarchical structures may have had a much wider, deeper and more lasting impact on German society than is generally assumed. It is surely not without significance, for example, that both Franz von Papen and Kurt von Schleicher (the two Chancellors in 1932–3 who helped pave the way for Hitler) began their careers as royal pages at the Kaiser's court.

As well as the political and social hierarchies, the Kaiser stood at the apex of a third, quite separate hierarchy which was undeniably important in the *Kaiserreich*, namely the military. However incompetent Wilhelm may have been as the 'supreme war lord' and coordinator of Germany's armed forces, there was constitutionally no scope for any political interference in his 'power of command'. Indeed, effective political control over the army could only be exercised through the monarch, aided by his military cabinet. The army swore loyalty and obedience exclusively to the Kaiser, and the political significance of this relationship can scarcely be exaggerated. Invariably appearing in military uniform and surrounded by military men, Wilhelm often chose generals in preference to bureaucrats to head offices of state and, unlike ministers, generals had the right of direct access to the monarch whenever they wished. The German Foreign Office always suspected the influence of the Kaiser's military and naval attachés who had the potential to run a kind of parallel diplomatic service, circumventing the official diplomatic channels. Moreover, after the homosexuality scandals of 1906–9 ensured that Wilhelm's closest civilian friends in the so-called 'Liebenberg circle' were banned from court, the influence of the Kaiser's military entourage was unrivalled. Repeatedly, when it came to a clash between civilian and military authority, the Kaiser took the army's side. The plight of the 'responsible government' in 1913 during the Zabern affair, when Wilhelm insisted that the Chancellor, Bethmann Hollweg (1909–17) defend army transgressions in the Alsatian town and the Reichstag impotently passed a vote of no confidence, is a salutary reminder of the extent to which Wilhelmine Germany remained a military monarchy rather than a constitutional state.

The hereditary Prussian monarch thus continued to enjoy political, military and social power in Wilhelmine Germany and the significance of his prerogatives should not be underestimated. Transposing modern political categories and concepts on to pre-1914 Germany leads to distortions unless it is remembered that national state structures were relatively undeveloped, that the 'government' consisted exclusively of crown appointees and that, unlike the Kaiser, neither the political parties nor the bureaucrats warranted a mention in the imperial constitution. Moreover, despite occasional objections from modern historians to the term 'Wilhelminism' as a description of the era between 1890 and 1918, there can be little doubt that Wilhelm II's personality impressed itself on German politics and society, whether to inspire enthusiastic dreams of a new kind of 'imperial monarchy' or prompt intensely gloomy forebodings about the burden his reign placed on Germany's political development.

Finally, in Europe before 1914 monarchies still outnumbered republics as systems of state organization, and dynastic ties continued to exert an influence both on German foreign policy and on relations between the German federal states, most of which continued to be headed by monarchs and princes. A strong monarchy was seen as the single, proven, viable alternative to parliamentarism and (as Dominic Lieven has pointed out with respect to the Russian autocracy) it was the rational choice of government for all those, often highly intelligent people who resisted the latter. Before 1914 there was little real pressure, even from the people's elected representatives, for a full parliamentarization of the German political system. Even in October 1918, after four years of unsuccessful war, the evident nervous collapse of Wilhelm II and the establishment of a virtual dictatorship by the military, only a tiny minority within the left of centre political parties were republicans who wished to see the abolition of the monarchy altogether. After the establishment of the Weimar Republic, officials, judges and military officers continued to talk and behave 'in the old style', disaffected royalists were actively disloyal and the post-war crisis encouraged many to look back nostalgically on the 'good old days' before 1914. To understand fully the role of the monarchy before 1918, we must also research more thoroughly into the effects of its collapse.

III   Armaments, foreign policy and war

The controversy over Germany's role in unleashing the First World War has largely been laid to rest by German historians. However much blame may be apportioned to the other protagonists in the July crisis of 1914 and whatever the significance of longer-term diplomatic, political, social, economic and intellectual forces in propelling Europe towards war in 1914, the direction of German policy in these crucial weeks is clear. The decision-makers in Berlin undoubtedly escalated the crisis after the assassination of the heir to the Austrian throne, the Archduke Franz Ferdinand, and his wife in June 1914. Their so-called 'blank cheque', assuring Austria of German support if she chose to deal energetically with Serbia (whom they immediately suspected was implicated in the murder), their pressure on Vienna to act speedily and decisively, their quashing of mediation attempts by other powers, and their secret preparations for war, all bear out the view, widely expressed within the imperial ruling elite, that Germany believed the moment had arrived to break out of her perceived encirclement by a hostile coalition of Entente powers. Kaiser Wilhelm II declared that it was 'now or never' for Austria to deal with the Serbs;[6] the Chancellor, Bethmann Hollweg, believed his hardest duty was to take this 'leap in the dark';[7] and the military began preparations for the two-front war which, in accordance with the dictates of the Schlieffen plan, would begin with the invasion of Belgium. After the Austrians began shelling Belgrade across the Danube on 29 July, Germany still insisted officially that the developing conflict should remain localized, yet she sacrificed the interests and security of her ally unashamedly. Austria was allowed neither the time nor the opportunity to achieve her objectives against Serbia before Berlin's declaration of war, and strategic planning ensured that she was called upon to relieve pressure on Germany by opening the Galician front. Only five days after Germany, and under pressure from her ally, Austria reluctantly declared war on Russia on 6 August.

There is also overwhelming evidence that Germany's rulers were fully conscious of the implications of their actions for the peace of Europe in 1914. Since the Balkan Wars of 1912–13, they had been preoccupied with the possibility of a general European war resulting from a crisis in the Balkans, a war which (as the Kaiser made clear to his military and naval advisers in December 1912) would almost certainly number Britain among Germany's enemies. Yet they were obviously prepared to risk such a war in 1914 not least because, given the scale of the arms race over the previous decade, they were convinced that their chances of victory would diminish if they procrastinated. Having secured Reichstag acceptance of two army bills in 1912 and 1913, the second of which constituted an unprecedented increase of military strength in peacetime, Germany was presented with a 'window of opportunity' before the effects of changes to the French and Russian military programmes made themselves felt by about 1917. Convinced that Germany was still a match for her enemies in 1914, the Chief of the German General Staff, Moltke, proposed to the German Foreign Secretary a few weeks before the Sarajevo assassinations that he 'should conduct a policy with the aim of provoking a war in the near future.'[8] On hearing the news of Russian mobilization at the end of July 1914, the Bavarian military plenipotentiary rushed to the Prussian War Ministry and recorded: 'Beaming faces everywhere. Everyone is shaking hands in the corridors: people congratulate one another for being over the hurdle.'[9]

If the material evidence of Germany's role as the pacemaker in the July crisis of 1914 is irrefutable, the twin issues of Germany's motivations in pressing for war and how best to interpret the general thrust of German diplomacy in the previous decades remain highly controversial. Germany's actions in 1914 have variously been seen as the logical consequence of a planned policy of aggression to achieve territory and world power (Fischer, Röhl), as the product of much more inchoate and ill-defined strivings for equality of status with the other imperial powers in Europe (Nippperdey), and as an extreme 'social imperialist' response to the Reich's domestic predicament by 1914 (Wehler, Berghahn). Similarly, assessments of German foreign policy between 1890 and 1914 shift uneasily between condemnation of her naval programme and diplomatic bullying, acknowledgement of a large measure of confusion and drift behind the aggressive posturing, and a preoccupation with the domestic determinants of foreign policy, sometimes to the extent that international relations are denied any significant degree of autonomy or inherent dynamism.

Germany's role in the origins of the First World War must be set within the wider context of the impact of German unification on the European state system from 1871. Prussia's spectacular military victories in the period 1864–71 not only presented the established European powers with a *fait accompli* which few had foreseen, but also signified the consolidation of a powerful new Reich in a part of central Europe which had traditionally served as a kind of defensive 'shock-absorber' within the state system. Moreover, Germany's military superiority from 1871, her burgeoning population and her growing industrial strength were all likely to be construed as potentially threatening by her neighbours, irrespective of the foreign policies her leadership pursued. The 'War in Sight' crisis of 1875, when the renewal of Franco-German tension prompted British and Russian warnings to Berlin that they could not tolerate another subjugation of France, is often seen as the first collective attempt by the European powers to contain Germany. The development of Bismarck's famous 'alliance system' which isolated France is also usually interpreted as his attempt to stave off the consequences of German unification, motivated by the need to prevent the formation of a hostile coalition and preserve his new creation.

Recent work by Lothar Gall and others has tended to downplay the longer-term significance of Bismarck's treaties and alliances and to question the extent to which even the Dual and Triple Alliances were integral parts of a wider 'system' which was meant to endure. Yet, if anything, this has rather heightened the impression that Bismarck's foreign policy was largely an exercise in crisis management. Despite his emphasis on the preservation of peace, his insistence that Germany was a 'satiated state' after 1871 and his effort to maintain the status quo in the Balkans through the creation of a balance of power, Bismarck's policies were subjected to new diplomatic, economic and domestic pressures from the late 1880s which called into question his conservative assumptions. In 1890 Germany may have 'lost control of the system' (Schroeder) when Bismarck's successors failed to renew the secret Reinsurance Treaty of 1887 with Russia (an omission which foreshadowed the formation of the Franco-Russian alliance of 1894). However, given the changed conditions in which foreign policy had to be conducted in the 1890s, with the rise of mass politics, the growth of nationalism and the renewed focus on imperial rivalries, some kind of realignment within the European state system was probably inevitable.

The Reich (which encompassed not only the territory of the reunited Germany of today but also territories which are now part of Poland, Lithuania, Denmark, Belgium and France) enjoyed a 'latent hegemony' in Europe between 1871 and 1890, and there were some optimistic, self-confident voices in the Wilhelmine era (such as the industrialist, Hugo Stinnes) prepared to predict that sooner or later Germany would come to dominate the continent of Europe even without a war. Yet Imperial Germany, like its Nazi successor, ultimately represented a threat to the peace and stability of Europe, not merely because of its size, strength or geographical location, but because of the foreign policy it pursued and its very nature as a state. How far German foreign policy before (and after)

1914 was conditioned by the way in which Germany was unified, how far the values of militarism and nationalism were integral to the self-identity of the new German state, and how far the Reich's status as a 'belated nation' ultimately served to propel her on to an aggressive course are ambitious and difficult questions to which there can probably be no satisfactory or conclusive answers. Yet, without adopting an overly fatalistic or determinist view about the Reich's development from 1871, there seems little doubt that the notion of a short, successful war as a panacea for all domestic and foreign ills penetrated deeply into the psyche of at least some of those who, having experienced the Prussian constitutional conflict and wars of unification as adolescents and young men, went on to assume high office in the Wilhelmine era. Long before he became State Secretary of the Foreign Office, Bülow (who had volunteered to fight in the Franco-Prussian War) extolled the virtues of the 'national idea' as an integrative device, insisted that Germany's fate depended above all on 'the sharpness of the Prussian sword' and called for the harnessing of all the nation's military and moral forces in preparation for the decisive great struggle which would probably come at the turn of the century.[10] The memoirs of men like Tirpitz, the State Secretary of the Navy Office (1897–1917), and Einem, the Prussian War Minister (1903–9), uniformly begin with accounts of their formative experiences during the wars against Austria or France and approvingly note the beneficial effects of the military victories on Prussian prestige. In July 1911 the Chancellor, Bethmann Hollweg, surveyed the national mood during the Second Moroccan Crisis and concluded, 'The people need a war.'[11]

The willingness of the 'men of 1914' to embark on a policy of war can be seen as the most extreme manifestation of a defensive, 'social imperialist' strategy to stabilize and legitimize the position of the ruling elite at a time when its power was increasingly threatened by democratic and socialist forces. 'I am putting the main emphasis on foreign policy', the new Foreign Secretary, Bülow, wrote rather self-evidently in December 1897, adding the much-cited words, 'Only a successful foreign policy can help to reconcile, pacify, rally, unite.'[12] The social imperialist interpretation of German foreign policy effectively circumnavigates the problem of defining the concrete objectives of German imperialism before 1914, seeing the pursuit of *Weltpolitik* (world policy) and naval armaments from 1897 as primarily serving an integrative function. Moreover, it usefully focuses attention on some of the more fearful and pessimistic assumptions within the ruling elite in July 1914 which seem to belie the dominance of a warmongering mentality. In this context, however, it should be noted that one important source which was used to draw a more sympathetic portrait of the *Angst*-ridden Chancellor in 1914, the published diaries of his private secretary, Kurt Riezler, can no longer be regarded as wholly reliable. In 1983 it was revealed that significant portions of the original Riezler diaries had been destroyed prior to publication and that the entries for July 1914 were significantly different in form from the rest of the diary.

Recent work (notably by Blackbourn and Eley) has tended to undermine the socioeconomic basis of the social imperialist thesis and challenge the dichotomy drawn between the forces of progress and reaction in the *Kaiserreich*. For example, it is now difficult to argue that the policies of the ruling elite were supported by the powerful coalition of conservative economic interests which had first emerged in 1878–9. The alleged deal which was brokered between the agrarians and big industrialists in 1897–8, whereby an ambitious programme of *Weltpolitik* and naval armaments (to bring material benefits to the workers and divert attention away from the need for domestic reform) was coupled with the promise of a highly protectionist tariff, barely survived the 1898 elections and could not form the basis of a lasting anti-socialist *Sammlung* (rallying) of forces which supported the state. In addition, especially between 1898 and 1902, the government came into sharp conflict with the agrarians who played a major role in thwarting the Prussian canal bills of 1899 and 1901. The government felt under no obligation to pander to their interests when steering the tariff legislation through the Reichstag in 1902. Bülow was even prepared if necessary to negotiate new commercial treaties without a new tariff law.

It is also difficult to see the navy as serving the interests of a domestic *Sammlung* or primarily as an instrument of domestic policy. While the fleet did prove unexpectedly popular, the financial cost of building a huge navy of battleships ultimately put enormous strain on the Reich's constitutional, fiscal and social fabric and eventually encouraged dissension within the ruling elite. The anti-parliamentary implications of the navy laws of 1898 and 1900, which provided for a fixed number of ships to be built each year and their automatic replacement at the end of their lifetime, were more than outweighed by the effects of the growing Reich deficit. The significance of the Reichstag's power of the purse was even more apparent after the decision in 1906 to build dreadnoughts and enter into an openly hostile arms race with Britain. The huge profits expected to be made by German industries involved in the naval programme also never materialized. The government maintained its political control over both the planning and the implementation of the programme, never allowing the initiative to pass to economic interest groups. It successfully squeezed the profit margins of the armaments industry through encouraging an uneconomic expansion of private shipyards and competition for government contracts.

The political and strategic assumptions of the 'Tirpitz plan' clearly indicate that the State Secretary of the Navy Office was intent on building a fleet of huge battleships, ships which were unsuitable for colonial or commercial purposes but could present an effective challenge to the British Royal Navy. Historians may dispute the extent to which Tirpitz's aims were known and appreciated by the Reichstag, the wider German public and even within the ruling elite itself. In 1907, after the formation of the Bülow Bloc parliamentary coalition of liberals and conservatives, Tirpitz himself lamented to Bülow that 'the most knowledgeable and hence most dangerous experts on the true significance of the Navy Law, which at the moment is still not completely understood by most politicians . . . sit in the Centre Party',[13] a party which was now opposed to the government. Yet the drive to build the second strongest navy in the world cannot be dismissed as irrational by the standards of the time nor as a mere means to maintaining the domestic status quo. Rather, the 'Tirpitz plan' was the core of Germany's bid for 'world power' before 1914 and it involved subordinating the interests of German foreign and domestic policy to the needs of naval armaments. Supported by the Kaiser, Tirpitz refused to be deflected from his aims even after his strategic assumptions had been overtaken by the formation of the Triple Entente in 1907 (which suggested that the Royal Navy could no longer be viewed in isolation). Both Bülow and Bethmann Hollweg as Chancellor came to question the rationale of the naval programme, and in 1912, for the first time since the adoption of the Tirpitz plan, the army was given priority with respect to resources. But significantly the naval programme was never abandoned despite all the difficulties and Germany was only prepared to limit her battleship building before 1914 if Britain agreed unconditionally to remain neutral in a continental war.

Arguments that the ruling elite 'fled forwards' (Wehler) to escape its domestic problems in 1914 are also undermined by the manifest lack of a revolutionary situation or even an acute domestic crisis on the eve of 1914. Notwithstanding the SPD's gains in the 1912 elections, its agitation for Prussian suffrage reform and the rash of strike activity in 1912, there is also evidence of its commitment to radical reformism, a new willingness to cooperate with the government and, indeed, its integration into the state (although it must be stated that all of these developments were anathema to conservatives). The SPD voted for Bülow's failed financial reform in 1909 and the new constitution for Alsace and Lorraine (which included universal suffrage) in 1910. Moreover, however unwelcome the development was to members of the ruling elite, its support, along with that of the left liberals, was vital in securing the tax reform (including a capital gains tax on property) which financed the Army Bill of 1913. In July 1914 Bethmann

Hollweg correctly calculated that if Russia, the autocratic *bête noire* of Europe's left, was made to appear the aggressor, then the SPD would rally patriotically behind a war of national defence. SPD deputies unanimously voted for the war credits on 4 August and the overwhelming majority welcomed the Kaiser's proclamation of a 'civil truce'.

Nor can it be said that the Reichstag posed a particularly serious democratic challenge to the ruling elite in the last years of peace. In the 1890s the clashes between monarchy and parliament had precipitated much talk of a *Staatsstreich* (*coup d'état*) within the ruling elite, but after 1900 relations between executive and legislature became far more routine and cooperative. The Reichstag augmented its power before 1914 and achieved significant concessions such as measures to ensure the secret ballot in elections, remuneration for parliamentary deputies, and procedural changes to allow votes of no confidence. Yet there is little evidence to suggest that the Reichstag wished to use its legislative power to institute parliamentary government in Germany before 1914 or that parliamentary considerations appreciably entered into the calculations of Germany's leaders in the July crisis. The fact that the arms bills of 1912–13 were passed by a conservative-centre majority and the financial cover by a centre-left majority also undermines assertions that there was a complete domestic stalemate by 1914.

If there was a crisis in Germany on the eve of the First World War it was a perceived crisis rather than one based on an objective evaluation of prevailing conditions, having more to do with the fears of an increasingly fragmented right than the reality of the 'progressive challenge'. Moreover the complex of anxieties, hopes and expectations prevalent within the different groupings on the right needs to be analysed precisely. Fears about Russia's future military strength, the prospects for the next Reichstag elections due in 1917, the democratizing effects of further military expansion, the continuing vitality of state particularism, the implications of industrial capitalism, the odds for a renewal of the tariff law in 1917, the progressive collapse of the patriarchal order, all might combine with an enormous confidence in German military power, belief in the infallibility of the General Staff and expectations of a decisive Teutonic victory in the future battle against the Slavs. Evidence that individual conservatives within the bureaucratic elite felt 'besieged' in 1914 may be better explained with reference to the radical nationalist challenge, their declining influence within their profession or, indeed, their sense of isolation within an increasingly imperialist culture, rather than to the threat posed by socialism and democracy.

German foreign policy from 1890 remains notoriously difficult to interpret, not least because the Bismarckian consensus that the Chancellor controlled this sphere of the state's activities came under challenge and there were no effective constitutional means for resolving conflicts over Germany's aims or interests. Thus it is possible to detect the broad outlines of German policy at different junctures – the hopes of the New Course to replace the 'wire to St Petersburg' with a *rapprochement* with Britain, the misplaced confidence of Holstein, a leading official in the Foreign Office, in Germany's ability to pursue a 'free hand' policy between Britain and the Franco-Russian combination from the mid-1890s, the desire of Bülow to exploit Russia's difficulties in 1904–5 to bully her into concluding a continental alliance against Britain. But such policies often overlapped and were contradictory, or they were never pursued consistently and unequivocally. Moreover, it is always possible to discern divergent tendencies, whether within the Foreign Office or between the Kaiser, Chancellor and foreign secretary, to highlight the failure of coordination at the highest level and illuminate what appears to be a zig-zag course after Bismarck's departure. Hence even the personnel and policy changes of 1897 and Bülow's highly publicized call in the Reichstag that Germany, too, should have 'a place in the sun' have left many unconvinced about the extent of Germany's aggressive ambitions before 1914.

At a time when most of the earth's territories were already accounted for, the aims of German *Weltpolitik* were bound to be left vague and unspecified. Moreover, from 1898 the need to bring the navy safely through the 'danger zone' when it was particularly vulnerable to a British attack, ensured that German foreign policy, far from actively pursuing overseas possessions, had to be practised with restraint. To a considerable extent German foreign policy was reactive in the decade after 1900, whether seeking to test the Anglo-French entente, exploit the Russo-Japanese war or support the Austrian annexation of Bosnia-Herzegovina in 1908–9. In 1905 Germany had a good case in seeking to maintain the 'open door' policy in Morocco and in an era of prestige politics could legitimately assert her equal right to be consulted about the future of the North African state. But the execution of her policy during the First Moroccan Crisis was clumsy, heavy-handed and inconsistent. Her determination to test the Anglo-French entente resulted in her isolation and humiliation at the Algeciras conference of 1906, giving rise to the first complaints that she was encircled.

In the decade before 1914 Germany's interests undoubtedly grew in areas of the world such as the Balkans, the Middle East and Africa where it had been possible for Bismarck (notwithstanding his brief foray into colonialism in the mid-1880s) to profess with some justification that Germany was disinterested. Yet how far the desire to extend those interests underscored German policy in 1914 remains in dispute, as does the very nature and significance of German imperialism before the First World War. One recent study by Woodruff D. Smith has explored the origins of *Weltpolitik* as an imperialist ideology of modernity, with broad support within the bureaucracy and business community, and has argued that it aimed to promote German commerce and industry rather than to acquire colonies (although there was a colonial element). But it is maintained that *Weltpolitik* came into conflict before 1914 with a rival ideology of *Lebensraum*, which also had its proponents within the ruling elite (and notably within the radical nationalist associations) and aimed rather at the defence of traditional society against the effects of industrialization, for example through a migrationist colonialism in eastern Europe. Consequently those who supported *Weltpolitik* within the Foreign Office proved unable to assert their priorities from 1912, failing to persuade Wilhelm II and the conservative imperialists to agree to naval limitations with Britain in exchange for imperial agreements in Africa. But Smith does not directly consider the role of German imperialism in precipitating the First World War, primarily being interested in the ideological origins of Nazi imperialism.

In the 1960s the famous 'Fischer controversy', prompted by the publication of Fritz Fischer's books, *Germany's Aims in the First World War* and *War of Illusions*, not only focused attention on Germany's role in the July crisis but also prompted questions about the nature and status of Germany's extensive war aims after the outbreak of the hostilities. In asserting that the First World War was an aggressive war which was deliberately provoked by Germany, Fischer maintained that, unlike the war aims of the other belligerents, Germany's aims were formulated too quickly to be interpreted as the product of wartime exigencies. Five weeks after the outbreak of war and before the French 'miracle of the Marne' scuppered German hopes of a quick victory, Bethmann Hollweg drew up his 'September programme' which envisaged achieving 'security for the Reich in west and east for all imaginable time'[14] by such means as the military and economic subjugation of France and Belgium, the annexation of Luxembourg, the creation of a central European customs union (or *Mitteleuropa*) under German leadership, and the eventual fulfilment of Germany's war aims in colonial Africa and against Russia (these last being achieved when the punitive Treaty of Brest Litovsk was inflicted on the Bolsheviks in March 1918). However, while not denying that Germany developed concrete war aims during the First World War, proponents of the social imperialism thesis such as Wehler have preferred to see the numerous, megalomaniacal and boundless schemes of expansion, hatched not only by the imperial government and army but also by the leaders of the federal states, as yet another means of diverting attention from the issue of internal reform, an issue which inevitably became more pressing as the war continued. Only in 1918 did the opportunity arise for the 'unrestrained rhetoric' to become a reality. The establishment of a German Reich in the east in March 1918 was thus, in Wehler's view, 'the qualitative leap' which linked the foreign policy of Imperial Germany to that of Hitler, beginning 'the pre-history of the Second World War'.[15]

Important evidence which supports the thesis that the First World War was a premeditated war of aggression also relates to the so-called 'war council', which was summoned by the Kaiser to the Berlin Schloss on 8 December 1912. Historians now have several versions of this meeting at which the Kaiser discussed with his top military and naval advisers the possibility and desirability of a general European war arising over the Balkans. Moreover recent research by John Röhl has confirmed that the Chancellor was informed of the meeting within 24 hours (some historians such as Wolfgang Mommsen had concluded from his absence that the council was devoid of political significance) and that measures agreed on 8 December, such as the need to prepare the German public through the press for a war against Russia, were put into effect. At the war council the military urged an immediate war, but Tirpitz argued for 'a postponement of the great fight for one-and-a-half years' (until June 1914) when the Kiel Canal would be widened to allow the passage of dreadnoughts and the navy would be better prepared for a war against Britain. At the very least the council indicates why a general European war did not develop out of the Balkan wars of 1912–13. Germany proved willing to cooperate with the other powers to ensure the crisis remained localized.

Some historians, however, such as the Swiss historian, Adolf Gasser, have gone further and argued that the First World War was deliberately planned from December 1912. John Röhl has uncovered retrospective references over the ensuing weeks to the decisions taken at the council and also new evidence of Germany's economic and financial preparations for war between 1912 and 1914. The whole debate about this extraordinary event tends to lead back to the nature of decision-making processes in Germany on the eve of the First World War and historians' inability to agree on the answer to the famous question, posed by the Austrian Foreign Minister, Berchthold, in 1914, 'Who rules in Berlin: Bethmann or Moltke?'[16] Paradoxically, Mommsen, who has blamed the outbreak of the First World War on the 'weakness and confusion' within the ruling elite and Bethmann Hollweg's ultimate powerlessness to enforce his strategy against the military and the Kaiser's court, is most inclined to dismiss the war council because the Chancellor was not present. Others, however, emphasize the strength of the Chancellor's position in July 1914, deny there was a division between the military and civilian leadership, and see the war originating in a consensus which lasted until the military defeats of August and September 1918.

Ultimately the direction of German policy in the last months of peace, the extent to which it was supported by a domestic consensus or arose, rather, from military pressure or the isolation of the ruling elite, can only be clarified by further research. In Imperial Germany, as elsewhere in Europe, foreign policy remained an arcane sphere where decisions were taken by a handful of men. Few were privy to the assumptions of those men and it was a brave Reichstag deputy who used the occasion of the budget debate to criticize the conduct of foreign policy publicly. Yet the actions of the 'men of 1914' were not merely guided by their individual and collective concerns but also conditioned by their positions within the wider institutional and political structure. Only close examination of that structure can determine why it was, for example, that the Kaiser's 'now or never' response to the assassinations at the beginning of July served to pull the bureaucratic, diplomatic and military elements within the elite into line, while his recognition that 'every cause for war has vanished' and readiness to mediate for peace on 28 July could effectively be disregarded.[17]

For all the ambiguities in interpretations of German foreign policy before 1914, the impression it created in the chancelleries of Europe was disastrous. The aggressive rhetoric of Germany's rulers, the succession of misconceived and bullying policies, the persistent attempts to extract maximum advantage from international crises, the sheer inconsistency and unpredictability of German diplomacy in many areas, as well as the refusal to enter into any kind of naval arms limitation agreement, all created apprehension among Germany's neighbours and confirmed her role as the main disturber of the peace before 1914. In Britain, Foreign Office officials became convinced as early as 1907 that Germany was seeking to dominate the continent of Europe, and Churchill, as First Lord of the Admiralty in 1911, voiced his disquiet over the combined naval and military strength now at the disposal of a government which was not accountable to parliament. In Russia, five months before the outbreak of the First World War, a leading newspaper maintained that 'The foreign policy of Germany for forty years has consisted in a systematic frightening of her opponents with the prospect of war', and urged the government to stand firm in a subsequent crisis.[18] In France, too, the decision for war in 1914 was widely understood as a refusal to submit to German domination and the Balkan issue scarcely merited any public discussion.

The Entente powers thus had few doubts about the offensive nature of German diplomacy before 1914, just as they were of one mind in blaming Germany for starting the war. In 1919 they also had no qualms about including the 'war guilt' clause in the Treaty of Versailles. Drawing no distinction between the old *Kaiserreich* and the new republic, they made Germany and her allies accept responsibility for all the damage and destruction wrought by the war. Furthermore, they expected her to pay.

Notes:

1. Röhl, J. C. G., *Germany Without Bismarck. The Crisis of Government in the Second Reich, 1890–1900* (1967), p. 194.
2. Lerman, K. A., *The Chancellor as Courtier. Bernhard von Bülow and the Governance of Germany 1900–1909* (1990), pp. 139–40, 187–9.
3. *Ibid.*, p. 246.
4. Wehler, H.-U., *The German Empire 1871–1918* (1985), p. 64; cf. *Deutsche Gesellschaftsgeschichte, 3 vols, vol. 3 1849–1914* (1995), pp. 854–7.
5. Lerman, *Chancellor as Courtier*, p. 328.
6. Kaiser's marginalia on report from Tschirschky to Bethmann Hollweg, 30 June 1914, in I. Geiss, ed., *July 1914. Selected Documents* (1967), p. 64.
7. Erdmann, K. D., ed., *Kurt Riezler. Tagebücher, Aufsätze, Dokumente* (1972), 14 July 1914, p. 185.
8. Rohl, J. C. G., ed., *From Bismarck to Hitler* (1970), p. 70; F. Fischer, *War of Illusions. German Policies from 1911 to 1914* (1975), p. 402.
9. Pogge von Strandmann, H., 'Germany and the Coming of War' in R. J. W. Evans and H. Pogge von Strandmann, eds., *The Coming of the First World War* (1990), p. 120.
10. Bülow to Eulenburg, 23 December 1889, in J. C. G. Röhl, ed., *Philipp Eulenburgs Politische Korrespondenz* vol.1: *Von der Reichsgründung bis zum neuen Kurs 1866–1891* (1976), pp. 388–90.
11. Wehler, *Deutsche Gesellschaftsgeschichte*, vol. 3, p. 1151.
12. Röhl, *Germany Without Bismarck*, p. 252.
13. Lerman, *Chancellor as Courtier*, p. 185.
14. Fischer, F., *Germany's Aims in the First World War* (1967), p. 103.
15. Wehler, *German Empire*, p. 211.
16. See Taylor, A. J. P., 'The Ruler in Berlin', in *Europe: Grandeur and Decline* (1967), p. 159.
17. See Geiss, *July 1914*, pp. 64 and 256.
18. Spring, D. W., 'Russia and the Coming of War', in Evans and Pogge von Strandmann, *Coming of the First World War*, p. 76.

Select bibliography

Berghahn, Volker R., *Germany and the Approach of War in 1914* (1993).
Berghahn, Volker R., *Imperial Germany 1871–1914* (1994).

Berlepsch, Hans-Jorg von, 'Neuer Kurs' im Kaiserreich? Die Arbeiterpolitik des Freiherrn von Berlepsch 1890 bis 1896 (1987).

Blackbourn, David, Class, Religion and Local Politics in Wilhelmine Germany. The Centre Party in Württemberg before 1914 (1980).

Coetzee, Marilyn S., The German Army League. Popular Nationalism in Wilhelmine Germany (1990).

Eley, Geoff, Reshaping the German Right. Radical Nationalism and Political Change after Bismarck (1980).

Eley, Geoff, From Unification to Nazism. Reinterpreting the German Past (1986).

Elias, Norbert, Über den Prozess der Zivilisation. Soziogenetische und psychogenetische Untersuchungen, 2 vols. (1969). See also, J.C.G. Röhl, The 'kingship mechanism' in the Kaiserreich in The Kaiser and his Court. Wilhelm II and the Government of Germany (1994).

Epkenhans, Michael, Die wilhelminische Flottenrüstung 1908–1914 (1991).

Evans, Richard J., ed., Society and Politics in Wilhelmine Germany (1978).

Fischer, Fritz, Germany's Aims in the First World War (1967).

Fischer, Fritz, War of Illusions. German Policies from 1911 to 1914 (1975).

Gall, Lothar, Bismarck. The White Revolutionary 2 vols. (1986).

Gasser, Adolf, Preussischer Militärgeist und Kriegsentfesselung 1914. Drei Studien zum Ausbruch des Ersten Weltkrieges (1985).

Geiss, Immanuel, ed., July 1914. The Outbreak of the First World War: Selected Documents (1967).

Geiss, Immanuel, German Foreign Policy 1871–1914 (1976).

Hull, Isabel V., The Entourage of Kaiser Wilhelm II, 1888–1918 (1982).

Lerman, Katharine A., The Chancellor as Courtier. Bernhard von Bülow and the Governance of Germany 1900–1909 (1990).

Lowe, John, The Great Powers, Imperialism and the German Problem, 1865–1925 (1994).

Moeller, Robert G., ed., Peasants and Lords in Modern Germany (1986).

Mommsen, Wolfgang J., Imperial Germany 1867–1918. Politics, Culture and Society in an Authoritarian State (1995).

Nipperdey, Thomas, Deutsche Geschichte 1866-1918, vol. 2: Machtstaat vor der Demokratie (1993).

Retallack, James, Germany in the Age of Kaiser Wilhelm II (1996).

Retallack, James, Notables of the Right. The Conservative Party and Political Mobilization in Germany 1876–1918 (1988).

Röhl, John C. G., Germany Without Bismarck. The Crisis of Government in the Second Reich 1890–1900 (1967).

Röhl, John C. G., The Kaiser and his Court. Wilhelm II and the Government of Germany (1994).

Röhl, John C. G., and Sombart, Nicolaus, eds., Kaiser Wilhelm II. New Interpretations (1982).

Schoenbaum, David, Zabern 1913 (1982).

Schroeder, Paul, 'World War One as Galloping Gertie: A Reply to Joachim Remak', Journal of Modern History, XLIV, 3 (1972).

Smith, Woodruff D., The Ideological Origins of Nazi Imperialism (1986).

Sperber, Jonathan, The Kaiser's Voters. Electors and Elections in Imperial Germany (1997).

Stargardt, Nicholas, *The German Idea of Militarism. Radical and Socialist Critics 1866–1914* (1994).

Wehler, Hans-Ulrich, *The German Empire 1871–1918* (1985).

Wehler, Hans-Ulrich, *Deutsche Gesellschaftsgeschichte, vol. 3: Von der 'Deutschen Doppelrevolution' bis zum Beginn des Ersten Weltkrieges, 1849–1914* (1995).

11

Imperial Germany: cultural and intellectual trends

Matthew Jefferies

In the opening chapter of his classic essay *Weimar Culture. The Outsider as Insider*, Peter Gay makes a startling admission: 'the Republic created little', he writes, 'it liberated what was already there'.[1] In other words, much that is celebrated as 'Weimar culture' was not the fruit of liberal democracy at all, but first began to blossom in the very different climate of the Second Empire. Whether one regards Gay's claim as exaggerated or not, it is certainly true that the imperial era saw a growing pluralism, dissent and diversity in German cultural life, and ultimately demonstrated a dynamism and zest for innovation which was hardly apparent at the Empire's birth. In the light of this, it is perhaps surprising that the cultural and intellectual developments of the imperial era have not received more attention from historians.

Whilst there are many monographs on particular aspects of pre-First World War German culture, and a growing number of valuable essay collections too, the sort of general studies which have helped to raise the profile of Weimar culture are conspicuous only by their absence for the Bismarckian and Wilhelmine periods. It is understandable that historians should be wary of searching for some elusive, all-embracing *Zeitgeist*, especially for a time of increasing complexity and contradictions. Yet however incomplete and impressionistic it must be, an overview is still required, not least to complement the wide range of new perspectives cast on the political and social history of Imperial Germany in recent years.

It is unfortunate that some of the most widely read attempts to analyse the cultural and intellectual life of the *Kaiserreich* have been written by historians primarily concerned with the roots of National Socialism. The result has been, on the one hand, an exaggerated and misleading emphasis on 'cultural pessimism', anti-rationalism and *völkisch* mysticism; and, on the other, a preoccupation with the 'unpolitical German' and the 'feudalized' bourgeoisie. No one would deny that these are dimensions to Imperial German culture worthy of discussion, but the wider picture has sometimes been lost by historians whose approach has seemed dangerously teleological. It is important, therefore, to stress right at the outset that many of the themes and trends in German cultural and intellectual life were common, to a greater or lesser degree, to Europe as a whole.

The decades either side of 1900 witnessed a far-reaching revolution in painting, architecture, music, literature, and indeed in almost every other art form: an upheaval which did not stop at national borders and which coincided with – and was nourished by – a similarly radical questioning of previous assumptions in scientific and philosophical life. This dual revolution in the realm of culture and ideas, usually subsumed under the convenient if problematic term 'modernism', helped to transform a Europe already undergoing dramatic economic, social and technological change.

Modernism in the arts revolted against the limitations of established representational codes and historical convention. It took very different forms – including a revived interest in 'primitive' cultures and folk myths as well as the shock of the new – and led to a rapid turnover in stylistic approaches – impressionism, symbolism, naturalism, cubism, futurism, expressionism – as the classical canon splintered and the international art trade developed into an increasingly sophisticated commodity market. Changes in the nature of arts patronage were accompanied by a breaking down of barriers between 'high' and 'popular' culture, and between the various art forms themselves.

Both modernization in general (industrialization, urbanization, the growth of mass politics and the mass media), and modernism in particular, provoked hostility wherever they appeared, and not only from enemies of progress and reactionary philistines. The costs of modernity – such as the alienation and anonymity of the big city, the loss of traditional lifestyles and the many threats faced by the natural world – were very real; whilst the arrogance of many modernists, who claimed to have triumphed over history, was always likely to arouse a hostile response. Indeed, the attitude of *épater les bourgeois* was an integral part of most modernist movements.

By the 1890s, intellectual disdain for the emerging mass society and its culture was widespread throughout Europe amongst thinkers on both the left and right of the political spectrum. Almost all the values associated with nineteenth-century civilization – liberalism, materialism, positivism, rationality – were called into question, giving rise to a profound scepticism about the benefits of 'progress' and the mood of malaise popularly associated with the *fin de siècle*. 'Modernists' were themselves hostile to many aspects of the modern society which had spawned them, but by no means all were pessimists. Indeed, many expressed a youthful optimism for the future and became engaged in efforts to reform society through art, whilst others preferred to retreat into a cultish aestheticism or hedonistic decadence.

However, for all that was essentially pan-European in character, there was clearly something particularly remarkable about a German culture which in these years not only played a decisive role in the development of abstract art, atonal music and modern architecture, but also produced Nietzsche, Einstein and Freud. It was as if the trends and themes which shaped European culture as a whole affected Germany in a particularly heightened and acute form. Most historians suggest it was the unusually rapid and intense experience of modernization which made pre-First World War Germany, in Modris Eksteins's phrase, the 'modernist nation *par excellence*'.

The relationship between economic and social modernization and cultural modernism is far from straightforward, but in searching for the cultural and intellectual trends which shaped Imperial Germany one has to put responses to modernization at the top of the list. There were, however, other pervasive themes which were important in the German case, and one deserves particular mention: the national question. The fact that culture (*Kultur*) had served as an important focal point of national consciousness in the century or so before unification ensured that the writer or artist had a more central role in German life than in many other countries. This did not subside after 1871, and cultural issues continued to be debated with an intensity and vigour untypical of other national contexts: attempts to define what was distinctively German, and how it differed from other national traditions, remained a major preoccupation of cultural critics and producers. At the same time, however, the manner in which Germany had been unified reduced rather than increased the chances of Germany developing genuinely national cultural institutions. The smaller German states, fearful of Prussian domination, saw cultural policy as an important area of autonomy, and as a counterweight to Berlin's hegemony. Cultural affairs therefore remained largely under their own jurisdiction – the only major exceptions were press and copyright laws – and any attempt to increase the imperial role met with fierce opposition, from Bavaria in particular.

The polycentric nature of German cultural and intellectual life – rightly highlighted as a positive consequence of German particularism – therefore continued, despite the rise of Berlin as a capital city of increasing importance. Germany's other cultural centres fell into three main categories: the many *Residenzstädte*, the seats of royal courts, where rulers had provided theatres, museums and academies; the old university towns, such as Leipzig and Jena; and towns with thriving art markets. The most important of the latter were Munich, Düsseldorf, Dresden and – beyond the borders of the Reich – Vienna. Until the 1890s, however, this apparent abundance was not reflected in diversity.

I *Gründerzeit* culture

At the time of unification, and in the economically turbulent years which followed (the so-called *Gründerzeit*), the arts in Germany had a deserved reputation for being conservative and unadventurous. The Academies of Fine Art, whose annual exhibitions or 'salons' were the crucial marketplace for most artists (the turnover of the 1888 salon in Munich was over one million marks), were bastions of tradition, unwilling to accept innovation or deviation from established conventions. As anyone familiar with the trials and tribulations of the French impressionists will be aware, this was by no means unique to Germany, but even so, the insularity and conventionality of the German academies were frequently recognized by contemporaries. At a time when paintings were expected to tell a story, to inspire, and to reflect lofty ideals, the predilection was for historical, mythological and biblical subjects, packed with detail and highly composed, yet executed in a style that was intended to give an illusion of reality, so that any evidence of artifice – the strokes of the paintbrush, for instance – had to be hidden from view.

The most successful German painters of the day were men like Franz von Lenbach (1836–1904), who dominated the artistic life of Munich until the 1890s and was best known for his many portraits of Bismarck, and Anton von Werner (1843–1915), who held a similarly dominant position in the Berlin art world. Werner produced many large and pompous paintings for the Prussian state, depicting scenes from the Franco-Prussian War and most famously the proclamation of Kaiser Wilhelm I at Versailles, first painted in 1877. These 'princely painters' (*Malerfürsten*), who mixed with kings, chancellors and great industrialists, lived in a truly palatial style and were probably respected more for their wealth than their creativity. Certainly Hans Makart, a Viennese artist, is remembered for his imposing studio – piled high with artistic treasures, and open to the public for an hour each afternoon – rather than his paintings.

German painters of the mid- to late nineteenth century did not, on the whole, belong to movements or even loose associations. They were highly conscious of their individual reputations and were often scornful of their 'competitors', particularly if they felt their place in posterity was under threat. With the exception of Adolph Menzel (1815–1905), who was always something of a maverick, the leading German painters consciously emulated the styles and themes of the old masters, in large and opulent canvases full of theatricality and pathos. The German historians Richard Hamann and Jost Hermand have drawn parallels between the heroic postures of *Gründerzeit* art and the cult of genius which pervaded other areas of early imperial culture: academic work, for instance, often concentrated on the biographies of great men, and Friedrich Nietzsche attempted to embody the whole of his philosophy in a single individual, Zarathustra.

Of course, the work of the 'heroic' *Gründerzeit* artists was out of reach of all but the wealthiest individuals and institutions, but many of the leading painters also produced smaller genre scenes for more modest budgets and surroundings. Middle-class Germans could also obtain original works by joining one of the many *Kunstvereine* – by 1900 there were over 80 of these 'art clubs' – which were established in major towns during the nineteenth century and which usually allocated paintings to members by lottery. For the vast majority of people, however, art came in the form of reproductions, which were often of high quality. The demand for reproductions, the success of the *Kunstvereine*, the popularity of art history as an academic discipline and the high attendance figures at exhibitions all testify to a great hunger for art in late nineteenth-century Germany: indeed, historians such as Thomas Nipperdey have made much of art's role as a surrogate religion in an increasingly secular society.

The popularity of painting in the manner of the old masters was complemented by a vogue for heavy, highly ornamental furniture – antique or reproduction – and dark, wood-panelled rooms. This was due in no small measure to the proselytizing of the writer and publisher Georg Hirth (1841–1916), who vigorously promoted the German Renaissance as the most suitable historical tradition on which to base a national style for the new Empire. The long-running debate on what should be the German national style in design and architecture was complex, since the aesthetic arguments were clouded by political symbolism. For instance, Hirth, and other liberal enthusiasts of the German Renaissance, were principally attracted to the *Dürerzeit* by its image as a golden age of civic responsibility, in which the sturdy burghers of towns like Nuremberg had maintained a proud record of self-government. Architecture was similarly an issue of political identity for the Catholic politician and art critic August Reichensperger (1808–95), a founder of the Centre Party and the most vociferous champion of the Gothic style. He celebrated the completion of

Cologne cathedral in 1880 as a fitting symbol for the new Empire, but fought in vain for the new Reichstag building also to be designed in what he termed the 'German style'. For others, however, it was essentially an economic issue: with the growing internationalization of trade, they argued, Germany would need to develop some sort of distinctive style of its own, if it was to compete with the established identities of British or French goods.

It was largely in response to the poor impression made by German applied art in the shop window of the great world fairs that a major exhibition was held in Munich's Crystal Palace in 1876. Visitors had to pass through a display of 3,000 pieces of historic German furniture and *objets d'art* under the banner of 'Our Fathers' Works', before they could reach the contemporary exhibits, most of which were in historical styles. The message of the exhibition was that German designers should study the work of their forefathers and continue in their traditions, even if machines had largely replaced the craftsman's hands.

However, with manufacturers always eager to outshine their rivals' products, and with designers anxious to show off their mastery of a range of historic styles, gained at a growing number of colleges of applied art (*Kunstgewerbeschulen*) or technical colleges, no uniform national style emerged. Whilst each historical style had its own rules and conventions, these became increasingly blurred in the later nineteenth century, with particular problems caused by objects and buildings with no historical prototype, such as telephones and cookers, railway stations and department stores. More often than not, the result was the sort of eclectic historicism which was by no means unique to Germany, but which became a prime target for German cultural critics at the turn of the century.

Taking their cue from these early modernist critiques, contemporary historians have tended to portray the *Gründerzeit* as a period of cultural and moral decline: as a time of nouveau riche speculators and their tasteless attempts at upward mobility (the sort of characters portrayed in Sternheim's *The Snob*, Fontane's *The Adulteress* or Heinrich Mann's *Man of Straw*); of paintings made by and for vulgar upstarts; of pygmies posing as giants; of a superficial architecture and design, which hid shoddy workmanship behind a veneer of surrogate sophistication. There is a good deal of truth in all this, but such generalizations can be overplayed and it would be wrong to dismiss all the cultural products of the post-unification period as pompous and overblown *kitsch*. It is perhaps instructive to note that houses and apartment blocks from this era are highly sought after in contemporary Germany, and even reproduction German Renaissance furniture can now demand high prices at auction.

It is more doubtful whether the official art and architecture of the Empire will ever be regarded with much affection. The major imperial building projects – Paul Wallot's Reichstag building, completed in 1894; the Imperial High Court in Leipzig, designed by Ludwig Hoffmann and completed in 1895; or Raschdorff's new Berlin cathedral, built between 1894 and 1904 – were impressive only in their monumental scale. Similarly, the numerous statues and memorials erected in the name of Germania or (more frequently) Borussia were imposing rather than imaginative, and few would dispute Gordon Craig's assertion that 'the victory over France and the unification of the German states inspired no great work of literature or music or painting'.[2] Several of the largest monuments to unification, such as the Victory Column in Berlin (started in 1865 as a memorial to the war against Denmark, and finally unveiled in revised form on Sedan Day in 1873) or the Hermann Monument near Detmold (started in 1838 but not finished until 1875) were completed only with the financial assistance of the Emperor but, in general, neither Wilhelm I nor Bismarck showed much interest in culture.

This all changed with the accession of Wilhelm II in 1888. Wilhelm had dabbled in art since childhood, and went on to design trophies, uniforms, furniture and statues and to paint numerous pictures, under the tutelage of Anton von Werner. Although it is difficult to gauge the true extent of his influence, it is clear that – as in other areas of policy – Wilhelm tried to pursue a much more 'hands-on' approach to cultural affairs than his predecessors. As King of Prussia he was able to wield considerable influence through his powers of patronage and appointment in Berlin's cultural institutions. Several episodes are well known: in 1898 he denied the recommended award of a gold medal to Käthe Kollwitz because he disliked both the style and content of her work; in 1904 he interfered with the selection of paintings to be shown in the German pavilion at the St Louis World Fair, prompting a parliamentary outcry; and in 1909 the director of the National Gallery in Berlin, Hugo von Tschudi, was forced to resign after the Kaiser vetoed the purchase of some paintings by the French artists Courbet and Daumier, though the benefits of German particularism were once again demonstrated when von Tschudi was immediately invited to take up a similar position in Munich.

Wilhelm was also able to use his wealth and influence to pursue grandiose projects, including a wave of equestrian monuments to mark the hundredth anniversary of his grandfather's birth (contributing to a total of some 400 memorials to Wilhelm I and a staggering 700 to Bismarck erected during the Wilhelmine period), and an 'avenue of victory' (*Siegesallee*) in Berlin. The *Siegesallee* was an ambitious double row of 32 marble statues, designed to venerate the history of the Hohenzollerns, but which quickly became a target of satire and abuse (the writer Alfred Döblin condemned its 'byzantine emptiness and falseness of spectacle'). After its completion in 1901, Wilhelm invited the sculptors and artists who had worked on the project to court, where he addressed them with a speech on the role of art in society. In it he described art as a body of unchanging, eternal values, which could be used to uplift and educate the German nation, and especially the working class, to appreciate truth and beauty.

II   Cultural critics and reformers

By the time Wilhelm made this speech, however, it was clear that he was already swimming against the tide. The idea that cultural values were somehow permanent and unchanging, that the rules of art had been laid down centuries before and would only be challenged by fools and charlatans, was increasingly difficult to uphold at a time when a broadly based movement for cultural renewal was advancing on many fronts. The groundwork for the reformers was laid by a multitude of cultural critics, whose attacks on *Gründerzeit* values came from very different angles, but often ended up hitting the same targets.

The most biting and brilliant of the critics was undoubtedly Friedrich Nietzsche (1844–1900), a master of German prose and a philosopher whose aphoristic style was unusually brutal and direct ('philosophizing with the hammer'), but unsystematic and frequently contradictory: his most enduring ideas, the 'Death of God', the 'Superman' and the 'Will to Power', continue to arouse controversy today. Nietzsche once described himself as the great 'seducer and pied piper', and he has certainly been cited as an influence by numerous very different movements and individuals. However, since he viewed creative people as the vanguard of humanity – he wrote that the world was only justified as an aesthetic phenomenon and that only art could make life bearable – it is not surprising that artists, writers and composers were amongst his most devout followers. Nietzsche was a fierce critic of almost every aspect of Imperial Germany and its culture, and anyone who sought change could draw inspiration from his highly emotive language.

Another inspirational figure with a problematic legacy was Nietzsche's one-time friend, and later sworn enemy, Richard Wagner (1813–83). Wagner's influence on late nineteenth-century Europe has been described by Norman Stone as 'immense', and not just because of his music – which was far more innovative than the Germanic mythology of his librettos might suggest – or his works of theory and criticism, which were full of anger and spite. Wagner's music dramas gained a permanent home at Bayreuth in

1876. In 1882 the festival theatre was 'consecrated' with the première of his last work, *Parsifal*, which Wagner believed should be performed nowhere else. More a religious rite than an opera, *Parsifal* was an initiation ceremony for a theatre that was fast becoming a temple. The huge and fanatical audiences which flocked to Bayreuth in a spirit of holy communion every year thereafter were drawn by the prospect of seeing a total work of art, the *Gesamtkunstwerk*: a concept which was to hold a particular fascination for succeeding generations of German artists.

Amongst the many other cultural critics to emerge in the later nineteenth-century the writings of the *völkisch* 'cultural pessimists' (principally Paul de Lagarde and Julius Langbehn, although both Nietzsche and Wagner were also pulled into this sphere by their relatives and acolytes) have attracted particular attention from historians. Their work was first highlighted by a series of studies in the early 1960s by historians such as George Mosse and Fritz Stern, who argued that a distinctive 'Germanic ideology' developed in the second half of the nineteenth century, which was hostile to most aspects of the modern world, and which offered in its place a rag-bag of romantic, irrational and racist impulses, possessing a revolutionary dynamic, every bit as hostile to orthodox conservative thinking as it was to liberalism and socialism. It was suggested that these writers had a lasting and damaging influence on German society, and in particular on the educated middle class, the *Bildungsbürgertum*.

Ultimately, of course, the influence of particular writers and thinkers is extemely difficult to measure. The 'cultural pessimists' certainly had more readers than disaffected intellectuals on the fringes of academic life could usually expect, but the proponents of the 'Germanic ideology' thesis have been convincingly challenged on a number of levels. The intricacies of the debate cannot be entered into here, but it is significant for our narrative to note the way in which de Lagarde (1827–91), Langbehn (1851–1907) and others were savagely critical of historicism in the arts, and urged the development of new forms of cultural expression, based not on the pattern books of history, but derived from the soul and soil of the German *Volk*.

Langbehn, in particular, was an important figure for many German artists and architects. Not only did he reject the unthinking adaption of historical forms, but he also urged the reconciliation of utility and beauty in a way that echoed early twentieth-century functionalism; and although he was not in the same league as Nietzsche, he came up with some memorable aphorisms of his own, such as: 'the professor is the German national disease'; or 'the true artist can never be local enough'.

Langbehn's best-known work, *Rembrandt as Educator* (1890), helped to clear the way for a succession of widely read art pedagogues, who each in their own way tried to communicate to the general public the value of simplicity and spontaneity in artistic creativity, and to elevate the standing of folk art and vernacular traditions against the prevailing pomposity of imperial culture. These included Alfred Lichtwark (1852–1914), the long-serving director of Hamburg's *Kunsthalle*; Ferdinand Avenarius (1856–1923), the publisher of the popular cultural journal, *Der Kunstwart*; and Paul Schultze-Naumburg (1869–1949), whose writings on architecture and the landscape helped to sensitize many middle-class Germans to issues of town planning and conservation. The founding of artists' colonies in rural locations, such as one established in the 1890s on the windswept North German Plain at Worpswede, were a direct response to such pedagogic efforts.

The revolt against historicism inspired by this disparate group of cultural critics and pedagogues took a different guise in each of the arts, and nowhere was it clear-cut. The voices of renewal fell into two main camps: those who sought to re-establish continuity with folk values ('primitive' or naive art, vernacular architecture, folk tales, simple peasant clothing and so on); and those who looked for radically new approaches. Later, in the 1920s, these contradictions would become all too apparent, but for the time being, such distinctions were blurred by a shared contempt for the excesses of the *Gründerzeit* and a common vocabulary which placed emphasis on 'honesty' and 'sobriety'.

Chronologically, the first of the arts to experience the spark of revolt was literature. At the time of unification, in literature as in painting, it was believed that the ideal task of the creative artist was to depict what was uplifting, good and true. Thus, apart from Theodor Fontane's novels, which dealt in a rather subtle and subdued way with the stresses and strains beneath the surface of bourgeois life, German writers of the early imperial era showed little interest in social or political themes. This began to change in the 1880s when, inspired by Zola, Ibsen and others, a German variant of naturalism emerged in both Munich, where it was led by Michael Georg Conrad and revolved around the journal *Die Gesellschaft* and Berlin, where its leaders were the Hart brothers and Otto Brahm (1856–1912). Brahm was a co-founder and director of the so-called 'Free Stage' (*Freie Bühne*), where 'members only' performances allowed controversial plays to escape the censor. Naturalist writers brought contemporary social problems – such as the plight of the poor or the position of women in society – to the German stage for the first time, though the depth of their social engagement has often been questioned. The best known of the German naturalists was Gerhart Hauptmann (1862–1946), whose play *The Weavers*

(1892) was initially banned in Prussia and became the subject of a long court battle, which ultimately went Hauptmann's way on the grounds that the seat prices at the Deutsches Theater were too high for the sort of people who might be tempted to riot. Wilhelm II, who condemned the play, cancelled his box in protest.

Naturalism was also a trend in painting: Max Liebermann (1847–1935) painted artisans, peasants and housewives in an unsentimental, naturalistic style – his painting *Plucking the Geese* led to him being dubbed an 'apostle of ugliness' – before developing a lighter palette and falling under the influence of French impressionism. With another naturalist painter, Fritz von Uhde (1848–1911), Liebermann played a prominent role in the Secessions of the 1890s; a series of rebellions by German artists, who 'seceded' or withdrew from the art establishment in their state by refusing to show their work at the annual salon and establishing their own gallery space instead.

The Secessions, which effectively broke the stranglehold of the academies, and enabled modern art to establish a foothold in central Europe, began in Munich in 1892, and continued in Vienna (1897) and Berlin (1898). The exact combination of motives varied in each case: the conservative selection of works by salon juries; the hostility of juries to innovative foreign art; the cramped and insensitive ways in which pictures were hung; generational and organizational conflict, and so on. By no means all the Secessionists were modernists, and many were moved by economic rather than aesthetic motives, but this did not lessen the significance of their actions. The traditional importance of state patronage to artists in the German lands ensured that their rebellion against the art establishment also assumed a political character. This was especially the case in Berlin, where the Kaiser – who had nothing but baffled contempt for modern tendencies in art – became involved. As with many subsequent confrontations between modernism and the establishment, however, it was the latter which claimed to represent popular taste, and the Secessionists who were caricatured as 'elitist' and 'undemocratic'.

A number of the Munich Secessionists moved away from painting in the mid-1890s and turned to applied art and architecture. Thanks to former Secessionists like Peter Behrens (1868–1940) and Richard Riemerschmid (1868–1957), Munich for a time became a leading centre of the new style in design and architecture, known generally as *art nouveau*, but in Germany dubbed *Jugendstil*, after the graphic style of the journal *Jugend* (founded in 1896 by Georg Hirth, who embraced the new style every bit as enthusiastically as he had the German Renaissance). The close links between the Secessions and *art nouveau* were emphasized by the fact that in Vienna, where the architect J. M. Olbrich designed a purpose-built exhibition hall for the Secession, the new architecture and design was known as *Sezessionsstil*.

Jugendstil, like other manifestations of *art nouveau*, is regarded by design historians as a crucial transitional phase between historicism and modernism. The desire of its practitioners to find a fresh style, untainted by historical associations, led many to seek inspiration in the forms of the natural world: the result was the free-flowing, curvillinear style, which made an impact in most European states in the last years of the century. Many of the young designers who identified with the style had not enjoyed a formal academic training, and some like Henry van de Velde (1863–1957) expressed a social concern inspired by the British Arts and Crafts movement. If the new style was to integrate art and society, they argued, no object should be too small to be worthy of aesthetic concern, and wherever possible it should be made in workshops, where the artist had control over the whole production process and the worker was more than an alienated automaton. The workshop thus became the focal point of *Jugendstil* design, and the *Werkstätten* in Munich, Vienna and Dresden became large and profitable enterprises for a time, although their hand-crafted furniture was invariably too expensive for the working-class families which featured so prominently in the designers' rhetoric.

Jugendstil was quickly taken up by mass manufacturers and provincial builders, and it very soon became just another style in the pattern books; the artists' colony established at Darmstadt by the progressive Grand Duke Ernst Ludwig of Hesse as a 'document of German art', represented its swansong. However, although it blossomed only briefly, the new style brought forth a host of young talent, including individuals who were to remain at the forefront of German architecture and design for the next 30 years or more.

Gordon Craig has written that 'before 1914 it was only on rare occasions that German artists were interested, let alone stirred by political and social events and issues'.[3] As the example of the *Jugendstil* designers suggests, this view is easily challenged. Of course, aesthetic narcissism and the idea of 'art for art's sake' did exist; and some like the writer Stefan George (1868–1933) retreated into a rather precious private universe, but the stereotype of the unpolitical German artist, seeking *Innerlichkeit* ('inwardness') instead of social engagement, is unhelpful and inaccurate. On the contrary, artists and aesthetes often played a prominent role in the multitude of social and cultural reform movements to emerge in turn-of-the-century Germany.

The best known of these is probably the youth movement, with its numerous hiking associations (*Wandervögel*), but many others existed under the broad umbrella of the *Lebensreformbewegung* (literally, 'movement for the reform of life'). This term was first used in print around 1896, to denote a host of autonomous organizations active in a wide range of fields, but all aiming for a fundamental reform of lifestyles. Some of the groups targeted the individual (abstinence, naturism, vegetarianism, homeopathic medicine), while others focused on society at large (housing reform, land reform, clothing reform, conservation and environmental protection).

Typical of the latter group was the German Garden City Association (founded in 1902). Germany's first garden city, at Hellerau near Dresden, never developed much beyond a village, but still became a focal point for the Wilhelmine reformers and a place of pilgrimage for many individuals, including George Bernard Shaw, who recognized kindred spirits at work. The settlement was built to a plan by Richard Riemerschmid around the factory of Karl Schmidt's *Deutsche Werkstätten* – one of the leading furniture 'workshops' – and also featured workers' housing by progressive architects, and a centre for rhythmic gymnastics, where pioneers of dance such as Mary Wigman and Marie Rambert were amongst the students.

The Garden City Association was, like most of the *Lebensreform* organizations, overwhelmingly middle-class in character, but attracted a bizarre mixture of reformist socialists, progressive liberals, anarcho-libertarians and *völkisch* nationalists. It has already been stated that the Wilhelmine reform movements embraced people with very different aesthetic approaches; much the same could be said of their political character. For instance, the principal theorist of the garden city idea in Germany was the notorious anti-Semite and arch-reactionary Theodor Fritsch, but the association's leaders, the Kampffmeyer brothers, were supporters of the SPD. Just as the 1920s were to bring an aesthetic polarization, so the political climate of the Weimar Republic was to turn erstwhile colleagues into bitter enemies.

Nowhere was this more apparent than in architecture: the well-known and highly politicized arguments of the 1920s, between 'modernists' and 'traditionalists', were fought out largely by former friends and associates from the same Wilhelmine organization, the German *Werkbund*. Founded in 1907, the *Werkbund* sought to resolve the dilemma on which the *Jugendstil* designers had foundered: namely, the proper role of artists, craftsmen and designers in an age of machine mass production. The reconciliation between art and industry, which the organization proposed, was to be on the latter's terms. Its membership thus included major industrial firms as well as individual businessmen, politicians and designers, all hoping that an 'ennobling' of the modern industrial world would not only boost German exports, but would also increase the self-respect of industrial workers, and thereby help to restore social harmony to the German people. Peter Behrens's work with the electrical engineering giant AEG is the best-known example of the organization's ethos in action, and the man once dubbed 'Mr Werkbund' further secured his place in the history books by employing all three of the future giants of European modern architecture – Walter Gropius, Mies van der Rohe and Le Corbusier – in his studio near Potsdam before 1914. Gropius's own project, the 'Fagus' factory at Alfeld (1911–13) became an icon of modernism in its own right, and introduced many of the design principles he was to pursue as director of the 'Bauhaus' in the 1920s.

Not all the products of *Werkbund* design were so unashamedly modern, but even so, *Werkbund* architecture is well summed up by Nipperdey's phrase 'modern buildings for modern people, proud of their modernity'.[4] The organization's work found relatively widespread acceptance amongst the general population – its 1914 Cologne exhibition attracted over one million visitors – and it even had some support in governing circles, as the choice of Peter Behrens to design the new German embassy in St Petersburg (1912) indicates. New ideas in music, which evolved in a way curiously parallel to the development of architecture – from 'late nineteenth century bombast to disquieting severity' as Norman Stone has put it[5] – may have been more difficult for the public to accept, but one should not take the whistles and cat-calls that accompanied Schoenberg's moves towards atonality as necessarily representative of the concert-going public as a whole.

III Technological and intellectual change

Of course, many Germans had neither the time nor the inclination to involve themselves in cultural issues, and no doubt the more zealous *Lebensreformer* and outspoken modernists appeared rather crankish to the proverbial man or woman in the street, but whether they knew it or not, all Germans at the turn of the century were participating in a cultural revolution of unprecedented proportions. The rapid development of a commercial popular culture was made possible by technological change – the first telephones (from the 1870s), typewriters (late 1870s), Kodak cameras (1880s), Emil Berliner's gramophone (1887), radio broadcasts (1900s) – but predicated on changes in the organization of capitalism (mass production and consumption) and mass education.

New printing techniques and almost universal literacy facilitated an explosion of printed matter. Between 1885 and 1913, daily newspaper circulation in Germany doubled and the range of popular fiction (such as Karl May's adventure stories), illustrated magazines and satirical journals (like *Simplicissimus*, launched in 1896 and with a circulation of 85,000 by 1904) all expanded dramatically. The development of electric lighting helped a proliferation of cabaret, revue and nightclub shows, providing not only a venue for the music of the tango, the bunny-hug and the turkey trot, but opportunities for writers of the quality of Frank Wedekind (1864–1918), who was described as 'a genius of smut', but whose plays *Spring Awakening* (1891), *Pandora's Box* (1894), and *Earth Spirit* (1895) broke through the conventions of naturalist theatre and paved the way for expressionist drama.

Such subversive entertainment posed an obvious challenge to the censors. Laws on blasphemy, obscenity, incitement and 'gross mischief' were all used against the theatre and the press in Wilhelmine Germany – Wedekind himself spent some time in jail for 'insulting the monarch' – but efforts to introduce a new censorship law (the infamous 'Lex Heinze') met with impressive and largely effective opposition. In fact, as Robin Lenman has pointed out, the principal regulator of cultural production was now the market rather than the censor. In other words, avant-garde artists and writers were more worried about not finding buyers for their work than about police interference or stern lectures from the likes of Wilhelm II.

Rising levels of disposable incomes, and a gradual reduction in working hours, led to a growth in organized sport and increasing leisure opportunities. The institution which best represented this trend was the cinema. Gary Stark has claimed that a 'bioscope' performance at Berlin's Wintergarten in November 1895 was the world's first example of a film being shown to a paying audience; 10 years later there was still only a handful of permanent cinemas in Germany (the first films were shown in touring circus tents); but by 1914 there were some 300 cinemas in Berlin alone, and up to 3,000 in Germany as a whole. Of course, the movie was not yet regarded as an art form, but it was already an established and important leisure pursuit for millions of predominantly working-class Germans. In time, it would – along with other commercial entertainments – reduce the appeal of the vast mosaic of clubs and associations built up in the sociocultural milieu of the socialist labour movement. For the time being, however, workers' choral, theatre and reading societies continued to represent an important, if not exactly innovative, slice of German cultural life.

If the growth of a commercial mass culture was regarded with fear and suspicion by Germany's labour leaders, it was a similar story in the country's great seats of learning. German academics, struggling to cope with a four-fold increase in students between 1871 and 1914, felt that their authority, status and economic well-being were all under threat. Countless gloomy tracts were written to contrast the values of German *Kultur* with those of Anglo-Saxon *Zivilisation*, by which they meant the British 'shopkeeper mentality' or the cold commercialism of American life. However, despite the generally conservative outlook of most of their number – Craig describes professors at this time as the 'intellectual bodyguard of the Hohenzollerns'[6] – intellectual life did not stagnate in the Wilhelmine era. On the contrary, many German academics became preoccupied with trying to make sense of the atomization of modern life and its effects, which could be felt all around them. Thus it was in these years that sociology began to emerge as an academic discipline, with valuable contributions from Simmel, Tönnies, Troeltsch, and above all Max Weber (1864–1920), whose classic work on *The Protestant Ethic and the Spirit of Capitalism* (1904–5) explored the relationship between ideas and social development. Weber shunned both cultural pessimism and vulgar optimism, to produce a body of work noted for its subtlety, conceptual originality and methodological rigour. He perceived more clearly than most that whilst the modern world brought great benefits, it also posed new dangers of its own.

The most important intellectual milestones passed in these years, however, were in the natural sciences. After the discovery of X-rays (1895), radioactivity (1896) and the electron (1897), the physicist Max Planck (1858–1947) outlined what became known as quantum theory in 1900, and five years later, another future German Nobel prize winner, Albert Einstein (1880–1952), proposed his special theory of 'relativity'. Perhaps the most important aspect of Einstein's work was that it amounted to a denial of any absolute frame of reference, and thus called into question the very nature of scientific laws or, as Michael Biddiss has put it, 'opened up vast vistas of uncertainty'.[7]

Much the same could be said of the work of Sigmund Freud (1856–1939), the Viennese specialist in nervous ailments, who invented 'psychoanalysis' in the 1890s and whose publications *The Interpretation of Dreams* (1899) and *Three Essays on Sexuality* (1905), revealed the power of the subconscious. His work was epoch-making – even if *The Interpretation of Dreams* took eight years to sell its first 600 copies – because it called into question the entire conventional terminology of sanity, morality and rationality.

Freud's work on the subconscious mind was to have a great influence on the last major movement in Imperial German culture, expressionism. Much has been written on German expressionism in recent years, not least because an expressionist tendency – characterized by emotion, exaggeration and violent distortion – became manifest in every field of the arts at some point between 1905 and 1925. The principal expressionist groupings in German fine art, *Die Brücke* (founded in Dresden in 1905) and *Der Blaue Reiter* (founded in Munich six years later), produced some of the greatest paintings of the twentieth century, and two members of the latter group – Wassily Kandinsky (1866–1944) and Franz Marc (1880–1916) – were instrumental in the evolution of abstract art after 1910. In this, the relationship between expressionist art and music was very close: the first abstract artists cited music's lack of a 'subject' as justification for their move away from representational art, whilst the composer Schoenberg was also a noted portrait painter. The pursuit of the *Gesamtkunstwerk* led artists to use every available medium of expression.

German expressionists embodied many of the qualities and contradictions of modernism as a whole: proclaiming a new vision, yet turning to primitive folk art for inspiration; fiercely critical of bourgeois materialism, yet smart enough to secure the best prices for their work; anti-urban, yet fascinated by the city and unwilling to move far away from metropolitan life. The expressionists demonstrated that criticisms of rationality and materialism could be just as much an expression of modernity as of conservatism; and whilst much has rightly been made of the movement's apocalyptic strain, it is important not to lose sight of the more prosaic aspects of the expressionist phenomenon. As Thomas Nipperdey has pointed out, this revolution in art went hand in hand with a fundamental change in middle-class consciousness: modern art established itself in Germany not in spite of the middle classes, but because of them. New private art dealers – like Paul Cassirer in Berlin – and many new patrons – like the bankers Karl Ernst Osthaus and August von der Heydt, in the industrial towns of Hagen and Wuppertal respectively – were vital for the breakthrough of expressionism, just as other bourgeois patrons commissioned buildings from *Werkbund* architects, and attended concerts by Schoenberg.

If nothing else, therefore, study of the cultural life of Imperial Germany can help to revise the still-popular cliché of the 'feudalized' German bourgeoisie, aspiring to nothing more than reserve officer status and an attractive duelling scar.

Notes:

1. Gay, P., *Weimar Culture* (1974), p. 6.
2. Craig, G., *Germany 1866–1945* (1978), p. 215.
3. *Ibid.*

4. Nipperdey, T., *The Rise of the Arts in Modern Society* (1990), p. 20.
5. Stone, N., *Europe Transformed, 1878–1919* (1983), p. 400.
6. Craig, G., *Germany 1866–1945*, p. 205.
7. Biddiss, M., in P. Hayes, ed., *Themes in Modern European History 1890–1945* (1992), p. 88.

Select bibliography

Essay collections

Behr, S., Fanning, D., and Jarman, D., eds., *Expressionism Reassessed* (1993).

Chapple, G., and Schulte, H., eds., *The Turn of the Century. German Literature and Art* (1981).

Forster-Hahn, F., ed., *Imagining Modern German Culture 1889–1910* (1997).

Rogoff, I., ed., *The Divided Heritage, Themes and Problems in German Modernism* (1991).

Stark, G., and Lackner, B. K., eds., *Essays on Culture and Society in Modern Germany* (1982).

Teich, M., and Porter, R., eds., *Fin-de-Siècle and its Legacy* (1990).

Essays and monographs

Abrams, L., *Workers Culture in Imperial Germany. Leisure and Recreation in the Rhineland and Westphalia* (1992).

Allen, A. T., *Satire and Society in Wilhelmine Germany. Kladderadatsch & Simplicissimus, 1890–1914* (1984).

Campbell, J., *The German Werkbund. The Politics of Reform in the Applied Arts* (1978).

Craig, G., 'Religion, Education and the Arts', in *Germany 1866–1945* (1978).

Dube, W.-D., *The Expressionists* (1972).

Eksteins, M., *The Rites of Spring, the First World War and the Birth of the Modern Age* (1990).

Harrison, T., *1910. The Emancipation of Dissonance* (1996).

Heskett, J., *Design in Germany, 1870–1918* (1986).

Jefferies, M., *Politics and Culture in Wilhelmine Germany. The Case of Industrial Architecture* (1995).

Jelavich, P., *Munich and Theatrical Modernism* (1985).

Jelavich, P., *Berlin Cabaret* (1993).

Lenman, R., *Artists and Society in Germany 1850–1914* (1997).

Lewis, M., *The Politics of the German Gothic Revival: August Reichensperger* (1993).

Makela, M., *The Munich Secession. Art and Artists in Turn-of-the-Century Munich* (1990).

Nipperdey, T., *The Rise of the Arts in Modern Society* (1990).

Pascal, R., *From Naturalism to Expressionism: German Literature and Society, 1880–1918* (1973).

Paret, P., *The Berlin Secession. Modernism and its Enemies in Imperial Germany* (1980).

Rose, P. L., *Wagner. Race and Revolution* (1992).
Schorske, C., *Fin-de-Siècle Vienna: Politics and Culture* (1981).
Schwartz, F., *The Werkbund. Design Theory and Mass Culture before the First World War* (1996).
Stern, F., *The Politics of Cultural Despair* (1961).

12

The First World War

Roger Chickering

The summer of 1914 marks the pivot of modern German history. The popular reaction to the news of war was, as recent research has made clear, a great deal more complex than the general euphoria that was suggested in the famous crowd scenes in Berlin, Munich and other German cities. Still, whether they regarded it with enthusiasm or anxiety, Germans of all descriptions hoped in 1914 that war would resolve the many problems that had vexed their country since unification in 1871. A great common exertion in the name of national defence might, in this reasoning, heal the open sores of class conflict, confessional tension, political division, cultural uncertainty and international insecurity. These were the expectations to which the Kaiser gave voice when he exclaimed on 4 August that he henceforth 'recognized no parties, only Germans.'[1]

In the event, the war had no such effect. Instead, the conflict that began in August 1914 exacerbated all these problems amidst prodigious, unanticipated strains that eventuated, in the fall of 1918, in military and political collapse. The legacy of the First World War thereafter tormented the first German republican experiment, preoccupied the National Socialist dictatorship that followed, and survived in political divisions that disappeared only in 1989. The repercussions of this war, which George Kennan has called '*the* great seminal catastrophe' of the twentieth century, thus far transcended Germany's history.[2]

I War without end

The dynamic that governed the broad impact of war in Germany was military in a strict sense. The armies that went to war in 1914 were composed and equipped in ways that rendered impossible a swift decision

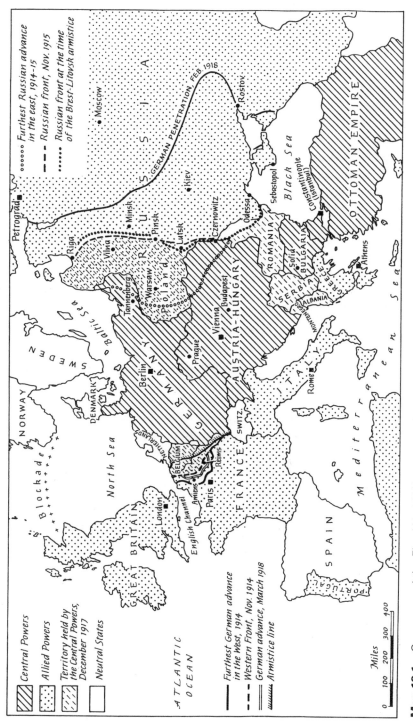

Map 12.1 Germany and the First World War in Europe

at arms. In the aftermath of the Franco-German war of 1870–71, the armies of all the European powers had instituted universal military service, which drove the expansion of each of these bodies into millions of men. Industrial technologies thereupon placed lethal weapons – long-range, rapid-firing rifles, machine-guns and field artillery – into the arsenals of all these armies. The effect of these technologies was to provide forces on the defensive with tactical advantages so overpowering that they frustrated every attempt to mount effective offensive operations, until the advent of armoured vehicles at the end of the war signalled a new dynamic of combat.

The German plans for this war were by no means blind to the challenges that attended the movement of mass armies in an industrial age. The Schlieffen Plan, which in its basics governed the German campaign in 1914, was predicated on the impossibility of a simultaneous attack against the French and Russian armies, as well as on the difficulty of a frontal assault on French lines. The most promising solution to this problem, Schlieffen reasoned, was to concentrate the bulk of Germany's land forces for a swift operation in the west, which would exploit the speed and efficiency of German mobilization to envelop the French forces in a vast flanking manoeuvre that led through Belgium. Victory over the French army would then liberate the bulk of the German forces for service in the east against the Russians, whose mobilization was supposed to be much more ponderous.

Schlieffen's plan amounted to an enormous gamble on a quick victory, and the first five weeks of combat appeared to vindicate his expectations. The German mobilization proceeded according to plan, and the advance of the German armies through Belgium and northern France portended the great decisive battle that Schlieffen had anticipated. This battle took place in early September 1914, but in circumstances that the German general had not foreseen, as staggering difficulties of supply and communication disrupted the coordinated movement of the German forces. At the Marne River, to the east of Paris, French and British forces halted the German advance.

The Battle of the Marne was the decisive moment of the war; and a case can be made that the Germans were henceforth destined to lose. Neither the initial German successes in the eastern theatre, which culminated in dramatic victories at Tannenberg and the Masurian Lakes, nor the ensuing 'race to the sea' in the west could disguise the failure of the German gamble in 1914 – a strategic defeat of catastrophic proportions. In the west the opposing armies now faced one another across a continuous front, which stretched for more than 400 miles from the Channel coast to Switzerland. Offensive operations perforce meant frontal attacks by unprotected foot soldiers against elaborate entrenched positions, which bristled with weapons and were fortified to withstand artillery bombardment. For most of the war, the unhappy role of attacking such positions fell to the Allied forces, which faced the challenge of dislodging the Germans from French and Belgian soil. Repeated Allied offensives in Flanders and northern France bought acres of barren land at a cost of tens of thousands of lives. A German strategic reprise came against the French fortress at Verdun in 1916. Here, in a battle that epitomized the war's frightful immobility, German and French armies locked for 10 months in a military rite of futility, in which they together sacrificed three quarters of a million soldiers.

To the east, the war featured more mobility, but it, too, defied a rapid military decision. In equipment, organization and training, the German forces were superior by a wide margin to their Russian antagonists and their Austro-Hungarian allies alike. Thanks to these disparities and the immense expanses of territory that defined the eastern war, German offensive operations succeeded on a scale unknown in the west. By the end of 1915, German armies had advanced hundreds of miles eastward to seize control of Poland and the Baltic lands. Still, victory eluded them. For all the disadvantages they faced, the Russian armies could tap massive reserves of manpower, which kept huge armies in the field to mount offensives in 1916 and 1917.

Although its operational modes differed in the two theatres, military paralysis thus descended on both the eastern and western fronts. The war became a question of attrition, a dreadful stalemate in which the basic issue was the capacity of the contending sides to endure staggering losses. In these circumstances, the opposing forces were fated to feed the war's insatiable demands for men and material, until the capacities of the one side or other were exhausted. This logic remanded the decision to the home front, for it turned the conflict into a titanic contest to mobilize human and material resources for military use. Ultimately, however, the same logic assured the defeat of Imperial Germany.

II Mobilization of the German home front

The mobilization of Germany's resources for this ordeal commenced the moment the troops began their march to the front in the summer of 1914. On 4 August, the Reichstag established the legislative framework for the whole undertaking. In a dramatic demonstration of patriotic unity, which quickly became known as the *Burgfrieden* (an allusion to the peace that reigned in medieval castles during times of war), the parties in the Reichstag delegated legislative authority to the Bundesrat, which was henceforth empowered to pass emergency laws that were binding at all levels of government. While the Reichstag retained the powers to veto any such laws, it never chose to do so. Instead, for most of the war, its role was reduced to convening every six months to approve the bond issues that financed the German military effort.

For their implementation, laws decreed by the Bundesrat descended into an administrative labyrinth that bore the imprint of a much older piece of legislation. The Prussian Law of Siege was the administrative foundation of German mobilization. It had been framed in 1851 and incorporated into the Prussian constitution; it then passed, with minor modifications, into the constitution of the German Empire in 1871. Upon the outbreak of war, this law stipulated that the country's 24 military districts (*Wehrkreise*) become the fundamental units of home-front administration; and it vested the commanders of the army corps, which were based in these districts, with comprehensive, near-absolute executive powers. As these commanders departed with their units for the front, however, their powers devolved onto their deputies. These 'deputy commanding generals' were henceforth the pivotal figures in the governance of the German home front. They were charged in the first instance with ensuring the orderly supply and reinforcement of all the front-line units associated with their corps. This responsibility extended well beyond the recruitment, training and deployment of replacement soldiers. It included ·basic matters of civilian life, including all facets of the transportation system in their corps' district. The deputy commanding generals were responsible for maintaining domestic security and order, so the police and judiciary systems fell within their jurisdiction, too, as did questions of censorship and public morale. With a vast array of responsibilities to discharge on the home front, these soldiers became the most powerful officials in the country.

The exercise of these powers, however, encountered important practical constraints. Upon the outbreak of war, offices of military administration settled like an ill-fitting template atop existing institutions of the public bureaucracy. Any hope that military administration could provide coordination to the bureaucratic fragmentation of Imperial Germany quickly proved illusory. The hybrid system that emerged was the characteristic German response to the domestic challenges of war, and it required the coordination and cooperation of thousands of civilian officials, from the provincial *Oberpräsident* to the municipal secretary, whose own powers and prerogatives were now massively circumscribed by military authority. For the duration of the war (and to the extent that they were not themselves called to military service) officials at all levels of the civilian bureaucracies remained at their posts, now in the role of auxiliaries to the soldiers. In keeping with guidelines laid down by the army, civilian policemen censored newspapers, letters, brochures, posters and the cinema; they kept watch, too, over political assemblies and those people, like the members of the German Peace Society, who were suspected of subversion. Civilian officials in the state railways provided essential services in moving troops through Germany and beyond, while municipal officials had to confront the immense difficulties of administering the civilian food supply.

The difficulties in the tangled administrative system that emerged lay paradoxically less in the practical limits that it placed on the powers of the deputy commanding generals than in the absence of constitutional limits on the same powers. The lines of authority that defined the powers of the military were themselves military; the deputy commanding generals were responsible alone to their superior in the chain of command, which meant in practice the commander-in-chief of the German army, the emperor William II. This monarch, however, was notoriously unable and temperamentally disinclined to supervise his home-front commanders, let alone impose uniform policy guidelines on them. Hence the deputy commanding generals ruled their districts like independent satrapies for most of the war. They could resist policy initiatives from the War Minister in Berlin no less than from the civilian provincial president in a place like Düsseldorf. Communications from the War Ministry typically arrived on their desks not as orders or directives, but as supplications, 'entreaties', or 'recommendations'. Nor could the Bundesrat, a civilian body, issue orders to them. As a consequence, significant jurisdictional irregularities perplexed the military administration of the German home front. Pamphlets or newspaper articles that were routinely banned from the empire of the Second Army Corps, in the environs of Stettin, could circulate freely in Baden, the domain of the Fourteenth Army Corps.

These disparities symptomized another problem, which also had to do with the autonomous powers of the military commanders. The boundaries of the *Wehrkreise* did not, as a rule, correspond to the major civilian bureaucratic jurisdictions. The district of the Fourteenth Army Corps included not only the Grand Duchy of Baden, but also the two Prussian principalities of Hohenzollern, which lay in the midst of Württemberg, which in turn lay in the dominion of the Thirteenth Army Corps. The Prussian Rhineland, the bureaucratic terrain of a single civilian provincial president, was dissected into four separate *Wehrkreise*. Given even the best of intentions, civilian and military officials found this proliferation of incongruent jurisdictions a growing source of conflict, confusion and delay.

The German military's bureaucratic design for the home front was, like its operational plans in 1914, geared to a short war. The chief administrative concern behind the Law of Siege was to maintain domestic order in the interest of funnelling supplies and reinforcements to the front during what was foreseen, in the script provided by General von Schlieffen, to be a well-delineated period of crisis, as the apocalyptic battle of the first hours was fought – and won. In this regard at least, the administration of the home front functioned well in the initial phase of the war; and the inability of the German field armies to win the apocalyptic battle could not be blamed on deficiencies at home. From Königsberg to Freiburg, cooperation between military and civilian agencies was exemplary; the dispatch of men and resources to the front proceeded with remarkable precision, popular support for the war proved near-unanimous and subversion non-existent.

The failure of the war to end as planned laid bare all the institutional flaws in the military design for home front rule. With the prolongation of combat, maintaining domestic order and providing supplies and reinforcements to the front posed colossal, unforeseen administrative challenges. Soldiers discovered that industrial war demanded new skills of them. These had much less to do with command or operational virtuosity than with economic planning and tedious negotiations with producers, wholesalers, consumers and civilian bureaucrats. Mounting shortages, which were driven by the British blockade and the natural limits of Germany's human and material resources, lured bureaucratic oversight into phases of life that had hitherto been regulated by market forces. Popular discontent was a major product of the ensuing regimentation of economic life at home, and it called forth its own administrative response, which led to the attempted regimentation of morale. The army thus became the central, pervasive force in the bureaucratic nightmare that defined the war on the German home front.

The challenges were several; and they were compounded by the absence of any systematic pre-war German planning for economic mobilization. In the first place, equipping the German armed forces demanded the mobilization of resources to produce the weapons and munitions that this war consumed in staggering quantities. This undertaking proved to be vast and complex, for it involved the wholesale sectoral redistribution of resources. The most intractable of these resources were human. Not only did industry compete directly with the army for its supply of male labour, but workers of every description had, like the soldiers, to be fed from limited stocks of food. Each of these challenges called forth its own bureaucratic apparatus, in which soldiers occupied central roles.

The effort to mobilize the raw materials to produce weapons and munitions registered the greatest success. The bureaucratic means to do so took shape in the first weeks of the war with the establishment, by the Bundesrat, of the 'War Raw Materials Section' (*Kriegsrohstoffabteilung*) within the War Ministry. This new agency, which was the inspiration of the German industrialist Walther Rathenau, was authorized to coordinate the procurement and distribution of all war-related raw materials. To this end, its officials herded the pertinent sectors of the economy into some two dozen semi-public 'War Raw-Materials Corporations', each of which was charged with purchasing available stocks of the materials in question and then allotting them to the companies with which the War Ministry had negotiated contracts to produce military equipment. 'War Metals, Inc.', for example, gathered together the twenty-two leading metal-processing firms in the country. The resulting corporation took charge of the supplies of all non-ferrous metals, which it then provided to the industrial firms that processed these metals for military use. The most striking feature of this arrangement, which was soon replicated in chemicals, iron and steel, cotton and other textiles, rubber, leather, and other sectors, was to encourage a marriage of public and private corporate power, in which private entrepreneurs operated with the financial support and bureaucratic authority of the state. In every case, the war corporations comprised the firms that dominated the sectors in question and held the bulk of the war contracts. It thus bred the further concentration of an industrial base that was already the most cartelized in Europe.

Mobilizing the raw materials of war proved to be easier than assembling the labour to process these materials into the weapons of war. The dilemma lay in basic limits of Germany's demographic base and in the fact that many of the soldiers who marched to war had pursued peacetime occupation in mines and factories that were central to the production of munitions and weapons. The appeal to women, who could quickly be employed in less-skilled positions, offered one way to address this problem; and by the war's end, women made up more than a third of the industrial workforce. Still, the war's voracious appetites required the War Ministry constantly to balance the competing demands for able-bodied males in the army and industry. Guidelines for the exemption or reclamation of labour from the army accompanied the war contracts issued in Berlin; but because the War Ministry could not enforce these guidelines, industrialists who held the contracts found themselves regularly in negotiations with the deputy commanding generals, who could.

Whether they served in the army or industry, these men had to be fed; and in this respect, they resembled every other German who experienced the war. The food supply was the most difficult administrative challenge of all. In this sector, the problems of bureaucratic control were far more daunting, given the variety of goods and the millions of small producers who had to be regulated. The situation became immediately urgent, however, as the British blockade of the North Sea coast cut Germany off from overseas imports, which in 1914 had provided about a quarter of the country's food supply (and fertilizers). The difficulties were compounded by the privileged claims that the army enjoyed on the food supply, as well as the resistance of German farmers to regulation. The resulting difficulties débuted in the first moments of the war and led to shortages of basic foodstuffs, from flour and meats to potatoes and eggs.

Public agencies on all levels struggled in vain to improvise effective solutions to these problems, which poor harvests rendered ominous at several junctures, particularly during the dismal winter of 1916–17, after the potato crop failed. The attempt to control prices locally merely drove agricultural goods to other localities. This experiment quickly yielded to national price ceilings, which the Interior Ministry administered; but price ceilings tempted farmers to withhold the controlled products or to steer them to the black market. Impressed with the success of the war corporations in the industrial sector, officials in the Interior Ministry moved early in 1915 towards a national system of rationing, which entailed the entire cycle of agricultural production and consumption in bureaucratic regulation. An Imperial Grain Corporation set the pattern. It resided in the Interior Ministry and comprised leading grain farmers and wholesalers, who were empowered to purchase the country's entire grain crop at controlled prices and then to distribute it through a network of agencies to local governments, which in turn rationed it at controlled prices to their hungry citizens. Soon some forty of these corporations reigned over food stores of every description, from potatoes to sauerkraut.

The failure of these agencies reflected the natural limits of Germany's agriculture as much as it did the bureaucratic morass. It registered not only in the shortages, but also in the unremitting inflation of food prices. A ingenious array of 'ersatz' products addressed the shortages of meat, sugar, potatoes, and other precious goods, while ways no less ingenious were found to 'stretch' still others, from bread and milk to coffee and beer. Food shortages remained none the less the single most omnipresent dimension of life on the German home front, and they hit urban dwellers with particular force.

Like no other feature of the war, the failure of public agencies to deal well with food shortages undermined public morale and confidence in the country's leadership. The state intervened massively into the life of every man, woman and child; hence the institutions of the state were directly implicated in the war's every frustration and disappointment. The prolongation of the war thus gnawed away at the state's very legitimacy.

The problem became critical during the second half of the war, but the administration of morale occupied the government from the beginning. Initial support for the war was genuine and deep. It reflected the conviction, which the government skilfully manipulated, that Germany had been attacked in 1914 by its envious enemies, who were determined to deny the country its rightful place in the world and to destroy its cultural achievement. This conviction supplied a moral consensus and sense of purpose that seemed, in the early stages of the war, to eclipse the uncertainties that had hovered over German cultural life on the eve of the war. The war would, proclaimed the philosopher Rudolf Eucken in August 1914, 'bring about the sweeping purification and edification of our soul'.³ From Max Weber to Thomas Mann, the country's cultural elites – scholars, writers, artists and composers alike – subscribed to this understanding of the war with near unanimity, and neither they nor the country's schoolteachers and clergy needed the government's encouragement to propagate it. During the first half of the war, overt opposition to the war of any kind remained sparse and fragmented, so most deputy commanding generals found their powers of censorship and monitoring public opinion to be ample.

The year 1916 represented in this and most other respects the war's turning point. The full dimensions of Germany's material disadvantages became apparent in the monster battles at Verdun, the Somme, and in the east, where the Russian Brusilov offensive brought the Austrian army to the brink of collapse. The growing strains visited on the German home front by strategic stalemate, the lengthening casualty lists, industrial mobilization and hunger all registered in growing discontent and eroding support for the war. In these circumstances, the supreme command of the army passed in the summer of 1916 to Paul von Hindenburg and Erich Ludendorff, the two soldiers who had presided over the German triumphs in the eastern theatre. Behind Hindenburg's authority and prestige, which quickly eclipsed that of the Kaiser, Ludendorff exercised the real power in the combination. The war, he believed, had become 'total'; it demanded the removal of every restraint on the mobilization of economy and society.

In the fall of 1916, the announcement of the 'Hindenburg Programme' signalled Ludendorff's designs. A 'Supreme War Office', with General Wilhelm Groener at its head, amalgamated the powers of several existing agencies in hopes of re-energizing industrial mobilization. Equipped with the authority at last to direct the deputy commanding generals in these economic matters, Groener's office presided over a ruthless purge of the economy, which shut down firms that were not immediately involved in war production. An 'Auxiliary Service Law', which the Reichstag passed in

December 1916, then provided for a civilian draft, whose object was to mobilize, into the army or the war industries, the entire male workforce between the ages of 17 and 60. In this way, an additional 3 million workers were to be channelled into industrial production – a feat that would, Ludendorff insisted, double the army's munitions stores and treble its supplies of artillery and machine guns.

The pendant to this effort was the army's intensified attention to public morale. As signs of disaffection, defeatism and subversion mounted, they persuaded Ludendorff that attending to morale required intervention more proactive than censorship, monitoring public opinion, or supervising suspicious organizations. Accordingly, in the fall of 1916 the army launched a far-flung campaign of 'patriotic instruction'. Its target in the first instance was the soldiers, in the barracks at home as well as in the trenches; but 'popular enlightenment' was soon served up to the civilian populace as well. Its goal was to smother doubts about the wisdom of the war in a flood of propaganda, in which assurances of success mixed with predictions of doom in the event of defeat.

The Hindenburg Programme failed to achieve most of its goals. Its institutional apparatus only exacerbated the bureaucratic confusion, while the limits of Germany's resources defied even Ludendorff's energy and determination. The army's campaign of 'popular enlightenment' was heavy-handed and largely ineffective in the face of material conditions that worsened significantly in 1917. None the less, the Hindenburg Programme represented, at least in the eyes of those who presided over it, the essential prelude to a final German attempt to win the war on the battlefield.

III   The social impact of war

Mobilization for war had immense social repercussions. It unsettled several orders of group relationships, principally those that were defined by class, gender and age. The wrenching reorganization of the economy for war, the abrupt redefinition of essential goods and services, and the manner in which the German government chose to pay for the war all fanned social tensions that had been defined in the era before the war.

The war meant the planned and systematic demolition of social resources. Men and materials were mobilized in pursuit of their own destruction. The consequence of four and a half years of this enterprise was to breed general immiseration. The social costs came in the form of direct material expenditures, depleted investments, a near-incalculable birth-deficit, and over 6 million military casualties. By a mechanism that was insidious, because it was largely unanticipated and misunderstood, these costs reduced the real wealth of practically every German who endured the conflict. The government financed the war primarily by means of domestic borrowing, which took the form of regular flotations of war bonds and other unsecured instruments of indebtedness. The practical effect was to finance the war by printing money, in the expectation that the country's defeated enemies would foot the entire bill at the war's conclusion. In the meantime, inflation was the result, as the money supply exploded and precious goods, like food and shoes, became scarce. Between 1914 and 1918, the index of food prices more than doubled, and the general cost of living more than trebled.

All Germans faced the consequences of inflation, but some were better able to cope with them than others. The mobilization of the economy put a premium on the production of weapons, munitions and other goods whose employment in combat was immediate. The result was to steer massive amounts of both capital and labour into the war industries, in the first instance those that processed metals and chemicals. Businesses in these sectors thrived, to the comparative benefit of those who worked in them. Not only did the war encourage further centralization and the accumulation of capital here, but labour in the war industries was also better situated to deal with the ravages of inflation. Because workers here were essential to the war effort, the War Ministry sought to keep them satisfied and loyal. One means to this end was to accommodate their wage demands. Another was to encourage them to organize, in the calculation that trade unions, even if they were Socialist, would promote discipline on the shop floor. The unions were happy to support the war in this fashion – to the extent that they participated in the administration of the Auxiliary Service Act. The power of organized labour increased substantially during the war, while unionized workers in the core sectors were to a degree shielded from inflation. Although their wages failed to keep up with the rate of inflation, they fell less behind the cost of living than did wages and salaries in the other sectors of the economy.

Those who worked in the sectors that were marginalized by the war and the Hindenburg Programme were the hardest hit. This fate befell enterprises that produced for consumer or other 'non-essential' needs – like textiles, food-processing and printing – and to smaller enterprises of nearly all descriptions. While wage-rates lagged here, small business-people were driven out of work for want of labour, capital, or coal, which Groener's office rationed in its efforts to purge the economy of non-military production. The position of the 'white-collar' lower middle-class of clerks, secretaries, teachers and salaried officials was especially precarious, for these people typically subsisted on fixed incomes, which they invested in war bonds whose value shrivelled in step with inflation; and they were reluctant to organize. The war thus assaulted one of the hallowed measures of social status in Imperial Germany, as it left this clerical middle class worse off materially than the organized sectors of the 'blue-collar' industrial proletariat.

Women faced similar material pressures, which were often compounded by the need to provide for families in the absence of a male breadwinner – an occupation that involved most of them in endless waits in queues for scarce goods. The mobilization of millions of men for the front resulted in the wholesale feminization of the home front, the assumption by women of critical positions in industry and administration. Women of the upper classes became prominent in charity and local government. The war encouraged the migration of millions of working-class women into the war industries, where many of them joined trade unions. Women of the lower-middle class who were employed in clerical positions experienced the same material disadvantages as their male colleagues, except that their pay, like the wages of working-class women, was lower to start. In all events, the contribution of women to mobilization was essential and extensive enough that granting them suffrage at war's end seemed a fitting tribute.

The departure of male parents for armed service and female parents for the assembly lines left millions of children in the care of grandparents, siblings, or no one at all, particularly as the lack of fuel for heating and the conscription of male teachers abbreviated the school year in many parts of the country. While the army beckoned to young males in their late teens, thousands of other teenagers of both sexes found occupation in the factories – and with it wages and more liberated lifestyles that aroused the concern of their elders. The absence of adult supervision was of growing concern to the police and courts, too, as young people turned increasingly, whether out of material need or the lure of adventure, to criminal behaviour.

Alarming increases in the rate of youth criminality were but one index of the tensions that mounted on the home front with the prolongation of war. The ferment in class and gender relations spawned widespread anxieties and recriminations – resentments between poor and rich, farmers and city-dwellers, Bavarians and Prussians. Resentments grew as well between Protestants and Catholics, particularly once Catholic politicians joined the critics of the war-effort. One of the most ominous symptoms of distress was also confessional; it lay in the growing popular association of Jews with slackers and war profiteers. Jews served, died, and otherwise contributed in fact to the German war effort with as much dedication and determination as any other sector of the population, Protestant or Catholic. Jews were, however, one convenient and well-practised target of antagonisms that became rife as the *Burgfrieden* dissolved during the final two years of the war.

IV   Polarization and collapse

The mood of unity and commitment that accompanied the war's outbreak rested on a pervasive belief, which was captured in the idea of the *Burgfrieden*, that Germans were fighting a defensive war. In many sectors of German society, this belief sustained support for the war effort until the end. The difficulty was that 'defensive war' meant different things to different people; and as soon as debate turned to the specific aims for which the country was fighting and to the makeup of the German constitution after the war's end, agreement collapsed. During the first half of the war, the government preserved a tenuous consensus by proscribing debate over Germany's war aims. When Ludendorff removed the wraps in the fall of 1916, public debate began in earnest. Because it bred on the increasing privations of life on the home front, the debate became increasingly bitter, to the point where it threatened the *Burgfrieden* itself.

From the Conservatives on the right to the Social Democrats on the left, the entire spectrum of German politics rallied to the defence of the Fatherland in the summer of 1914, as the Reichstag voted unanimously in favour of the bond issue to finance the war. The failure of the war to end in the fall of 1914, however, invited closer scrutiny into the reasons why Germans were being asked to bear the ever heavier burdens of industrial war. Two opposing views quickly emerged, even as their loudest champions struggled with the censors. One camp argued that the outbreak of war had revealed the full extent of Germany's vulnerability in Europe, and that the peace settlement should make forever impossible any future military attack on the country by its many enemies. The solution proffered by this camp comprised far-flung German annexations in Western and Eastern Europe, as well as in Africa. Germany was to retain control of Belgium and northern France, as well as Poland, the Baltic lands and areas of western Russia. In the eyes of the people who embraced this vision, such acquisitions offered tangible rewards to the German people for their sufferings. Not incidentally, a victorious peace of this character was also calculated to emphasize the superiority of the semi-authoritarian German constitutional system, in which the prerogatives of the Kaiser's government, particularly in military and foreign affairs, remained beyond parliamentary control.

An alternative position took shape in another camp, where discussions dwelt less on foreign conquests than domestic constitutional change. In the view of leaders of this camp, the Allies figured less as objects of demonization, and demands for security-guarantees were as a rule less extravagant. Here, too, the conviction reigned that the German people were to be rewarded after the war for their sacrifices, but the rewards were to come primarily in the shape of constitutional reforms, which meant above all government responsible to democratically elected parliaments, not only at the federal level but also in Prussia and the other German states.

The contours of these contending views of the war corresponded to the positions occupied by their proponents in the pre-war structures of social and political power. The annexationist camp was populated in the main by the country's elites – aristocrats and leaders of the propertied and educated middle classes. These men were leading figures in public bureaucracies, universities, the Protestant churches, and the armed forces. They were at home in the political parties of the right – the Conservatives, Free Conservatives, and National Liberals – as well as in the patriotic societies, like the Pan-German League and the German Navy League, that served as the most vociferous proponents of a draconian peace. The other camp was home to the parties of the left – the Progressives and, most critically, the Social Democrats – who represented the sectors of German society that were bearing the greatest material burdens of war. In addition to the labour movement, the Reichstag – the most democratic institution in the land – was the principal locus of their power, particularly as the pivotal Catholic Centre party began in 1916 to gravitate in their direction, providing a parliamentary majority to the reformist forces.

Caught between two increasingly irreconcilable camps was the federal Chancellor, Theobald von Bethmann Hollweg, who attempted to steer a tortuous path between the two by making both think that he was an ally. These vacillations have made him a controversial figure, thanks in no small part to Professor Fischer, who has portrayed him as a ruthless annexationist.[4] Bethmann's sympathy for the annexationists' thinking was doubtless genuine, but it was tempered by an awareness of the overwhelming difficulties that confronted Germany in a war against a vastly superior combination of forces. His political strategy during the first years of the war was accordingly to appease all shades of opinion at home, while he explored cautiously the prospects of a negotiated peace with one or more of the country's antagonists. The coming of Hindenburg and Ludendorff to power in 1916 soon made this political strategy untenable. The two soldiers had little patience for opposition or moderation of any kind; and they quickly became themselves the symbols of uncompromising victory, or, as it became known, a 'Hindenburg Peace'. In their eyes, the role of the Chancellor was to manage the Reichstag and keep the critics docile, as the army's leadership led the war effort to a successful conclusion. The growing power and prestige of the army's supreme command made it an unequal match for the Chancellor, whose position depended ultimately on the support of the Kaiser.

The showdown came in 1917. After the Allies had rejected a tentative German offer to negotiate in December 1916, the initiative in Berlin passed to the soldiers, who were relieved but not surprised by the Allies' refusal of the German overture. The next month they persuaded the Kaiser and a reluctant Bethmann to begin unrestricted submarine warfare against all Allied maritime traffic – in the full knowledge that this step would bring the United States into the war against Germany. The submarine campaign represented another military gamble, as well as a gesture to the German right. The entry of the United States into the war eventuated in April 1917; and it followed within weeks the news of revolution in Russia. Both events profoundly altered the complexion of domestic politics in Germany. The American intervention came in the name of a 'world safe for democracy' and a 'war to end all wars'. In so far as they suggested a formula for a compromise peace, these gallant slogans provided encouragement to the German left at a time of great anxiety. In Berlin and other industrial centres, German workers responded to news of the Russian revolution with a wave of strikes, in which calls for higher food rations mixed with demands for an end of the war. It was a sign of the alarm within the government that Bethmann could persuade the Kaiser to issue a proclamation on Easter Sunday that promised, albeit in vague terms, constitutional reform at war's end. On the same Sunday in April, the left wing of the Social Democratic party, which had become increasingly appalled over a war that was difficult to portray as defensive any longer, formally broke away to form another party. The new one was united only in calling for an immediate end of the war, but a radical faction within it, the so-called Spartacus League, advocated social revolution to achieve this end. The split of the SPD into two separate parties, the new Independent Social Democratic Party and the old one, which became known as the Majority Social Democratic Party, signalled the end of Socialist unity in Germany, the great ideal that had animated the Socialist labour movement almost from its birth.

In July 1917 the political ferment migrated to the Reichstag. Here, in defiance of the government, a parliamentary majority of Progressives, Majority Socialists, and members of the Catholic Centre Party passed the 'Peace Resolution', which renounced annexations and called for a negotiated end of the war. The response of Hindenburg and Ludendorff to this affront was to force the resignation of Bethmann Hollweg and replace him with a pliant non-entity, of whom few Germans had ever heard.

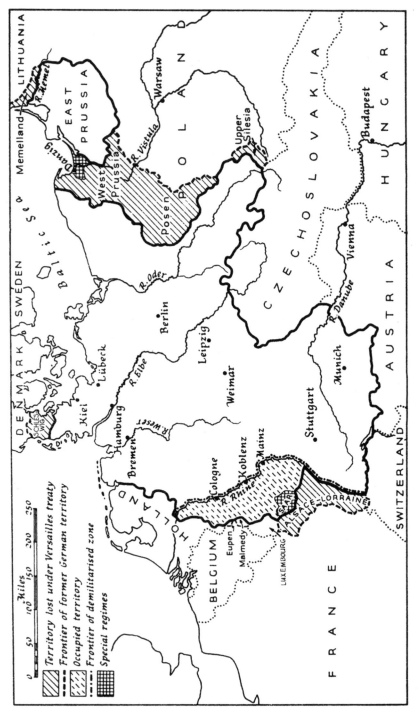

Map 12.2 Germany in 1919

Scale legend:

Miles
0 50 100 150 200 250

▨ Territory lost under Versailles treaty
▤ Frontier of former German territory
▨ Occupied territory
▦ Frontier of demilitarised zone
▦ Special regimes

With this step, German domestic politics settled into the uneasy pattern that prevailed until the fall of 1918. To speak of a 'military dictatorship' exaggerates the situation only a little, for Ludendorff was now effectively in control of executive powers, civilian as well as military.[5] His power was not unfettered, however, for the government remained beholden to the Reichstag for its funds. The last months of the war thus witnessed the full-scale polarization of German politics. The right coalesced around the high command. To lend moral support to the idea of a Hindenburg Peace, the high command gave its blessing to a massive new patriotic society, the Fatherland Party, which came to life in September 1917 and soon attracted over a million members. One of its principal objects was to intimidate the parties of the left in the Reichstag, which was now home to all manner of popular disaffection with the war, as well as with a government that insisted on the war's uncompromising prosecution.

By early 1918 it was clear to all that the resolution of the domestic stalemate would depend entirely on the outcome of the war – the circumstances in which the stalemate was brought to an end on the battlefront. Ludendorff had reason for optimism, for in late 1917 his armies won the war in the east. The peace treaty that emerged in early 1918 gave form to the wildest aspirations of the annexationists, for it left Germany in control of vast stretches of territory in eastern Europe. The general could take further comfort in the fact that a majority in the Reichstag voted in favour of the Treaty of Brest-Litovsk, which formalized this peace, for the settlement in the east seemed to mock the ideals of the Reichstag's Peace Resolution. Only the Independent Socialists voted against it, while the beleaguered Majority Socialists abstained, fearful of the repercussions of further identification with the cause that Ludendorff symbolized. They had good reason for concern. In January 1918, thanks in part to the accurate perception that the high command was dragging out negotiations over the eastern peace, the largest and most alarming strikes of the entire war had broken out – in defiance of the Socialist unions – throughout Germany's industrial centres.

Late in March 1918, Ludendorff threw the dice a final time. Reinforced by troops recently transferred from the east, as well as by the fruits of the Hindenburg Programme from home, his armies in the west lashed out against the forces of France, Britain and – for the first time – the United States. Dramatic gains in several sectors of the front breathed hope on the German home front, but the offensive lacked both the strategic direction and, despite all the exertions of the home front, the material resources to sustain it. By the early summer, the 'Ludendorff Offensive' had been halted, and the Allies unleashed a series of counter-offensives, which were spearheaded by armoured vehicles. These attacks set the German armies into terminal strategic retreat.

By the end of September, even Ludendorff had concluded that the German military cause was lost. At this moment he undertook a shrewd, fateful political manoeuvre. To the Kaiser he insisted that political power be turned over to the Reichstag, that the civilian executive be made responsible to this body, and that the suffrage be democratized in Prussia and the other German states. By Imperial decree these changes, which fulfilled all the basic demands of the democratic reformers, were quickly enacted. In early October, a new, responsible cabinet was cobbled together out of the leftist parties in the Reichstag. General Ludendorff had brought revolutionary changes to Germany, once again, as in 1866–71, from above. The circumstances that faced the new democrats could hardly have been more daunting, however, for their first task was to bring the war to an end and to prevent the spread in Germany of revolutionary unrest, the possibility of which loomed in the spectre of Soviet Russia. In October, peace overtures went out from Berlin to the President of the United States, Woodrow Wilson, whom the Germans believed to offer the best chances for a moderate peace. This expectation was disappointed, and the armistice, which was concluded on 11 November 1918, was harsher than the Germans had hoped. By now, however, the situation in Germany urgently required an end to the war, for the institutional collapse of the Imperial German political system, which had forfeited its legitimacy in the military collapse, had begun.

Ludendorff watched these events from exile in Sweden, where he had fled after resigning his post at the head of the army in October. He had none the less led the German armies to defeat on the battlefield. He also bequeathed an exhausted and dispirited home front, which had been pushed to heroic limits in an ordeal for which it lacked the resources to prevail. The general's final legacy was to fashion a perverse connection between the home front and military defeat. In this reasoning, the home front – riddled by slackers, pacifists, Jews and Marxist revolutionaries – had stabbed the German army in the back, surrendering to the Allies while the soldiers stood unvanquished in the field. It was a bald lie, but it threw a dark shadow over the new republican government, which had to contend with the material and emotional rubble of the First World War.

Notes:

1. Quoted in Wolfgang J. Mommsen, *Bürgerstolz und Weltmachtstreben: Deutschland unter Wilhelm II. 1890 bis 1918* (1995), p. 566.

2. Kennan, George F., *The Decline of Bismarck's European Order: Franco-Russian Relations, 1875-1890* (1979), p. 3.
3. Quoted in Kurt Flasch, *Die geistige Mobilmachung: Die deutschen Intellektuellen und der Erste Weltkrieg: Ein Versuch* (2000), p. 21.
4. Fischer, Fritz, *Germany's Aims in the First World War* (1967).
5. Kitchen, Martin, *The Silent Dictatorship: The Politics of the German High Command under Hindenburg and Ludendorff* (1976).

Select bibliography

Chickering, Roger, and Stig Förster, eds., *Great War, Total War: Combat and Mobilization on the Western Front, 1914–1918* (2000).

Chickering, Roger, *Imperial Germany and the Great War, 1914–1918* (1998).

Daniel, Ute, *The War from Within: German Working-Class Women in the First World War* (1997).

Davis, Belinda J., *Home Fires Burning: Food, Politics, and Everyday Life in World War I Berlin* (2000).

Feldman, Gerald D., *Army, Industry and Labor in Germany, 1914–1918* (1966).

Feldman, Gerald, *The Great Disorder: Politics, Economics, and Society in the German Inflation, 1914–1924* (1993).

Fischer, Fritz, *Germany's Aims in the First World War* (1967).

Herwig, Holger, *The First World War: Germany and Austria–Hungary, 1914–1918* (1997).

Kitchen, Martin, *The Silent Dictatorship: The Politics of the German High Command under Hindenburg and Ludendorff* (1976).

Kocka, Jürgen, *Facing Total War: German Society, 1914–1918* (1984).

Ritter, Gerhard, *The Schlieffen Plan: Critique of a Myth* (1958).

Stevenson, David, *Armaments and the Coming of War: Europe, 1904–1914* (1996).

Stevenson, David, *The First World War and International Politics* (1988).

Whalen, Robert Weldon, *Bitter Wounds: German Victims of the Great War, 1914–1939* (1984).

Wheeler Bennett, John W., *Brest-Litovsk: The Forgotten Peace, March 1918* (1938).

Appendix 1: Some basic statistics for Germany, 1815–1918

Statistics for 'Germany' before 1871 are confusing. Some figures are for the area which was to become the territory of the German Second Empire in 1871. Such statistics are only of limited use for long-run comparisons because that geographical unit made no sense whatsoever before 1871. Some statistics are for the territory of the German Confederation. However, that territory excluded part of the population of Prussia (the provinces of East and West Prussia and the Grand Duchy of Posen) and the eastern half of the Habsburg Empire as well as its Italian possessions. Furthermore, some collections still exclude the Austrian part of the Confederation, although there is no possible excuse for so doing. Some statistics are for the area covered by the German Customs Union (*Zollverein*). Even statistics for individual states are a problem. Figures for the Napoleonic period have not been included because the territories of individual states changed with bewildering rapidity, so much so that some cartographers largely gave up compiling political maps and turned their attention to such things as 'natural frontiers'. Even in the stable period after 1814–15 there are some difficulties. Prussia was greatly expanded by annexation in 1866 while Austria lost Lombardy in 1859 and Venetia in 1866. Statistics were not always gathered by the same methods. This point should particularly be borne in mind when comparing labour force statistics before and after 1871 and one should also note that the different states before 1871 would not have used precisely the same methods or applied them with the same degree of accuracy. Prussia was always noted for her superiority in this regard. Finally, one should note that statistics are generally more reliable the later they are compiled. The pre-1871 statistics in particular provide little more than orders of magnitude, sometimes involve estimates, and frequently do not add up.

1. Population before unification

The German Confederation

Total population (in millions)

1822	39.6
1843	49.4
1864	53.7

Individual states in 1841: population in the German Confederation (in millions)

Austria	16.6
Bavaria	4.4
Hanover	1.7
Saxony	1.7
Württemberg	1.7
Baden	1.3

None of the other states had a population of over 1 million; their total population amounted in 1841 to about 5.5 million, ranging from about 734,000 inhabitants in Kurhesse to some 28,000 in Schaumburg-Lippe.

The table does not include Prussia, figures for which are given below for its whole territory, both within and outside the Confederation. It is, however, worth providing the population of the Habsburg territories within the Confederation as this was always regarded as the 'German' part of the empire.

Prussia

1820	10.3
1840	14.9
1870	19.4*

*This excludes the additional 4.5 million subjects gained by annexation in 1867.

Austria–Hungary

1820	25.5
1870	34.8

2. The German Second Empire

Population (in millions)

1870	40.8
1880	45.0
1890	49.2
1900	56.0
1910	64.6

Composition of the labour force for the territory of the subsequent German Second Empire

Date	Primary sector	Secondary sector	Tertiary sector
1800	62	21	17
1825	59	22	19
1846	57	23	20
1861	52	27	21
1871	49	29	22

Composition of the labour force for the German Second Empire

Date	Primary sector	Secondary sector	Tertiary sector*
1882	41.6	34.8	23.7
1895	35.0	38.5	26.5
1907	28.4	42.2	29.4

*This includes the unemployed and those on unearned incomes.

Appendix 2: Chronology: Germany, 1800–1918

1799	Coup brings Napoleon to power as First Consul in France.
1801	Austria makes peace with France.
1802	Britain makes peace with France.
1803	France gains the left bank of the Rhine; the larger German states receive compensation on the right bank, resulting in the destruction of many small states.
1804	Francis II, Holy Roman Emperor, assumes title of Francis I, Emperor of Austria; Napoleon crowns himself Emperor.
1805	Bavaria and Württemberg become kingdoms. Third war of coalition (including Austria, Britain and Russia) against France. French victories over Russia and Austria (Austerlitz). French naval defeat at Trafalgar. Peace of Pressburg: Austrian territorial losses.
1806	End of Holy Roman Empire. Napoleon establishes the Confederation of the Rhine. Fourth war of coalition pits Prussia, Russia and Britain against France. French victories over Prussia (Jena and Auerstadt). With Berlin Decree Napoleon initiates blockade of Britain.
1807	Peace of Tilsit between France and Russia ends war. Prussia reduced to rump state; her lost territory is used to form Grand Duchy of Warsaw in the east and Kingdom of Westphalia in the west. Stein appointed First Minister in Prussia and begins process of reforms with the October Edict emancipating the peasantry. Napoleon tightens blockade with Milan Decree and founds an order of imperial nobility.
1808	Stein dismissed on Napoleon's insistence; Spanish uprising against Napoleon.

1809	Fifth war of coalition (Austria and Britain against France). Austrian defeat (Wagram) leads to further territorial losses and to appointment of Metternich as Austrian Chancellor.
1810	Napoleon marries Marie-Louise, daughter of Francis I. Hardenberg appointed Prussian Chancellor.
1811	Prussia joins military alliance with France.
1812	June: Napoleon invades Russia. French retreat begins in October. Yorck, the Prussian general, signs agreement with Russian army in December (Convention of Tauroggen).
1813	March: Prussia declares war on France. Austria declares war on France in August. October: France defeated in 'Battle of the Nations' at Leipzig.
1814	March: Allies enter Paris. May: first Peace of Paris. Peace Congress convened in Vienna agrees territorial settlement of German lands.
1815	March: Napoleon lands in France. June: Napoleon defeated at Waterloo. Final Act of Congress of Vienna. German Confederation established. Otto von Bismarck born.
1817	German Students' Associations (*Burschenschaften*) organize nationalist festival at Wartburg.
1818	Constitutions granted in Baden and Bavaria. Hegel appointed Professor at the University of Berlin.
1819	Murder of Kotzebue by a nationalist student in March leads in September to proclamation of the Carlsbad decrees by the German Confederation to enforce political restrictions on the German states. October: Prussia signs first trade treaty (with Schwarzburg-Sonderhausen).
1820	Vienna 'Final Act' establishes greater control of Confederation over affairs of individual states.
1823	Provincial diets established in Prussia.
1826	Start of publication of *Monumenta Germaniae Historica*, edited by Stein and intended to cultivate a love and knowledge of German history through the publication of medieval documents.
1830–1	Revolts in Hesse, Brunswick and Saxony lead to granting of constitutions.
1832	Nationalist festival in Hambach. Death of Goethe.
1833	Establishment of *Zollverein* (German customs union).
1834	Launch of Young Germany movement.
1837	Hanoverian constitution of 1833 suspended by new king.
1840	Frederick William IV becomes King of Prussia. 'Rhine crisis' with France.

1841	Friedrich List publishes *National System of Political Economy* advocating a programme of economic protectionism and nationalism.
1842	Consecration of Cologne Cathedral in presence of Frederick William.
1847	Meeting of the Prussian United Diet in Berlin.
1848	Outbreak of revolution in the German lands, other territories of the Habsburg Empire and elsewhere. German National Assembly convenes in Frankfurt in May; Prussia goes to war with Denmark over issue of Schleswig-Holstein; a truce agreed in August. December: Franz Joseph becomes Emperor of Austria. The Prussian National Assembly is dissolved and Frederick William issues his own constitution.
1849	April: Frederick William IV rejects offer of hereditary emperorship of Germany under terms of constitution drawn up by German National Assembly. Spring and early summer: counter-revolution, including use of Prussian and other troops against rebels in smaller states, Habsburg troops in Italy and Hungary, and Russian troops in Hungary.
1850	March: Frederick William IV summons a German parliament to Erfurt. July: peace agreed between Prussia and Denmark. November: Prussia backs down over Hesse-Cassel, abandons its 'Erfurt Union' plan and agrees to accept the authority of the Confederation. December: Austrian Chancellor, Schwarzenberg, abandons plan to include all of Habsburg Empire in Confederation.
1851	Confederation formally restored; Bismarck appointed first Prussian ambassador to Federal Diet.
1852–3	Formation of Germanic National Museum in Nuremburg.
1853	*Zollverein* renewed for a further 12 years. Austria unable to form Austro-German customs union and has to settle for commercial treaty with *Zollverein*.
1854–6	Crimean War signals final breakdown of the 1814–15 alliance system: Austria neutral but anti-Russian; Prussia neutral.
1858	Agreement between France and Piedmont to act against Austria. William appointed Regent in Prussia.
1859	War of France and Piedmont against Austria. Austria cedes Lombardy to Piedmont; Piedmont later cedes Savoy and Nice to France. The German National Association (*National Verein*) established. Bismarck appointed Prussian ambassador to Russia.

1860   Prussian Minister of War, Albert von Roon, introduces military reforms into Prussian parliament.

1861   Death of Frederick William IV; William I becomes King of Prussia.

1862   September: Bismarck recalled from his recent appointment as Prussian ambassador to France and appointed Minister-President in midst of constitutional conflict. October: Bismarck delivers his 'blood and iron' speech.

1863   March: Denmark incorporates Schleswig. October: German Diet votes for action against Denmark. December: Hanoverian and Saxon troops enter Holstein.

1864   February–July: War of Austria and Prussia against Denmark. By Treaty of Vienna (October) Denmark cedes Schleswig and Holstein to Austria and Prussia. November: Confederation agrees Prussian and Austrian forces should remain in sole charge of Schleswig-Holstein.

1865   August: by terms of Convention of Gastein, Austria and Prussia occupy and administer Holstein and Schleswig respectively. October: Napoleon III and Bismarck meet at Biarritz.

1866   January: renewal of *Zollverein* on low tariff basis which ensures continued exclusion of Austria-Hungary. April: secret three-month alliance between Prussia and Italy. June: start of war of Italy and Prussia against Austria. July: Prussian victory at Königgrätz. August: Treaty of Prague – Austria agrees to her exclusion from Germany. October: Treaty of Vienna – Austria cedes Venetia to Italy. Prussia annexes Schleswig-Holstein, Hanover, Hesse-Cassel and Frankfurt. The North German Confederation established.

1867   February: Constitution agreed for North German Confederation, including a lower house (Reichstag) elected by universal manhood suffrage. May: Bismarck acts to block French acquisition of Luxembourg. July: customs agreement between Confederation and the south German states.

1868   Establishment of a customs parliament.

1870   July: Hohenzollern candidacy (for the throne of Spain) made public; outbreak of war of Prussia and other German states against France. September: German victory at Sedan and Paris placed under siege. October: capitulation of French fortress of Metz.

1871   January: German Second Empire proclaimed at Versailles – William becomes German Emperor. March: first imperial

Reichstag convenes and agrees a constitution in April. May: Treaty of Frankfurt by which France cedes Alsace and Lorraine to Germany and agrees to pay a large war indemnity. July: beginning of the *Kulturkampf* (the campaign against Catholics).

1872   June: expulsion of Jesuits from Germany.

1873   May Laws increase power of Prussian state over education and appointment of clergy.

1873–4   End of the economic boom ushers in a period of reduced growth and price deflation.

1875   Pius IX condemns German government for persecution of Catholics. Formation of the Reichsbank. 'War in Sight' crisis.

1878   Bismarck shifts policy: introduces anti-socialist law following two assassination attempts on William I. Reichstag elections weaken the largest party, the National Liberals.

1879   Bismarck meets a papal envoy of the new Pope, Leo XIII. Bismarck able to form new parliamentary coalition with one section of the National Liberal party along with conservative deputies. Introduces a general protective tariff.

1882   May: Germany, Austria-Hungary and Italy form Triple Alliance. December: Colonial League formed.

1882–4   A period of active colonial policy by Bismarck.

1884   Reichstag elections held with great emphasis by Bismarck on colonial issues.

1887   February: 'cartel' elections to Reichstag leading to majority for the governmental parties (Free Conservatives, Conservatives, National Liberals). June: Reinsurance Treaty with Russia.

1888   March: Death of William I. Short reign and death of his son, Frederick, in June leads to the accession to the Prussian crown and German emperorship of Frederick's son, William II.

1890   February: Reichstag elections undermine the Bismarckian 'cartel' majority; anti-socialist law not renewed. March: Bismarck resigns and General von Caprivi appointed Chancellor. June: the Reinsurance Treaty with Russia is allowed to lapse.

1891   Formation of Pan-German League.

1893   Formation of Agrarian League in response to a series of bilateral treaties reducing grain tariffs.

1894   January: formation of Franco-Russian alliance. October: Caprivi resigns as Chancellor and is replaced by Prince von Hohenlohe.

1896   William II congratulates President Kruger of the Boer Republic on the failure of the Jameson Raid.

1897	Conservative reconstruction of government with three key appointments: von Tirpitz as Secretary for the Navy; von Miquel as Prussian Minister of Finance; and Bernard von Bülow as Secretary for Foreign Affairs.
1898	March–April: breakdown of Anglo-German talks on resisting Russian expansion in the Far East. April: passage of first Navy Law through the Reichstag; formation of the Navy League. June: Reichstag elections produce poor results for the right. September: Fashoda crisis between Britain and France.
1899	Anglo-French agreement on Africa.
1900	June: second Navy Law. October: Bernard von Bülow becomes Chancellor.
1902	Britain and Japan sign defensive alliance. Implementation of a new protective tariff.
1903	Reichstag elections see major socialist party success.
1904	Formation of Entente Cordiale between Britain and France. Commercial treaty between Germany and Russia. War between Russia and Japan.
1904–5	Naval defeats in Russo-Japanese war precipitate crisis and revolution in Russia.
1905	February–July: First Moroccan crisis.
1906	January–April: Algeciras Conference settles Moroccan crisis. February: Britain launches its first Dreadnought in response to German navy building. June: third Navy Law.
1907	January: Reichstag 'Hottentot' elections see socialist setback and a parliamentary majority (the 'Bülow bloc') of pro-colonial parties against Centre Party and SPD. Naval talks between Britain and Russia lead to agreement. June–October: Germany rejects disarmament proposals at The Hague. July: Triple Alliance renewed for six years.
1908	The *Daily Telegraph* affair. October: Austrian annexation of Bosnia-Herzegovina. Fourth Navy Law.
1909	March: collapse of 'Bülow bloc'; June: final defeat of the financial reform programme that had led to collapse. July: Bülow resigns and is replaced as Chancellor by von Bethmann-Hollweg.
1910	Failure of scheme to reform Prussian three-class franchise for elections to the lower house (Landtag).
1911	Second Moroccan crisis.
1912	February: Haldane mission to Germany fails to end naval race. March: new Navy Law published along with an Army Bill. First

Balkan War. Reichstag elections: SPD becomes largest party with 110 seats and over one-third of the popular vote.

1913   Second Balkan War. June: Army Finance Bill to pay for massive expansion of army. France also passes an Army Bill to expand its army.

1914   28 June: assassination of Archduke Franz Ferdinand of Austria leads to the July crisis. Austrian ultimatum to Serbia issued on 23 July. The first declaration of war was Austria on Serbia (28 July). Seven further declarations of war by 12 August saw a general state of war in Europe. On 4 August, in a demonstrative display of national unity, all the parties in the Reichstag vote for war credits. September: first battle of Marne halts German advances into France; Russian defeat at the Masurian Lakes. Falkenhayn replaces Moltke as German Commander-in-Chief. November: Hindenburg appointed Commander-in-Chief on the eastern front.

1915   February: Germany declares blockade of Britain. War on western front settles into pattern of inconclusive trench warfare.

1916   February: battle of Verdun. July: battle of the Somme. August: Hindenburg appointed Chief of General Staff with Ludendorff as Quartermaster-General. December: Auxiliary Service Law.

1917   February: revolution in Russia. April: USA declares war on Germany; William II promises universal suffrage for Prussian elections. July: Bethmann-Hollweg replaced as Chancellor by Michaelis; mutiny in German navy; Reichstag passes motion in favour of peace. October: Bolshevik seizure of power in Russia leads in November to opening of peace negotiations between Russia and Germany. December: hostilities suspended on Eastern Front; Michaelis replaced as Chancellor by Hertling.

1918   January: strikes in Berlin. March: Brest-Litovsk treaty between Russia and Germany gains territory in the east and provides basis for a renewed offensive on the western front (March–April). July: third and last German offensive on western front. September: the Army Command admits the war is going badly and calls for an armistice; Hertling replaced as Chancellor by Prince Max von Baden. October: Germany requests armistice from President Wilson of USA; dismissal of Ludendorff; William agrees to the appointment of a chancellor based on a Reichstag majority and a democratic reform of the

German constitution; sailors' mutiny. November: revolution; abdication of William II; armistice signed; proclamation of a republic under the SPD leader, Ebert. December: Reich Congress of Workers' and Soldiers' Councils in Berlin; foundation of KPD.

Notes on the contributors

Volker Berghahn is J. P. Birkelund Professor of European History at Brown University, Providence, RI. His recent publications include *Otto A. Friedrich, Ein Politischer Unternehmer, 1902–1975* (1993); *Imperial Germany, 1871–1914* (1995); and (ed.) *Quest for Economic Empire* (1996).

John Breuilly is Professor of Modern History at the University of Birmingham. His main interests are in nationalism, modern German history, and comparative urban and cultural history in modern Europe. His recent publications include: *The Formation of the First German Nation-State, 1800–1871* (1996) and (co-ed. with G. Niedhart and A.D. Taylor) *The Era of the Reform League: English Labour and Radical Politics 1857–1872* (1995) *Nationalismus und moderner Staat Deutschland und Europa* (1999).

Roger Chickering has been Professor of History at the BMW Center for German and European Studies at Georgetown University since 1993. He has held research fellowships from the Guggenheim Foundation, the Fulbright Commission, the Institute for Advanced Study at Princeton, and the Woodrow Wilson Center in Washington. His publications on German history include: *Imperial Germany and a World without War* (1976); *We Men Who Feel Most German* (1984); *Karl Lamprecht* (1993); and *Imperial Germany and the Great War, 1914–1918* (1998).

Christopher Clark is Fellow and Lecturer in Modern European History at St Catharine's College, Cambridge. He is the author of *Politics of Conversion. Missionary Protestantism and the Jews in Prussia 1728–1941* (1995), and *Kaiser Wilhelm II* (2000).

Karin Friedrich is Lecturer in History at the School of Slavonic and East European Studies, University of London. She is currently working on early modern urban history (Poland and Prussia) and on the history of political ideas and national identity. Her most recent publication is the *The other Prussia: Royal Prussia, Poland and liberty 1569–1772* (2000).

Matthew Jefferies is Lecturer in German History at the University of Manchester. He is author of *Politics and Culture in Wilhelmine Germany. The Case of Industrial Architecture* (1995) and recently completed *A Cultural History of Imperial Germany*. He is currently working on the history of German naturism and nudism.

Robert Lee is the Chaddock Professor of Economic and Social History at the University of Liverpool. He has published widely on the demographic, economic and social history of Germany. His recent publications include: (ed. with Richard Lawton) *Urban Population Development in Western Europe from the Late-Eighteenth to the Early-Twentieth Century* (1989); (ed. with Pat Hudson) *Women's Work and the Family Economy in Historical Perspective* (1990); *German Industry and German Industrialisation. Essays in German Economic and Business History in the Nineteenth and Twentieth Centuries* (1991); (ed. with Eve Rosenhaft) *State, Social Policy and Social Change in Germany, Oxford and New York* (1997); and (ed. with Richard Lawton) *Population and Society in Western European Port Cities* c. *1650 to 1939* (2000). He is currently completing two projects on the demographic and socio-economic development of Bremen and Stralsund in the nineteenth century.

Katharine A. Lerman is Senior Lecturer in Modern European History at the University of North London and her publications include *The Chancellor as Courtier: Bernhard von Bülow and the Governance of Germany 1900–1909* (1990). She is currently writing a book on Bismarck and researching into the genealogy and position of women within the imperial German ruling elite.

Wolfram Siemann is Professor of Modern and Contemporary History at the University of Munich. His recent books include *Die deutsche Revolution von 1848/49* (1985; English translation, (1998); *Gesellschaft im Aufbruch: Deutschland 1849–1871* (1996); *Vom Staatenbund zum Nationalstaat Deutschland 1806–1871* (1995); (ed. with Ute Daniel) *Propaganda. Meinungskampf, Verführung und politische Sinnstiftung 1789–1989* (1994).

Joachim Whaley is a University Lecturer in German and Fellow of Gonville and Caius College, Cambridge. He is the author of *Religious Toleration and Social Change in Hamburg, 1529–1819* (1985) and is currently working on a study of early modern Germany.

Index